Digital Transformation and Economic Development in Bangladesh

"Dr. Monzur Hossain's factual analysis on the role of digital transformation in the development framework of a lower middle-income country (LMIC) such as Bangladesh is a must-read for anyone working at the confluence of development economics, information technologies, and public policy. After having had the opportunity to shape the ICT Policy framework of Bangladesh adopted in 2009 and continuing to this day, I had the distinct pleasure of co-authoring a book titled 'Going digital: realizing the dreams of a digital Bangladesh for all' published by the University Press Ltd. in 2011. Hossain's book is the first major publication in a decade since that delves into the hopes, aspirations, and ground realities of the digitalization initiatives of a nation whose youthful population is highly expectant on the power of technology to bring them economic freedom."

—Habibullah N. Karim, *The founding secretary general and a past President of the Bangladesh Association of Software and Information Services (BASIS)*

"The Digital Bangladesh Vision has gained impetus and delivered benefit to the people of the low-income country. Why does this big-push approach not disintegrate in mid-air? How is the digital divide overcome? The author's lucid exposition of careful analyses of policies and impacts makes this book a must-read handbook for leapfrogging economic development."

—Tetsushi Sonobe, *Dean and CEO, Asian Development Bank Institute, Tokyo, Japan and Professor, National Graduate Institute for Policy Studies, Tokyo, Japan*

Monzur Hossain

Digital Transformation and Economic Development in Bangladesh

Rethinking Digitalization Strategies for Leapfrogging

palgrave
macmillan

Monzur Hossain
Bangladesh Institute of Development
Studies
Dhaka, Bangladesh

ISBN 978-981-19-2752-2 ISBN 978-981-19-2753-9 (eBook)
https://doi.org/10.1007/978-981-19-2753-9

This Palgrave Macmillan imprint is published by the registered company Springer Nature Singapore Pte Ltd.
The registered company address is: 152 Beach Road, #21-01/04 Gateway East, Singapore 189721, Singapore

This book is dedicated to my mother, Pakia Khatun, who died on August 10, 2016. Her smile was like sunshine to me, and she was the source of all my inspiration and hard work. She instilled in me to live a life with integrity, self-respect, and perseverance. As I am as old as the independent nation that we live in today, this is an opportune moment to dedicate a book to a mother who struggled to raise a newborn in the bloody war of 1971.

Preface

I have planned this book to be a token of commemoration for 50 years of independence, highlighting the role of digital transformation in the country's development framework. This book is the first of its kind that considers digital transformation as a strategy for leapfrogging toward a developed nation in the quickest possible time, embarking on the power of the youth. Having the demographic dividend in place, this is an opportune moment for Bangladesh to utilize its youth in the digital transformation process to march toward faster growth trajectories. A successful digital transformation will lead to a knowledge society, which is crucial for economic freedom and justice. The book has thus not restricted its analysis to different aspects of digitalization only; it also analyzes digitalization from a broader development framework.

Bangladesh celebrates its 50 years of independence in 2021 with high admiration from various quarters for its impressive economic and social performances over the last 50 years. The achievements are commendable for many reasons. The country by now has overcome the prevailing pessimistic outlook with its innovative development policies encompassing both public and private sectors and hard work and aspirations of the people, which are reflected in hard-earned remittances from abroad, a significant rise in readymade garments (RMG) exports that accommodated over 4 million female labor force, adopting modern agricultural technologies, and so on. Bangladesh achieved self-sufficiency in food production a decade ago. The country has reached the lower-middle-income status in 2015 and set to attain graduation from LDC status by 2026 and developed nation status by 2041. Though various reform policies, such as trade and financial reforms undertaken in the 1980s and 1990s, have uplifted the economy from the bottom, further progression requires some innovations and productivity gains to escape from development traps. This calls for a technology-driven development strategy.

In this context, the Bangladesh government adopted a digitalization strategy in 2009 as a key development strategy by pledging to achieve middle-income status by 2021, which is fifty years of its independence. Digital Bangladesh has become a buzzword of development over time as the digitalization targets are aligned with development targets. Under the "Digital Bangladesh" vision, the government undertook a massive digitalization process by investing in e-governance, ICT infrastructure, ICT parks, skills development programs, and so on. The Digital Bangladesh vision is an innovative policy framework of the Bangladesh government that may be considered a shifting development strategy in the context of the declining importance of traditional growth drivers, such as readymade garments, agriculture, etc. If properly harnessed, broader digital transformation could help the country avoid development traps and leapfrog into the next level of development. As a shifting development strategy, it is thus important to assess the context, relevance, and achievements of Digital Bangladesh policy in terms of the digital transformation of the economy. This book makes a modest attempt to evaluate the Digital Bangladesh Policy from these contexts, and its likely impact on economic growth and development.

Information and communications technologies (ICTs) could provide leverage to developing nations like Bangladesh to catch up with industrialized nations through at least three channels: (i) increasing efficiencies in product and process by reducing transaction costs reinforcing the "death of distance"; (ii) facilitate innovations through the adoption of software and information technologies that facilitate productivity gains across the board, and such productivity gains contribute to total factor productivity and hence higher economic growth; and (iii) the development of the IT industry with a skilled labor force that helps capture a part of growing outsourcing businesses from the developed world with low-cost labor advantage. Low-income countries like Bangladesh have comparative advantages to gain from adopting ICTs. For example, as the ICT sector mainly relies on human capital and a low level of investment, it is easier for Bangladesh to build necessary capabilities faster with its current demographic dividends.

A certain degree of digital transformation of the economy has occurred by now with the substantial adoption of digital technologies. Digital transformation takes place with the adoption of the digital technology built on telecommunications networks, computer technologies, software engineering, and so on. Nonetheless, ICT infrastructure is the precondition to achieving digital transformation. Though ICT infrastructure by now taking better shape in the country, the affordability and accessibility of digital services do matter. Furthermore, the spillovers resulting from their use have robust bearings on economic development. The book draws upon the supply-side and demand-side perspectives and policy diffusions that are instrumental to the digital transformation. The chapters are benefitted from the author's long-standing research works on the topic. The importance of the book lies in the fact that it examines a first-hand developing country experience that aspires to embark on a higher development trajectory with a "big push" policy for digitalization.

The chapters are thematically organized in three parts. Part I encompasses chapters highlighting development perspectives of "Digital Bangladesh," achievements, and policy and regulatory frameworks. The chapters provide a snapshot of the digital Bangladesh vision, associated investments in ICTs, and the current state of digitalization from both national and regional perspectives. Part II focuses on the supply-side aspect of digital transformation. This part provides a detailed discussion on the current state of the ICT industry, its performances, and challenges, including the ICT sector's contribution to service exports, ICT products, and services, types and nature of ICT firms, etc. It also reviews the policy of building ICT parks in various districts from the perspectives of agglomeration economies. In addition, this part provided a detailed analysis of the existing human resources and skills gap in the sector. Part III focuses on digital transformation and its impact on productivity and growth. Both micro- and macro-level analyses are done in this part of the book. The firm-level analysis focuses on innovations, market access, and financial access. From a macro perspective, ICTs' role in economic growth, particularly total factor productivity growth, has been assessed. ICTs' role in digital finance and sustainable development has also been highlighted here. Finally, the book draws conclusions based on the findings in various chapters and identifies the areas where more focus needs to be given to expedite the development outcomes. Though it is somewhat an earlier attempt to assess the digitalization policy in its ten years of inception, the analysis in this book could serve as a basis for further evaluation of digitalization policy as a shifting development strategy in the coming years.

Dhaka, Bangladesh Monzur Hossain

Acknowledgments

The book consists of chapters based on my long-standing research works in the areas of ICTs and knowledge economy. In particular, I use data collected from various surveys conducted by the Bangladesh Institute of Development Studies (BIDS) under my leadership with funding support from the SEIP, JICA, ADB, and others. The datasets are used to generate further knowledge, and interpretations and the findings provided in the book do not necessarily reflect the views of the sponsoring institutions. I sincerely thank them for the data. I also thank BIDS and all the relevant institutions for their support in steering research in these important areas. I also express my sincere gratitude to the BASIS, BCS, BACCO, and ISPAB for providing necessary information and extending their support to us as and when we sought.

I sincerely express my gratitude to Professor Dr. Shamsul Alam, State Minister for the Ministry of Planning, Professor Tetsushi Sonobe, Dean and CEO, Asian Development Bank Institute (ADBI), and Mr. Habibullah N. Karim, former President of BASIS for writing endorsements for this book. Their endorsements will help readers understand the importance of the book. I thank Afrin Mahbub for her excellent research assistance.

My sincere appreciation goes to Sandeep Kaur, Managing Editor of the book, and Hemapriya Eswarth, Project Coordinator, from Palgrave Macmillan for their continuous support in the process of publishing the book.

Finally, I thank my wife Farhana and daughters, Maisara and Mahpara for their encouragement and support while working on this book project.

Contents

About the Author

Monzur Hossain is a Research Director at the Bangladesh Institute of Development Studies (BIDS), Dhaka. He holds a Ph.D. in International Economics from the National Graduate Institute for Policy Studies (GRIPS), Tokyo, Japan. He worked with the Bangladesh Bank (central bank), academia, and research institutes. With extensive research focus on evaluating and analyzing development interventions and economic policies, his area of interests mainly concentrate toward the macro-financial domain. He has also interests in some emerging development issues pertaining to ICTs and knowledge economy, SME development, green finance, and renewable energy. The content of the book draws on his long-standing research works on ICTs and economic growth in Bangladesh. He has published extensively in nationally and internationally accredited journals and he has also to his credit numerous other publications in the forms of research reports and edited volumes. Recently he edited a book titled "Bangladesh's Macroeconomic Policy", which was published by Palgrave Macmillan, in February 2020.

Abbreviations

2SLS	Two-Stage Least Squares
3D	Three Dimensional
4IR	Fourth Industrial Revolution
AC	Assistant Commissioner
ADB	Asian Development Bank
ADP	Annual Development Program
ADR	Advance Deposit Ratio
AEZ	Agro Ecological Zone
AFI	Alliance for Financial Inclusion
AI	Artificial Intelligence
A2I	Access to Information
a2i	Aspire to Innovate
AICC	Agriculture Information and Communication Centre
AIPW	Argued Inverse Probability Weighted
AMIS	Agricultural Market Information System
AMR	Automated Meter Reading
ANU	Active Network Unit
APO	Asian Productivity Organization
ARDL	Autoregressive Distributed Lag
ASEAN	Association of Southeast Asian Nations
ASP	Active Server Pages
ATE	Average Treatment Effect
ATM	Automated Teller Machine
ATT	Average Treatment Effect for the Treated
B2B	Business to Business
B2C	Business to Consumer

BACCO	Bangladesh Association of Call Center & Outsourcing
BASIS	Bangladesh Association of Software and Information Services
BBS	Bangladesh Bureau of Statistics
BCC	Bangladesh Computer Council
BCS	Bangladesh Computer Society
BCS	Bangladesh Computer Samity
BEFTN	Bangladesh Electronic Fund Transfer Network
BGA	Ball Grid Array
BHTPA	Bangladesh Hi-Tech Park Authority
BIDS	Bangladesh Institute of Development Studies
BIID	Bangladesh ICT in Development
BIOS	Basic Input/Output System
BIT	BASIS Institute of Technology
BITM	Bangladesh Association of Software and Information Services Institute of Technology & Management
BNDA	Bangladesh National Digital Architecture
BPO	Business Process Outsourcing
BSCCL	Bangladesh Submarine Cable Company Limited
BSCIC	Bangladesh Small and Cottage Industries Corporation
BSCL	Bangabandhu Satellite Company Limited
BSRS	Bangladesh Shilpa Rin Sangstha
BTCL	Bangladesh Telecommunication Company Limited
BTEB	Bangladesh Technical Education Board
BTRC	Bangladesh Telecommunication Regulatory Commission
BTTB	Bangladesh Telegraph and Telephone Board
BUET	Bangladesh University of Engineering and Technology
C2B	Consumer to Business
C2C	Consumer to Consumer
CAD/CAM	Computer-aided design & computer-aided manufacturing
CAGR	Compound Annual Growth Rate
CCA	Controller of Certifying Authority
CD	Compact Disk
CEO	Chief Executive Officer
CER	Cyber Emergency Response
CISCO	Commercial & Industrial Security Corporation
CMMI	Capability Maturity Model Integration
CMSP	Coastal and Marine Spatial Planning
ComDev	Communication for Development
COVID	Corona Virus Disease
CRS	Constant Returns-to-Scale
CSE	Computer Science and Engineering
CSS	Cascading Style Sheet
CUET	Chattogram University of Engineering and Technology

DAM	Department of Agricultural Marketing
DB	Database
DBA	Database Administrator
DBMS	Database Management System
DC	Deputy Commissioner
DFS	Digital Financial Service
DLMS	Digital Land Management System
DLRS	Department of Land Records and Surveys
DLS	Department of Livestock Services
DOT	Digital Opportunity Task
DSA	Digital Security Act
DSS	Decision Support System
e-Auction	Electronic Auction
EDGE	Enhanced Data for Global Evolution
EEF	Equity and Entrepreneurship Fund
EEF	Equity Entrepreneurship Fund
EFT	Electronic Fund Transfer
EGCD	Esoko Ghana Commodity Index
E-Gov	Electronic Governance
e-Government	Electronic Government
EO	Export Oriented
EOU	Export-Oriented Unit
EPB	Export Promotion Bureau
e-Planning	Electronic Planning
ERP	Enterprise Resource Planning
e-services	Electronic Services
ET LMIS	Ethiopian Livestock Market Information System
EU	European Union
FAO	Food and Agriculture Organisation
FD	Forest Department
FDI	Foreign Direct Investment
FGD	Focus Group Discussion
FINTECH	Financial Technology
FIT	Fashion Institute of Technology
FM	Frequency Modulation
FRRMIS	Flood Risk and Response Management System
FTTX	Fiber to the x
G2C	Government to Citizen
G-8	Group of Eight
GDP	Gross Domestic Product
GIS	Geographic Information System
GMM	Generalized Methods of Moments
GPS	Global Positioning System

GPT	General-Purpose Technology
GSM	Global System for Mobile
GVA	Gross Value-Added
HAL	Hindustan Aeronautics Limited
HIES	Household Income and Expenditure Survey
HMT	Hindustan Machine Tools
HSC	Higher Secondary Certificate
HSPA	High Speed Packet Access
HTML	Hyper Text Markup Language
HTP	Hi-Tech Park
HTP	High Technology Park
IBAB	Institute of Bioinformatics and Applied Biotechnology
ICT	Information and Communication Technology
ICT4D	Information and Communication for Development
ICX	Interconnection Exchange
ID	Identification Document
IDI	ICT Development Index
IDLC	Industrial Development Leasing Company
IHE	International Institute for Hydraulic and Environmental Engineering
IIG	International Internet Gateway
IIMB	Indian Institute of Management-Bangalore
IISc	Indian Institute of Science
ILDTS	International Long Distance Telecommunications Services
IOC	Intergovernmental Oceanographic Commission
iOS	iPhone Operating System
IoT	Internet of Things
IPB	ICT Price Basket
IPCC	Intergovernmental Panel on Climate Change
IPR	Intellectual Property Rights
IPTV	Internet Protocol Television
IPW	Inverse Probability Weighted
ISO	International Organization for Standardization
ISP	Internet Service Provider
ISPAB	Internet Service Provider Association Bangladesh
IT	Information Technology
ITC	International Terrestrial Cable
ITES	Information Technology Enabled Services
ITI	Indian Telephone Industries
ITO	Information Technology Outsourcing
ITO	IT-Outsourcing Market
ITP	Information Technology Park
ITU	International Telecommunication Union

IV	Instrumental Variable
J2ME	Java 2 Platform, Micro Edition
JRC	Jamilur Reza Chowdhury
JSP	Jakarta Server Pages
KPO	Knowledge Process Outsourcing
KUET	Khulna University of Engineering and Technology
LDC	Least Developed Country
LED	Light Emitting Diode
LEDP	Learning and Earning Development Project
LFD	Local Financial Development
LICT	Leveraging Information and Communication Technology
LINUX	Lovable Intellect Not Using XP
LIS	Land Information System
LTE	Long-Term Evolution
M&A	Mergers and Acquisition
M.A.	Master of Arts
MBA	Masters of Business Administration
M.Sc.	Master of Science
MDGs	Millennium Development Goals
MFS	Mobile Financial Service
MGI	McKinsey Global Institute
MIMAP	Micro Impacts of Macroeconomy and Adjustment Policies
MIS	Management Information Systems
MNC	Multinational Corporation
MNO	Mobile Network Operator
MoPTIT	Ministry of Posts, Telecommunications and Information Technology
MS SQL	Microsoft Structured Query Language
MSME	Micro Small and medium-sized Enterprise
MSME	Micro, Small and Medium Enterprise
MSP	Marine Spatial Planning
NCBS	National Centre for Biological Sciences
NCST	National Council for Science and Technology
NDC	National Data Center
NDN	National Data Network
NEO	Non-Export Oriented
NEOU	Non-Export-Oriented Unit
NFC	Near Field Communication
NGO	Non-government Organization
NIIT	National Institute of Information Technology
NIUA	National Institute of Urban Affairs
NIX	National Internet Exchange
NLMIS	National Livestock Market Information System

NRB	Non-resident Bangladeshi
NRI	Network Readiness Index
NTP	National Telecommunication Policy
NTTN	National Telecommunication Transmission Network
NTTN	Nationwide Telecommunication Transmission Network
OCR	Optical Character Recognizer
OECD	Organisation for Economic Co-operation and Development
OFRS	Online Fertilizer Recommendation System
OII	Oxford Internet Institute
OLS	Ordinary Least Square
OPEC	Organisation of the Petroleum Exporting Countries
OTT	Over The Top
P2P	Person-to-person
PC	Personal Computer
PCA	Principal Component Analysis
PKSF	Palli Karma Sahayak Foundation
PM	Prime Minister
PMO	Prime Minister Office
POS	Point-of-sale
PPP	Public–Private Partnership
PROMIS	Procurement Management Information System
PSM	Propensity Score Method
PSTN	Public Switched Telephone Network
R&D	Research and Development
RADP	Revised Annual Development Plan
RBV	Resource Based View
RDD	Regression Discontinuity Design
REER	Real Effective Exchange Rate
RIMS	Resources Information Management System
RMG	Readymade Garments
RPA	Robotic Process Automation
RS	Remote Sensing
RTCC	Real Time Crime Centers
RTHD	Road Transport and Highway Division
RTI	Right to Information
SA	South Asia
SAARC	South Asian Association for Regional Cooperation
SDC	Swiss Agency for Development and Cooperation
SDG	Sustainable Development Goal
SEIP	Skills for Employment Investment Program
SEZ	Specialized Economic Zone
SME	Small and Medium-sized Enterprise
SMI	Survey of Manufacturing Industries

SMS	Short Message Service
SMW	South East Asia–Middle East–Western Europe
SMW-4	South East Asia–Middle East–Western Europe 4
SONAR	Sound Navigation and Ranging
SRDI	Soil Research Development Institute
STEM	Science, Technology, Engineering and Mathematics
STP	Software Technology Park
TBI	Technology Business Incubators
TCV	Total Contract Value
TFP	Total Factor Productivity
TFPG	Total Factor Productivity Growth
TP	Total Productivity
TV	Television
TVET	Technical and Vocational and Education and Training
UAE	United Arab Emirates
UDC	Union Digital Center
UISC	Union Information Service Centers
UK	United Kingdom
UMTS	Universal Mobile Telecommunication System
UN	United Nations
UNDP	United Nations Development Program
UNESCO	The United Nations Educational, Scientific and Cultural Organization
UNIX/UNICS	UNiplexed Information Computing System
UP	Union Parishad
US	United States
USA	United States of America
USAID	United States Agency of International Development
VAT	Value-Added Tax
VFX	Visual Effects
VoIP	Voice over Internet Protocol Services
VSAT	Very Small Aperture Terminal
WaPOR	Water Productivity Open-Access Portal
WARPO	Water Resources Planning Organization
WDM	Wavelength Division Multiplexing
Web.Dev	Web Development
WIMAX	Worldwide Interoperability for Microwave Access
WTO	World Trade Organization
XML	Extensible Markup Language
YoY	Year-Over-Year
YPSA	Young Power in Social Actions

List of Figures

Chapter 6

Chapter 7

Chapter 8

Chapter 9

Chapter 10

Chapter 12

List of Tables

Chapter 4

Chapter 5

Chapter 6

Chapter 7

Chapter 8

Chapter 9

Chapter 10

Chapter 11

Chapter 12

PART I

Digital Bangladesh Vision, Achievements and Policy

CHAPTER 1

Introduction

1 Background

> The ICT revolution fueled by the exponential progress of the semiconductor technology and the accelerated pace of globalization has become an important driver of economic growth across nations. In this rapidly changing landscape, the world economy is entering into a New Economic Order, in which developing Asia led by two fast-growing giant economies, China and India, will have much larger impacts on the world economy. (Jorgensen & Vu, 2016).

Being a close neighbor of India and China, Bangladesh aspires to capitalize on the ICT (Information and Communication Technology) revolution and leapfrog into the next level of development through a "big push" digitalization strategy, namely the "Digital Bangladesh Vision."[1] The digital Bangladesh vision was undertaken in 2009 with a vision to transform the economy into a digital economy by 2021, the year at which the country celebrates its fifty years of age. Under the

[1] The big push theory was initially introduced by P.N. Rosenstein-Rodan (1943) with an argument that a big thrust of a minimum size of investment is needed to overcome the various discontinuities and indivisibilities in the economy and offset the diseconomies of scale. As Bangladesh made a substantial investment and provided policy support to promote the ICT sector and digitalization, the Digital Bangladesh vision is consistent with the Rodan's big push theory.

M. Hossain, *Digital Transformation and Economic Development in Bangladesh*, https://doi.org/10.1007/978-981-19-2753-9_1

Digital Bangladesh Vision, the government made investments in ICT infrastructures, undertook various policies, and developed institutions. Following the IT-based development success stories, Bangladesh undertook significant digitalization efforts as its key development strategy to leapfrog into the middle-income status by 2021 and beyond, which has taken an important place in policy discourse. The digitalization policy of the Bangladesh government may be considered a shifting development strategy—a shift from traditional manufacturing-based development to service and technology-oriented development. In the context of the declining role of RMG, agriculture, and remittance in GDP growth, digitalization could help the country avoid the development trap by enhancing the productivity and efficiency of these sectors of the economy and the IT sector itself. Now the question is, could Bangladesh achieve the intended outcome from digitalization without having an industrial and robust human capital base like India and China? India's and China's experiences may provide a better understanding of the intricacies involved in the digitalization process. The development pathways of ICTs in India and China have some historical perspectives (van Dijk, 2005). An endowment of a robust human capital with a background in science and ICT originated from the need for heavy machine tool industries played a catalytic role in both countries to flourish ICT industries and digitalization processes in the absence of any particular big push strategy. Bangalore is an example (Parthasarathy, 2015). ICTs are considered an important driving force for their "compressed development," involving a dis-integrated and dispersed process of production. From the compressed development point of view, Bangladesh's digitalization policy could be deemed an important development policy.[2]

Historical anecdotes, dictated policy, international success stories, and other related issues could lead to a rethinking of ICT-based development strategy. In this context, the main objective of this book is to make a modest attempt to get the answer to the relevant questions by making a good review and analysis of the digitalization process in Bangladesh.

[2] While Japan and Korea are considered to be a "late development model," China and India are considered to follow a compressed development model. Late development model was based on vertical integration and flying geese pattern, however, compressed model involves a dis-integrated and dispersed process of production. This is why ICTs play an important role in the compressed development model (Whittaker et al., 2010).

Since the Digital Bangladesh Vision appears to be a big push for digitalization, this influential public policy warrants an in-depth analysis. The analysis is expected to serve as a benchmark for future evaluation of the digitalization process in Bangladesh, linking the development outcomes.

The complex and multi-dimensional problems of international development warrant new tools and processes that might contribute to overcoming traditional issues of development. In this context, the role of ICTs in development generates a renewed interest, particularly since the 1990s. Kofi Annan, then United Nations Secretary-General, observed in his Millennium Report, "New technology offers an unprecedented chance for developing countries to 'leapfrog' earlier stages of development. Everything must be done to maximize their peoples' access to new information networks." The underlying essence of this view lies not only in the potential benefits of ICT but also in the risks of being disconnected in this globalized economy. The Digital Opportunity Task (DOT) Force created by the G-8 summit in 2000 underscored the need for "mainstreaming" ICT as an essential component of overall development strategies "as a fundamental tool for reducing poverty and for spurring sustainable development" (Digital Opportunity Task Force, 2002). The digital divide between developed and developing countries and within-country has been increasing in the context of greater digitalization and therefore is getting prominence in development discourse. Then, determining the ICT policies' role in closing that gap is crucial in rethinking overall digitalization and development strategies.

Apart from the benefits accrued by the ICT industry, digitalization itself generates some benefits through internet use. The emergence of the internet at the beginning of the 1990s has opened up a new window for better communications and a host of debates about the costs and benefits of its use. Internet resolves the barriers of geography, leading to "new economic geography." Since ICT products and services can be used irrespective of physical distance and geographical borders, digital transformation could also overcome the barrier of distances (Cairncross & Cairncross, 1997; Quah, 2000). This will allow workers to work from anywhere, which has been evident in the face of the COVID-19 pandemic.[3] On the other side, information technology will reduce the involvement of human resources leading to unemployment jeopardizing

[3] The use of ZOOM and other online meeting and video conferencing platforms has increased manifolds during the Covid-19 pandemic worldwide starting from December

pro-poor development strategies. However, balancing approaches in the new aspect of the digital economy could promote development potentials and harness new development opportunities in more remote and economically lagging regions, leading to inclusive and balanced growth. The potential value of ICT in supporting development can be best ascribed in three underlying aspects (Steinberg, 2003): its inherent strength in bringing new ideas and thoughts generating social capital; its role in facilitating specific development goals; and fostering economic growth. The digital transformation that embraces the internet and information economy, thus, can bring benefits to the economy through several direct and indirect channels (Chavula, 2013; Hossain & Samad, 2020). After ten years of the Digital Bangladesh initiative, the progress made and the outcome achieved are not extraordinary and therefore need rethinking of digitalization strategies for leapfrogging in the years to come.

Though adoption of ICTs could enhance innovation and productivity, it is endogenous to economic growth. However, there are ample shreds of evidence that ICTs contribute to productivity and economic development in many countries, particularly in the postwar economic growth in the United States and elsewhere with appropriate policies. The IT-producing industries contributed 7.6% of postwar economic growth and 32.8% of postwar productivity growth in the USA (Jorgenson et al., 2016). In India, software service exports contributed to 45% of total e-service exports and 3.5% GDP (Erumban & Das, 2016). The McKinsey Report suggested that China is in the midst of a digital revolution, and its Internet economy stood at 3.3% of its GDP (McKinsey Global Institute, 2014). The report further predicted that the phenomenal use of the internet could add 0.3 to 1.0 percentage points to China's GDP growth rate from 2013 to 2025.

Since this book aims to analyze the digitalization policy at the advent of 50 years of independence, the brief development history of the country would be relevant to highlight at the outset. At the advent of 50 years of independence of Bangladesh in 2021, there are many reasons for the country to celebrate, particularly for its impressive and, to some extent, surprising development success. Looking back on history allows one to observe that starting from scratch, with a mere per capita income of about

2019 from Wuhan city of China. The use of ZOOM has increased 30-fold and its participants have increased to more than 300 million per day in virtual meetings. The company expects its revenue to reach more than $1.8b in 2020 (Sherman, 2020).

US$133 in 1971, the country is now dubbed as a development surprise or paradox with per capita income over US$2000 in 2021. The country has exceeded Pakistan, from which it had achieved independence after a nine-month-long bloody war in 1971, in terms of per capita income quite a few years ago, and recently India. It is now a lower-middle-income country and will be graduated in 2026 from LDC (Least Developed Country) status, delayed by two years from the actual year 2024 due to the Covid-19 outbreak. The country's development journey has a long history of deprivation, starting from British colonial rules to the Pakistani regime. The war-torn economy started its journey in 1971 with many problems like chronic poverty, high population growth, low literacy rate, and so on, that had led to pessimism about the country's existence and development. The then US national security adviser, Mr. Henry Kissinger, dubbed Bangladesh as a development "basket case," which became popular in some quarters. However, after 50 years of journey, the country has become a development surprise to many, proving Kissinger and others wrong (Asadullah et al., 2014; Hossain, 2020a, b, c).

Nonetheless, the development narratives of Bangladesh encompass a wide array of factors, including complex political, economic, and social dimensions. Despite political confrontations, the impressive economic progress has been underpinned by necessary but bold institutional reforms and macroeconomic stability. At its fifty years of independence in 2021, various authors and commentators highlight the underlying causes of Bangladesh's impressive growth and development (Basu, 2021; Hossain, 2020a; Mujeri & Mujeri, 2020). The country experienced faster growth in the 1990s and onward after undertaking massive institutional reforms in trade and financial sectors in the late 1980s and 1990s, which coincided with a transition to democracy after defying the military regime of General Hussain Muhammad Ershad in 1991 (Blair, 2020). The reforms undertaken, mainly with the suggestions of multilateral donors, paid off greatly because the country's ownership and interests were taken into cognizance. A gradual decline of the share of agriculture to GDP (Gross Domestic Product) with an increased role of industry and service in GDP reflects the economic transformation of the economy over time (Table 1). It is thought that remittances, RMG (Ready-made Garments) exports, and agricultural modernization with widespread NGO (Non-government Organization) interventions are the key drivers of growth and poverty alleviation, at least until recently with support from macroeconomic stability (Ahsan & Ahsan, 2018; Hossain, 2020a).

However, this book highlights an entirely different aspect—the digitalization approach of the government in the discussion of the country's impressive economic progress, particularly its role in fostering economic growth and development in the last decade.

There is no denying that rising income inequality, the regional disparity with high poverty pockets, the economic vulnerability of people, high concentration of RMG in exports, volatile international markets for migrant workers, high unemployment, weak governance institutions, etc., are some of the factors that pose a greater risk of sustainable development. While analyzing the growth episodes of the country, relatively higher growth in the 1990s and 2000s is thought to be the result of trade and financial reforms undertaken in the preceding decades (Hossain, 2020a). The decade of 2010 saw even higher GDP growth hovering over 7% without notable reforms. Moreover, the share of remittances, RMG exports, and agriculture in GDP has been declining over time with the growing importance of domestic-market targeted industries and service sectors in the economy. Total factor productivity appears to be increasing in this decade, with a growth rate of capital at 7% or more (Ahmed & Chowdhury, 2019). The economy's extraordinary performance in the last two decades is not just a paradox, rather is intrigued by some aspects that have not been fully unearthed yet. First, sound macroeconomic management and consequently long-term macroeconomic stability in terms of stable inflation, fiscal sustainability, and viable external sector are some of the contributing factors to these fascinating growth outcomes. Second,

Table 1 Some selected economic indicators

	GDP growth rate (%)	*Agriculture*		*Industry*		*Service*	
		Growth rate (%)	*Share to GDP (%)*	*Growth rate (%)*	*Share to GDP (%)*	*Growth rate (%)*	*Share to GDP (%)*
1972–1980	1.8	0.2	52.8	7.6	13.8	3.2	33.1
1981–1990	4	2.5	32	5.8	20.2	3.6	45.5
1991–2000	4.6	3.0	25.8	7.0	22.4	4.2	47.7
2001–2010	5.6	4.2	18.8	7.5	23.8	5.6	52.6
2011–2020	6.9	3.5	14.6	10.2	27.0	6.2	53.3

Source World Development Indicator, World Bank

political stability with a one-party regime provides some leeway of policy continuity with aspirations for mega infrastructure investments, which is another factor that may be consistent with the development pathways of the emerging Asian miracle economies in the earlier 1980s and 1990s (World Bank, 1993). Third, the adoption of massive digitalization under the "Digital Bangladesh Vision 2021" as a "shifting development strategy" since 2009 in the context of gradually declining importance of traditional sectors, such as the readymade garments, leather, etc., as the growth-driving sectors, to leapfrog into the next level of development.

The digitalization and associated investments in ICT infrastructure might have contributed to the incremental GDP growth in the 2010s and onward. How much digital transformation has taken place? What is its contribution to accelerating growth and development? What are the challenges that Bangladesh has been facing in its digitalization endeavors? What are the missing links that apprehend better outcomes of digitalization? These are pertinent questions that are aimed to be addressed in this book. This book makes a modest attempt to analyze these issues that have come up as of late, in the context of the policy shift toward the digital transformation of the economy with a focus on underlying benefits that this policy shift could have brought to the economy.

2 Organization of the Book

The book has 14 chapters. Chapter 1 highlights the context of the digitalization policy of the government, and discusses why and how this policy could serve as a shifting development strategy. It also gives an overview of the book highlighting the contents of the chapters. Chapter 2 discusses theoretical and conceptual issues on how digitalization could contribute to faster economic growth and help a country leapfrog to its next level of development. Chapter 3 provides an overview of the Digital Bangladesh Vision, highlighting various activities and investments undertaken to achieve Digital Bangladesh. Moreover, it reviews the achievements made so far toward the digital transformation. Chapter 4 is dedicated to reviewing the existing ICT policies and institutional and regulatory frameworks to achieve big push digitalization with affordable and safe access to ICT services. The chapter also provides a preface on Software Technology parks or Hi-Tech Parks to facilitate investments in IT and promote IT entrepreneurs. It also highlights the policies for human capital development, including the Skills for Employment Investment Program, and the significance to a2i, which supports research and technical provision, with the help of the ICT institutions and associations built to assist the development of information technology in Bangladesh. Chapter 5 provides an assessment of the current state of the IT and ITES sector. It gives a brief prelude to the IT industry, including the different sub-sectors that make up the IT industry, such as IT-enabled services, ISPs, call centers, the ICT hardware sector. Finally, the chapter discusses the challenges that persist in the IT sector, such as lack of a skilled workforce, limited access to finance, and problems related to IPR, foreign exchange regulations, and taxes.

Chapter 6 highlights the access, awareness, and perceived demand for IT services in rural households. Apart from the connectivity status in the rural areas, the chapter continues its outlook on the existing demand for e-information by rural households, such as information about agriculture, weather, education, health, employment, and government services or policies. Finally, the chapter provides an assessment of the facilities provided by the Union Digital Centre in rural areas. Chapter 7 provides a detailed analysis of the performance and productivity of the ICT service sector in the country. The chapter highlights firm growth theory and the fundamental features of the ICT firms in Bangladesh, followed by an econometric analysis of the IT firms' productivity, including their performance and dynamic capabilities. Chapter 8 analyzes the theoretical underpinning of the cluster-based ICT sector development policy and provides an international viewpoint highlighting Silicon Valley and Bangalore IT parks as examples of IT ecosystems. Highlighting the global experiences, the chapter highlights the challenges and opportunities of cluster-based ICT sector development in Bangladesh. Chapter 9 evaluates employment, the labor market, and the skills gap in the ICT sector. The chapter begins by highlighting the current status of the ICT labor market and the demand for IT professionals in various other sectors. It also provides insight into the contribution of women in the ICT sector and how occupations are distributed among IT professionals with additional dimensions regarding average wage and age, job switching patterns, and job placement of IT professionals. It signifies the shortage in skills in the ICT sector, followed by recommendations to mitigate the problem in question, and discusses that despite the growing demand, supply for IT professionals is limited, highlighting the level of IT education and training in Bangladesh.

Chapter 10 examines the transformative role of digitization on various sectors, including the service sector, manufacturing sector, and six other sectors in terms of productivity gains and GDP growth. It also provides insight into the efforts made to digitalize the agriculture, livestock, and fisheries sector and the effect of digitalization on job losses. Chapter 11 provides an analysis of SME innovations, market access, and consequent productivity through the adoption of ICTs and the complementary role of local financial development in improving the productivity and innovations of smaller firms. It includes an econometric analysis on the linkage between the local financial development and the firm's innovation and market access. Chapter 12 provides a theoretical discussion on the impact of digitalization on Total Factor Productivity and economic growth while providing a wide array of literature that correlates ICT development and its growth-enhancing effect on an economy. It also provides an empirical analysis for Bangladesh to assess the contribution of both ICT-producing and using sectors to the country's GDP. It highlights that ICTs significantly contribute to TFP growth in Bangladesh in the decade of 2010 onward.

Chapter 13 discusses the role of ICT in sustainable development in Bangladesh. It highlights the application of ICTs in the environment and natural disaster management and the preservation of natural resources, including the various ways ICTs can aid individuals, particularly those living in vulnerable areas, to adapt to climate change. It also highlights the usage of ICT in conserving biodiversity and ecosystem along with urban development. Finally, based on the discussions and findings of the chapters, Chapter 14 concludes that digital transformation is at the early stage with various policy and regulatory bottlenecks in place. Therefore, a rethinking of digitalization strategies is needed to facilitate the digital transformation to enhance economic outcomes through better use of ICTs by firms and individuals. The analysis in the book on the "big push" digitalization approach could serve as the basis for future research to gauge the impact of digital transformation on the economy in the coming days clearly and succinctly.

Appendix

See Table 2.

Table 2 Key macroeconomic indicators of Bangladesh, 1972–2020

Indicators/Year	*1972–1980*	*1981–1990*	*1991–2000*	*2001–2010*	*2011–2020*
Real GDP growth rate (%)	1.76	4.02	4.68	5.58	6.89
Tax revenue as % of GDP	–	–	–	7.14	8.76
Total government expenditure as % of GDP	4.78	4.22	4.78	5.15	5.61
Worker's remittance as % of GDP	0.97	2.70	3.15	7.14	7.67
Export as % of GDP	5.30	5.16	9.92	14.67	17.53
Imports as % of GDP	13.70	13.22	15.18	20.18	24.33
Trade as % of GDP	19.00	18.39	25.10	34.85	41.85
Current account balance as % of GDP	−3.01	−2.25	−0.38	0.90	−0.07
Inflation %		7.36	5.30	6.40	6.64
Infant mortality rate	142.04	115.72	79.34	48.73	30.86
Secondary enrollment rate	15.53	18.30	44.50	46.50	58.00
Poverty rate			48.90	35.75	24.3

Source Bangladesh Bank and Ministry of Finance

References

Ahmed, M., & Chowdhury, T. T. (2019). Total factor productivity in Bangladesh: An analysis using data from 1981 to 2014. *Bangladesh Development Studies, 42*(1).

Ahsan, S. M., & Ahsan, S. Q. (2018). One sunshine doth not a harvest market: An examination of the growth momentum in Bangladesh. *Bangladesh Development Studies, 41*(4).

Asadullah, N., Savoia, A., & Mahmud, W. (2014). Paths to development: Is There a Bangladesh surprise? *World Development, 62*, 138–154.

Basu, K. (2021, April 25). *Bangladesh at 50*. Project Syndicate. https://www.project-syndicate.org/commentary/bangladesh-independence-three-reasons-for-economic-success-by-kaushik-basu-2021-03

Blair, H. (2020). The Bangladesh Paradox. *Journal of Democracy, 31*(4), 138–150.

Bukht, R., & Heeks, R. (2017). *Defining, conceptualizing, and measuring the digital economy.* (Development Informatics Working Paper 68). Centre for Development Informatics Global Development Institute, SEED—University of Manchester.

Cairncross, F., & Cairncross, F. (1997). *The death of distance: How the communications revolution will change our lives.* (p. 302). Harvard Business School Press.

Chavula, H. K. (2013). Telecommunications development and economic growth in Africa. *Information Technology for Development, 19*(1), 5–23.

Digital Opportunity Task Force. (2002). *Digital opportunities for all: Meeting the challenge.* https://www.g7.utoronto.ca/summit/2002kananaskis/dotforce_reportcard.pdf

Erumban, A. A., & Das, D. K. (2016). Information and communication technology and economic growth in India. *Telecommunications Policy, 40*(5), 412–431.

Hossain, M. (2020a, October 16). Macroeconomic stability and economic resilience keep growth momentum afloat. *The Business Standard.* https://www.tbsnews.net/analysis/macroeconomic-stability-economic-resilience-keep-growth-momentum-afloat-146002

Hossain, M. (2020b). *Macroeconomic policy, economic growth and poverty reduction in bangladesh: An overview* (M. Hossain, Ed.). Palgrave Macmillan.

Hossain, M. (2020c). Trade liberalization policies and trade performances in Bangladesh: An empirical evaluation. In M. Hossain (Ed.), *Bangladesh's macroeconomic policy* (pp. 241–265). Palgrave Macmillan.

Hossain, M., & Samad, H. (2020). Mobile phones, household welfare, and women's empowerment: Evidence from rural off-grid regions of Bangladesh. *Information Technology for Development, 27*(2), 191–207.

Jorgenson, D. W., & Vu, K. M. (2016). The ICT revolution, world economic growth, and policy issues. *Telecommunications Policy, 40*(5), 383–397.

Jorgenson, D. W., Mun, S. H., & Samuels, J. D. (2016). The impact of information technology on postwar US economic growth. *Telecommunications Policy, 40*(5), 398–411.

McKinsey Global Institute. (2014, July). *China's digital transformation: The Internet's impact on productivity and growth.*

Mujeri, M. K., & Mujeri, N. (2020). *Bangladesh at fifty: Moving beyond development traps.* Springer International Publishing.

Parthasarathy, B. (2015). The ICT service industry in Bangalore, India. In H. Hirakawa, K. Lal, S. Naoko, & N. Tokumaru (Eds.), *Servitization, IT-ization and innovation models: Two-stage industrial cluster theory.* Routledge.

Rosenstein-Rodan, P. N. (1943). Problems of industrialisation of Eastern and South-Eastern Europe. *Economic Journal, 53*(210/211), 202–211.

Quah, J. K. H. (2000). The monotonicity of individual and market demand. *Econometrica, 68*(4), 911–930.

Sherman, N. (2020). Zoom sees sales boom amid pandemic. *BBC News*. https://www.bbc.com/news/business-52884782

Steinberg, J. (2003). Information technology and development: Beyond either/or. *Brookings Review, 21*(2).

Van Dijk, M. P. (2005). India-China: A battle of two new ICT giants. In A. Saith & M. Vijayabaskar (Eds), *ICTs and Indian economic development: Economy, work, regulation*. (pp. 441–459). Sage Publications Ltd.

Whittaker, D. H., Zhu, T. B., Sturgeon, T., Tsai, M. H., & Okita, T. (2010). Compressed development. *Studies in Comparative International Development, 45*(4), 439–467.

World Bank. (1993). *The East Asian miracle*. Oxford University Press.

CHAPTER 2

Digitalization and Economic Development: Policy, Context, and Theoretical Issues

1 What Do We Understand by Digitalization?

Digitalization is a process of transforming an economy into a digital and knowledge economy that must embark on a massive adoption of digital technology in the productions and services. Digital transformation, to be precise, is a combined process of generating, sharing, and transferring information with support from telecommunications networks, computer technologies, software engineering, and so on (Mićić, 2017). As Piazalo (2001) defines,

> a digital economy is an economy where both final output and intermediate input increasingly consist of information and where the modern (digital) ICT increasingly provide worldwide immediate access to any information made available. These new technologies might have the potential to enable an increase in the productivity of conventional business practices but also facilitate the establishment of new processes and products. Consequently, the evolution of the digital economy should not be considered as being restricted to the information sector, but as a far-reaching process that might alter and extend the products and production processes within the whole economy. (Piazolo, 2001, p. 30)

A narrow and broad perspective of the digital economy can be assessed from Fig. 1. The development of software, hardware, telecommunications, and information services will lead to the platform, sharing, and

M. Hossain, *Digital Transformation and Economic Development in Bangladesh*, https://doi.org/10.1007/978-981-19-2753-9_2

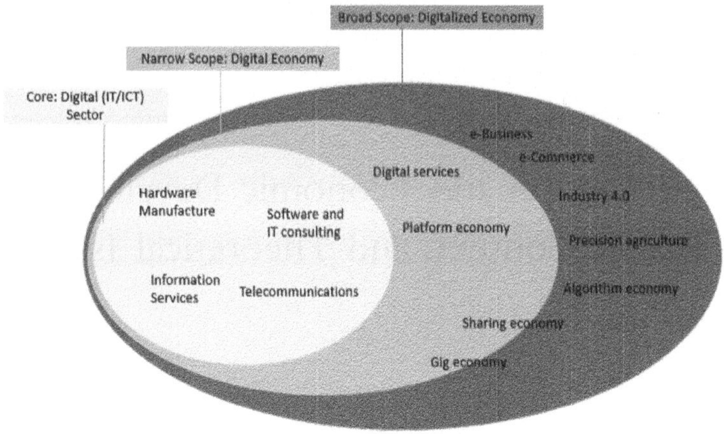

Fig. 1 Scopes of the digital economy (*Source* Bukht and Heeks [2017: 13])

the gig economy.[1] However, such a development will lead to a broader scope of the digital economy through e-business, e-commerce, industry 4.0, algorithm economy, etc. These are the pathways through which a transformation toward the digital economy might occur. Note that digitalization is a broader concept encompassing both ICT-producing and using sectors and services, which depends on many factors and is challenging to achieve in a short-term period.

2 The Digitalization Context of Economic Development

The context of digitalization should be perceived in multi-dimensional aspects that might foster the economic development of a country. Creating scopes for further digitalization is the key to materializing the digital economy. The essential elements of digitalization include:

[1] Gig economy is when individuals are paid for each project they take up rather than being compensated for on an hourly basis such as Information Technology (IT)-based projects and freelancing. Sharing economy enables individuals to rent out the assets they hold to others, such as Uber and Pathao (Gotley, 2020). Platform economy is the use of digital platforms to conduct digital interactions between individuals and businesses through the internet, such as OTT (Over The Top) media contents (Chan, 2018).

improving people's access to computers, mobile phones, particularly the smartphone, internet connectivity, useful online content, incentives for automation, and digitalization of private sector industries and services are essential to enhancing the maximum benefits of digitalization efforts. The key factors crucial for the ICTs' growth and development are highlighted briefly.

(i) **ICT infrastructure**: The government has to build the infrastructure required to connect most of the population and create opportunities to use the internet and digital content for broader economic development. This aspect includes policy, regulations, and incentives for both ICT firms and end-users.

(ii) **ICT industry development**: Private sector, mainly the ICT industry, has to deliver required services and products affordably. The development of the ICT industry and the export of e-services is thus essential for the country's leapfrogging to the next level of development. Innovations and productivity are critical aspects for the further development of the ICT industry.

(iii) **ICT human capital development**: Human capital is the primary input for developing ICTs. Therefore, to develop the ICT industry and attract FDIs (Foreign Direct Investment) in this sector, the existing skills constraints, such as the lack of adequate skills and skill mismatch, need to be identified. For that matter, a proper strategy for mitigating skills constraints need to be devised. The following three issues are important for skills development: an assessment of the current level of skills and the gap in terms of availability and quality; the supply-side capacity of the academic and training institutions to mitigate the skills gap; and emerging need in new areas of ICTs such as internet of things (IoT), artificial intelligence (AI), Robotics, etc.

3 Linking Digital Transformation to Economic Growth: Direct and Indirect Channels

The strength of ICT in fostering economic growth and development is well documented. ICT-supported sectors facilitate the growth of an economy through innovation and productivity. Digital transformation works through direct and indirect channels to foster GDP growth and development. Internet enhances transparency and competition that can lower prices and increase the quality of goods. The resulting savings improve welfare by enhanced consumption. ICTs can bring broader benefits to society by increasing social capital and enabling the government to deliver public services more efficiently.

Bangladesh has the potential to gain from the ICT industry with a widespread manifestation of this sector. Therefore, the industry could find its place in its key development strategies. The availability of trained and educated human capital and cheaper technologies are additional advantages for this sector to grow and overall economic growth. The investment and services from the adoption of ICTs and a more comprehensive broader application of ICTs might increase total factor productivity through increased efficiency of the capital that might contribute to higher economic growth.

There are at least two indirect channels through which ICTs contribute to growth. Firstly, ICTs increase economic efficiency and social capital and enhance financial inclusion; secondly, it improves productivity through innovations. The direct channels that contribute to economic growth and development are straightforward. The channels include (i) investment in ICT infrastructure, (ii) use of ICT in manufacturing, and (iii) products and services generated by the ICT industry. The channels are schematically shown in Fig. 2. A detailed discussion on the above direct and indirect channels is given below to understand these channels better.

3.1 Indirect Channels

(i) **Economic Efficiency, Social Capital, and Financial Inclusion**

The indirect channels by which ICT can influence growth and development could be attributed to at least three types of factors: (a) transaction cost and economic efficiency, (b) financial inclusion, and (c) information network and social capital. The use of mobile phones, the internet, and software reduces transaction costs and increases economic efficiencies leading to income gain of the households and firms from using ICTs. The second channel, financial inclusion through fintech, such as mobile financial services (MFS), allows firms and households to receive remittances, transfer and save money that broadly enhances access to finance affordably and quickly. Various studies suggest that such a role of

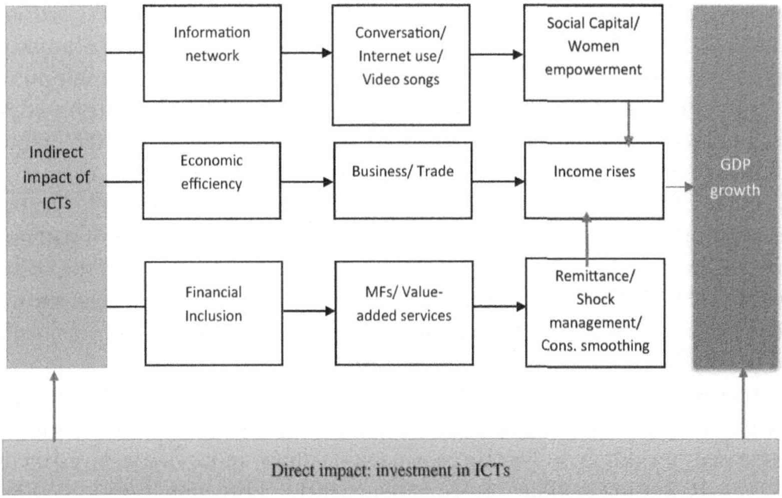

Fig. 2 A theoretical framework for understanding channels of ICT benefits (*Source* Modified from Hossain and Samad [2020])

fintech helps enhance the shock-absorbing capacities, including consumption smoothing leading to poverty alleviation (Jack et al., 2013; Murshid et al., 2020).

Information networks can help bring ideas and experience to even the most isolated community. As Hossain and Samad (2020) showed, rural households handicapped by physical infrastructure could benefit enormously from mobile phones and the internet. They can make a video call to their migrant family members outside the country, receive remittances quickly, and also connect to the mainland easily for any of their needs. ICT can also empower individuals and women, in particular, to participate in the social and political institutions of their community, as they can earn money, make many family decisions, and raise voices (Hossain & Samad, 2020).

(ii) **Productivity Gains Through Innovations**

ICT is often termed the General-Purpose technology (GPT), a new technology that changes the economy at micro and macro levels, ranging from production to policy. As a GPT, ICT also facilitates innovations in the production process that lead to productivity enhancements (Cardona et al., 2013). Ayyagari et al. (2011) observed from an enterprise survey of over 19,000 firms across 47 countries that imitation and adaptation of already-created and tested innovations benefit more than the cutting-edge technological innovations. A study in Bangladesh among 1200 manufacturing SMEs (Small and Medium-sized Enterprise) finds that ICT facilitates firms in undertaking simple training programs to sophisticated innovation activities, such as replacement of inputs, acquisition of patents, trademarks, and so on to remain competitive and productive in the niche market (INSPIRED survey, 2013). Firm-level studies have also shown that firms with high levels of ICT are more likely to grow and less likely to go out of business (Reenen et al., 2010).

Various studies show that ICT capital has a greater impact on productivity than non-ICT capital. For example, investment in ICT capital increased productivity by three to eight times more than investment in non-ICT capital (Plice & Kraemer, 2001). Hitt and Tambe (2006) showed that investments in ICTs generated spillover benefits about twofold. ICT's impact on productivity is partially due to its GPT nature, manifested in productivity benefits and spillovers (Rincon et al., 2013).

Apart from firm-level evidence, the adoption of ICTs has increased countries' productivity. For example, the United States. Between 1995 and 2002, ICT caused two-thirds of total factor productivity growth in the United States, and the development of labor productivity can also be attributed to ICT (OECD, 2004). Recent studies have found that approximately one-third of U.S. growth over that period is attributable to adopting ICT by organizations (Byrne et al., 2013).

Further, ICT-based solutions have already proved their value in addressing some Millennium Development Goals (MDGs) and supporting Sustainable Development Goals (SDGs). For example, in many countries, online health support is provided using an online health system in remote rural areas. Distance learning initiatives are another example of providing education to underserved and distant pupils. Similarly, Agriculture-based apps help farmers with the proper use of pesticides, seeds, and soil quality in many countries, including Bangladesh. What is important is to make these services accessible and cost-effective for poor people.

3.2 Direct Channels

(i) **Investment in ICT Infrastructure**

ICT can significantly contribute to economic growth and development by increasing investment in ICT infrastructures, manufacturing ICT products (hardware and software), and enhancing overall productivity. Recent evidence suggests that it can contribute significantly to economic growth (Erumban & Das, 2016; Jorgensen & Vu, 2016; Toader et al., 2018). ICT can improve total productivity by helping local producers develop networks with global markets. Estonia is an example that succeeded in achieving development objectives by promoting ICTs in its development strategies. A recent study analyzing the positive impact of access to mobile phones on income in rural Bangladesh has helped improve our understanding of how ICTs can contribute to overall development (Hossain & Samad, 2020).

(ii) **ICT Industry Development**

The ICT industry's importance[2] is widely recognized as a vehicle for achieving rapid growth and development of a country through technological advancement and innovation. ICTs help the services and manufacturing sectors that foster economic growth. The rapid expansion of telecommunication and reducing its costs over the last two decades facilitates ICT services from a remote location. Consequently, it has led to the emergence of the offshore/outsourcing industry. As a result, developing countries capture a bigger share of outsourcing activities, taking advantage of the ICT sector (such as computer, software, and internet) that is relatively cheaper and easier to absorb. The most important input for this sector is the IT-skilled labor force, which is also abundant in developing countries. This allows firms in low-income economies to build capabilities

[2] ICT is an umbrella term that includes "any communication device or application, encompassing radio, television, cellular phones, computer and network hardware and software, satellite systems, and so on, as well as the various services and applications associated with them, such as videoconferencing and distance learning." According to the OECD (Organization for Economic Co-operation and Development), ICT in manufacturing and service industry means that the industry must either perform information processing and communications by electronic means or use electronic processing to measure or control a physical process (OECD, 2003).

in outsourcing activities faster. The discussion here points to the fact that the development of the ICT sector depends at least on three factors: (i) IT infrastructure; (ii) human capital with specific ICT skills; and (iii) strategic alliance and networking ability of the firms, which can be facilitated by IT parks. However, we should not forget that these are not only the factors that can help a country achieve the desired goal; rather, as international experiences suggest, ICT sector development requires tailor-made strategies taking country advantages in cognizance, and only then a country perhaps could succeed in grabbing the benefits of digitalization.

4 Digital Bangladesh Vision: A Big Push for Digitalization

The theoretical discussion in the previous sections provides insight into how proper digitalization could help developing countries leapfrog to the next level of development. What is important is to have appropriate policies and appropriate investments in place. Inspired by the successes of some neighboring developing countries like India and China, the Bangladesh government, led by the Bangladesh Awami League, has undertaken a massive digitalization strategy called "the digital Bangladesh Vision program" in 2009 to push the digitalization of the economy as a shifting development strategy to achieve middle-income status expeditiously. By far, the digital Bangladesh vision is conceived as a big push for digitalization. Therefore, the government has made substantial investments in developing IT infrastructures, related institutions, IT parks, and formulating many more relevant policies. One of the objectives of this book is to evaluate the policies whether they are placed in the right direction and the intended outcomes are on track.

The digitalization process aimed at (i) ensuring 100% internet penetration among the populace; (ii) promoting public–private partnership for launching various e-services in the area of health, education, employment creation, and human rights mainly for the marginalized rural people; (iii) ensuring ICT literacy among the population; (iv) promote the ICT industry through infrastructure and policy; (vi) promoting e-commerce and automation of financial sector, and (vii) transferring into e-governance or mass digitization of government services. The targets, however, are set to embrace the characteristics of both the information and the internet economy that facilitate the products and processes with greater efficiency.

Within the broader scope of the digital economy, the digital Bangladesh vision sets four goals: connecting citizens, e-governance (e-governance is the complete digitization of the administrative and service wing of the government), human resource development, and ICT industry development. Except for e-governance, the other three goals are related to ICT infrastructure development and inputs of ICTs. E-governance is one of the outcomes of ICTs that could enhance public service delivery mechanisms. In this context, a brief account of digitalization in Bangladesh is briefly given below to understand the progress of the ongoing digitalization process.

Firstly, infrastructure in internet connectivity has been upgraded and enhanced to a great extent over the last few years. Bangladesh was connected with its second submarine cable network in 2017 that had significantly improved the country's bandwidth capacity, and is in the process of connecting with third submarine cables. 3G and 4G technologies have been adopted already, and the adoption of 5G is underway to enhance mobile internet connectivity. Almost 100 percent mobile phone teledensity has been achieved to date (though unique-subscription rate is lower). The government has developed over 5000 Digital Centres across the country at Union Parishads to provide various digital services to the citizens at the rural level (ICT Division, 2019). Bangladesh has so far issued over 100 million digital IDs (Identity) to citizens. Though these are essential investments in ICT infrastructure, the performance is poor in last-mile connectivity. Limited broadband connectivity at the mufassil and rural areas creates a digital divide because of higher prices and less reliability of mobile broadband internet. Bangladesh has made significant strides in fintech with great success in mobile financial services (MFS) since 2011. With the advancements in investments in internet connectivity, Bangladesh made considerable progress in the percentage of the population using the internet, from about 5% in 2012 to 24.8% in 2020, however, the country lags behind of its neighboring countries: India (34.5%), China (54.3%), and Asia (43%) (according to ITU statistics based on World Development Indicators, 2020).

Secondly, the government has developed the National Portal in 2014, which now houses over 45,000 websites and services of different government offices. Bangladesh National Digital Architecture has been developed to initiate interoperability. A Digital

Service Accelerator has been established to expedite and facilitate the e-services of all Ministries. The government has launched an e-nothi (e-notes) facility, a digital (paperless process) e-filing platform for storing, viewing, and sharing files among different levels of the government that has been instrumental for expeditious decision-making with more transparency and accountability. The online public procurement process (e-tender process) has been initiated to bring transparency and accountability to the public procurement process. These e-government services have facilitated government activities during the lockdown and afterward in the Covid-19 pandemic. Despite these developments, Bangladesh ranked 115th out of 193 countries with its e-Government Development Index value of 0.4862, remaining in the medium and low score groups (ICT Division, 2019). This questions the proper utilization of digital facilities and the accrued benefits of the facilities developed so far.

Thirdly, the development of the ICT industry, which includes Information Technology (IT) and Information Technology Enabled Service (ITES), has gained momentum with massive investments in ICT infrastructure. Currently, over 2000 IT firms have been employing about 50,000 IT professionals and exporting ICT products/services worth US$1 billion annually. The ICT industry as a whole, including ISPAB (Internet Service Provider Association, Bangladesh), call centers, MNOs (Mobile Network Operator), Hardware, and so on, employs about 0.30 million IT professionals. To make the ICT sector a driving force for leapfrogging, the ICT industry needs to capture a certain amount of global offshore businesses, ICT-cloud businesses, and effective use of ICTs in related industry development such as semiconductor, electrical, and electronics industries. Only application-based software development, which is now dominant, would not be enough to transform the sector into a game-changer one.

Finally, as human capital is the backbone of ICTs, various programs have been undertaken under the digital Bangladesh program to increase skills in information technologies. So far, over 65,000 IT-ITES professionals have been trained under multiple programs (ICT division, 2019). According to Oxford Internet Institute, Bangladesh has the second-largest pool of online workers in the world (Lehdonvirta, 2017). An unofficial estimate of BASIS (Bangladesh Association of Software and Information Services) suggests that about 0.65

million freelancers from Bangladesh are working in the outsourcing industry worldwide. Specialized labs have been established in 130 universities to create a dedicated talent pool. However, there exists a substantial skills gap and mismatch among the IT professionals in Bangladesh (Hossain, 2016). Through various programs to mitigate the gap between industry and academia in finding the right mix of the curriculum is underway with the help of private sectors and donors, the flow of quality human capital is still a big concern for the whole digitalization process. On top of that, the focus should now be on developing training and education programs on promising future technologies: IoT (Internet of Things), Blockchain, Artificial Intelligence, Big Data Analytics (ICT Division, 2019), and so on.

The progress on connectivity and other ICT indicators over the last decade has been phenomenal (Table 1). The increase in mobile phone penetration has been significant during 2000–2010, which further incremented to consequential peaks, 103% in 2020 (the ratio includes duplicate SIMs). However, in the case of internet connectivity, good progress has been made as the percentage of people connected to the internet has increased from 5% in 2012 to around 25% in 2020. Though the progress is satisfactory, it is not enough to create a significant impact on the internet economy. Therefore, both access to the internet and value-creation from internet use is critical for gaining benefits from the digital economy.

Table 1 Some selected ICT indicators for Bangladesh, 2000–2020

Outcome	*1995–1999*	*2000*	*2012*	*2020*
Internet connectivity (% of the population using the internet)	–	–	5.0	24.8
Mobile phone penetration (per 100 inhabitants)	0.04	0.2	64.36	103.31
Fixed broadband subscription	–	–	600,461	9,521,970
Secure internet servers (per 1 million people)	–	–	0.73	140.17
Number of submarine cables connected	0	0	1	2

Source ITU statistics based on World Development Indicators, World Bank

5 Conclusions

Digital Bangladesh has now become a buzzword of development in the development discourse of Bangladesh. This is, therefore, an influential policy agenda that needs to be evaluated succinctly. Bangladesh is poised to become a digital economy by exploiting its abundant pool of talented youths (with the virtue of its demographic dividend), favorable policy diffusions, and appropriate technological skills. Nonetheless, ICTs can make the best use of the country's youth population to foster economic growth through at least three channels: (i) increasing efficiencies in product and process development by reducing transaction costs reinforcing the "death of distance"; (ii) facilitating innovations through the adoption of software and information technologies that assist productivity gains across the board, which contribute to total factor productivity and hence higher economic growth; and (iii) developing IT industry with a skilled labor force that can capture a part of growing outsourcing businesses from the developed world with low-cost labor advantage.

It is true that low-income countries like Bangladesh have comparative advantages to gain from adopting ICTs and outsourcing IT and ITeS activities. Though Bangladesh made a sizeable investment in ICT infrastructure development, the digitalization process suffers from inadequate skilled human capital. Moreover, low levels of digital literacy, poverty, and to some extent, digital inequality are some of the bottlenecks for achieving digitalization at an expected level. Theoretically, it is easier for developing countries to build the necessary digitalization capabilities faster with affordable costs; in reality, all the countries invested in ICTs could not succeed equally. For example, the innovative activities and policies that helped Japan develop do not work nowadays for China and India (Lei & Dongsheng, 2013). These countries adopt new innovative strategies and policies. Therefore, homegrown innovative policies and strategies would be required to gain from the digitalization policy of the country.

References

Asian Development Bank. (2019). *Computer and software engineering tertiary education in 2018.*

Athreye, S. S. (2005). *The Indian software industry.* Oxford University Press.

Ayyagari, M., Demirgüç-Kunt, A., & Maksimovic, V. (2011). Firm innovation in emerging markets: The role of finance, governance, and competition. *Journal of Financial and Quantitative Analysis, 46*(6), 1545–1580.

Bukht, R., & Heeks, R. (2017). *Defining, conceptualizing, and measuring the digital economy* (Development Informatics Working Paper 68). Centre for Development Informatics Global Development Institute, SEED—University of Manchester.

Byrne, D. M., Oliner, S. D., & Sichel, D. E. (2013). *Is the information technology revolution over?* (FEDS Working Paper No. 2013–36). Divisions of Research and Statistics and Monetary Affairs. Federal Reserve Board.

Cardona, M., Kretschmer, T., & Strobel, T. (2013). ICT and productivity: Conclusions from the empirical literature. *Information Economics and Policy, 15*(3), 109–112.

Chan, D. (2018). *The rise of the platform economy*. Deloitte.

Erumban, A. A., & Das, D. K. (2016). Information and communication technology and economic growth in India. *Telecommunications Policy, 40*(5), 412–431.

Everest Group. (2017). *Betting on the future-The Bangladesh IT-ITeS industry is poised for growth*. Everest Group Research.

Gotley, I. (2020, July 22). *What's the difference between Gig economy and Sharing economy?* Spacer. https://www.spacer.com.au/blog/whats-the-difference-between-the-gig-economy-and-the-sharing-economy

Hossain, M. (2016). *Labor market and skills gap in the ICT sector in Bangladesh: An exploratory study*. Bangladesh Institute of Development Studies.

Hossain, M., & Samad, H. (2020). Mobile phones, household welfare, and women's empowerment: evidence from rural off-grid regions of Bangladesh. *Information Technology for Development, 27*(2), 1–17.

ICT Division. (2019). *e-Government master plan for digital Bangladesh*. Bangladesh ICT Division, Government of Bangladesh.

INSPIRED. (2013, June). *The survey of manufacturing SME sector in Bangladesh*. Mott MacDonald, The INSPIRED Bangladesh.

International Telecommunication Union. (2018). *Measuring the information society report volume 2*. ITU Publications.

Jack, W., Ray, A., & Suri, T. (2013). Transaction networks: Evidence from mobile money in Kenya. *American Economic Review, 103*(3), 356–361.

Jorgenson, D. W., & Vu, K. M. (2016). The ICT revolution, world economic growth, and policy issues. *Telecommunications Policy, 40*(5), 383–397.

Lehdonvirta, V. (2017). *Where are online workers located? The international division of digital gig work*. Oxford Internet Institute.

Lei, S., & Dongsheng, G. (2013). The change of the development model and its impact on innovative activity. In Hirakawa et al. (Eds.), *Servitization, IT-ization and Innovation models: Two-stage industrial cluster theory*. Routledge.

Mićić, L. (2017). Digital transformation and its influence on GDP. *Economics, 5*(2), 135–147.

Murshid, K. A. S., Khandker, S., Ali, K. S., Samad, H., & Hossain, M. (2020). *Impact of mobile financial services in Bangladesh: The case of bKash*. Bangladesh Institute of Development Studies.

OECD. (2003). *Information, Communication Technology (ICT) goods*. Organization of Economic Cooperation and Development (OECD).

OECD. (2004). *The economic impact of ICT: Measurement*. OECD Publishing.

Piazolo, D. (2001). Multilateral and European responses to e-commerce. *European Integration online Papers (EIoP), 5*(4).

Plice, R. K., & Kraemer, K. L. (2001). *Measuring payoffs from information-technology investments: New evidence from sector level data on developed and developing countries*. Center for Research on Information Technology and Organizations.

Reenen, J. V., Bloom, N., Draca, M., Kretschmer, T., & Sadun, R. (2010). *The economic impact of ICT*. The Enterprise LSE Ltd, Center for Economic Performance. Final Report. https://warwick.ac.uk/fac/soc/economics/staff/mdraca/cstudytheeconomicimpactofictlondonschoolofeconomics.pdf

Rincon, A., Vecchi, M., & Venturini, F. (2013). *ICT spillovers, absorptive capacity and productivity performance*. National Institute of Economic and Social Research.

Statista. (2021). *Global market size from outsourced services from 2000 to 2009*. https://www.statista.com/statistics/189788/global-outsourcing-market-size/

Tambe, P., & Hitt, L. M. (2006). Measuring information technology spillovers. *Information System Research, 25*(1), 53–71.

Teece, D. J., Pisano, G., & Shuen, A. (1997). Dynamic capabilities and strategic management. *Strategic Management Journal, 18*(7), 509–533.

Toader, E., Firtescu, B. N., Roman, A., & Anton, S. G. (2018). Impact of information and communication technology infrastructure on economic growth: An empirical assessment for the EU countries. *Sustainability, 10*(10), 3750.

World Bank. (2020). *Literacy rate, youth total (% of people ages 15–24)—Bangladesh*. World Development Indicators. https://data.worldbank.org/indicator/SE.ADT.1524.LT.ZS?locations=BD

Zaman, K. A. U., & Sarker, T. (2021). *Demographic dividend, digital innovation, and economic growth: Bangladesh experience*. (Working Paper 1237). Asian Development Bank Institute.

CHAPTER 3

Digital Bangladesh Vision and the Current State of Digitalization

1 Introduction

The Digital Bangladesh vision was laid down in 2009, which eloquently sets the goal to transform the country into a digital economy by 2021.[1] The digital Bangladesh Vision was first laid down in the Awami League's (AL) election manifesto in 2008 and subsequently, after formation of the government in 2009, it has come into effect as the government's priority policy agenda. The vision articulated "to expand and diversify the use of ICTs (Information and Communication Technology) to establish a transparent, responsive, and accountable government; develop skilled human resources; enhance social equity; ensure cost-effective delivery of citizen-services through public-private partnerships; and support the national goal of becoming a middle-income country within 2021 and join the ranks of the developed countries by 2041" (ICT Division, 2018)."Digital Bangladesh" has now emerged as a buzzword of development as it is

[1] The digital Bangladesh Vision 2021 was first laid down in the Awami League's (AL) election manifesto in 2008 and subsequently, after formation of the government in 2009, it has come into effect as the AL-led government's priority policy agenda. The vision articulated "to expand and diversify the use of ICTs (Information and Communication Technology) to establish a transparent, responsive, and accountable government; develop skilled human resources; enhance social equity; ensure cost-effective delivery of citizen-services through public–private partnerships; and support the national goal of becoming a middle-income country within 2021 and join the ranks of the developed countries by 2041" (ICT Division, 2018).

M. Hossain, *Digital Transformation and Economic Development in Bangladesh*, https://doi.org/10.1007/978-981-19-2753-9_3

aligned with the government's development plans. As part of mainstreaming digitalization, various targets and outcomes of digitalization have been incorporated in the country's various development strategies, such as five-year plans, Perspective plans 2021 and 2041, etc. For smooth implementation of digitalization strategies, the government amended the National ICT Policy 2002 several times (the National ICT Policy 2009, 2015, and 2018) and enacted the ICT Act, 2006 and amended it in 2009. The changes in policies were done to cater to the needs of emerging aspects of ICTs and bring dynamism in the policy.

The context of digitalization manifests in innovations and value creation in the economy. The digitalization strategies seek to exploit human capital and cheaper information and communication technologies based on computers and smart devices. The vision of being a developed country, or at least a middle-income country by 2041 as indicated in the Perspective Plan 2041, depends much on continued higher growth with massive investments in high-tech value-added manufacturing industries. Investment in ICT infrastructure can pave the way for high-tech value-added industry sectors, such as electronics, smart TV, smartphones, computer accessories, electric automobiles, etc., which are thought to be the next promising industries for Bangladesh after readymade garments (Hossain, 2020). Investments in ICTs will not only improve the digitalization process but also help create a pool of engineers and IT professionals that are important for the development of high-tech industries. Considering the current low development stage and lack of potential to promote heavy industries, Bangladesh has taken the right move for massive digitalization initiatives, exploiting its comparative advantage in acquiring soft but cheap technologies dependent on human capital and computers. As the country is hallowed with the abundance of the population with demographic dividend in place the gain from the ICT sector would be enormous if proper skills development policies are undertaken to take advantage of demographic dividend. Such human capital could also serve as the basis for high-tech industrialization. What is essential is to identify the right set of implementable policies in the right direction. Only then ICTs can support leapfrogging to the next level of development by skipping regular development stages, for which incorporating ICTs in the mainstream development strategy is crucial.[2]

[2] "ICT is an umbrella term that includes any communication device or application, encompassing radio, television, cellular phones, computer and network hardware and

This chapter provides an overview of activities and investments toward the country's digitalization under the Digital Bangladesh Vision during 2010–2021. It also discusses the extent of the resultant digitalization that has taken place during the same period. Further, Bangladesh's position in South Asia in terms of digitalization has also been discussed.

2 Government Policies on Digitalization

In the implementation of the digital Bangladesh agenda, the government has revised its initial target of achieving digital Bangladesh vision by 2021 according to the following timelines: short-term (by 2021), medium-term (2030), and long-term (by 2041), making it consistent with the government's perspective plan of becoming a developed country by 2041.

The spirit of Digital Bangladesh has been reflected in the country's *Seventh Five-Year Plan* (FY2016–FY2020), Perspective Plan 2021, Eighth Five-Year Plan (2021–2025), and Perspective Plan 2041 (Zaman & Rokunuzzaman, 2020). The ICT Policy 2018 features detailed strategies for applying ICT across ten areas: (i) Economic growth; (ii) Education; (iii) Youth empowerment; (iv) Equity; (v) Governance; (vi) Civil service; (vii) Judiciary; (viii) Law enforcement; (ix) Parliament; and (x) Environment (Fig. 1).

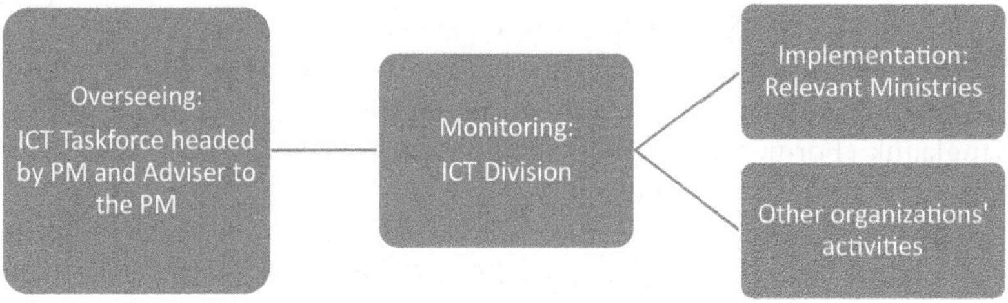

Fig. 1 Implementation of digital Bangladesh vision

software, satellite systems and so on, as well as the various services and applications associated with them, such as video conferencing and distance learning. According to the OECD, ICT in manufacturing and service industry means that the industry must either perform information processing and communications by electronic means or use electronic processing to measure or control a physical process" (OECD, 2003).

The ubiquity of mobile phones in the last two decades has brought some transformational changes in the digital landscape of Bangladesh.[3] In Bangladesh, out of 170 million mobile phone connections (almost equal to the whole population), about 90 million connections are unique, giving a penetration rate of 54% (GSMA, 2021). If duplicate connections are considered, the mobile phone penetration rate is over 100%. The GSMA Report 2021 also highlighted that despite having 95% coverage of a 4G network, only 28% of the population had 4G connections indicating a significant usage gap. This gap needs to be mitigated by increasing access to mobile broadband and a unique penetration rate with proper policies and incentives. Note, however, that the spectacular growth of mobile telephony across the country contributed significantly toward the development of the ICT sector and digitalization process, which is the outcome of the liberalization of Bangladesh's telecommunications sector that began with small steps in 1989 with the issuance of a license to a private operator for the provision of *inter alia* cellular mobile services in Bangladesh. Bangladesh entered the mobile phone world through the City Cell Company in 1993, though the company enjoyed monopoly market power until 1996 before Grameenphone got a license. The cost of a mobile phone connection from City Cell in the 1990s would require more than Tk. 0.1 million with a high tariff on talking time. That high costs obstructed people from the access to mobile phones. With the subsequent development of necessary ICT and Telecommunications policies, more MNOs (Mobile Network Operators) were allowed to enter the market, which helped significantly reduce the cost of mobile telephone services in a competitive environment. Later, Robi (Former Name Aktel), Banglalink (Former Sheba World), and Airtel (Former Name Warid) got licenses from the government.

Bangladesh also entered into the satellite club by launching the sole satellite, namely the Bangabandhu Satellite-1, in 2018, which gave Bangladesh control over the country's satellite bandwidth and related digital activities. However, the satellite's capacity in terms of its bandwidth remains underutilized due to the lack of diversification of its utilization within Bangladesh and a better marketing strategy outside Bangladesh (Sajid, 2021). This provides an important lesson that only developing

[3] https://www.itu.int/net4/wsis/forum/2016/Content/AgendaFiles/document/0ffca517-b27d-4f61-a21f-1da8541021f5/Bangladesh_BASIS_MRahman_WSIS2016.pdf.

infrastructure is not the solution, rather, complementary policies are essential to get the best result from the investments.

Establishing the Union Digital Center (UDC) in each Union Parishad (the lowest tier of the local government) is a remarkable initiative toward enhancing access to digital services and minimizing the digital divide in rural areas. Initiated in 2009 under a different name, Union Information Service Center (UISC), so far, a total of 3.91 million rural citizens have been directly receiving information and services from UDC that help UDCs generate revenue of about BDT 4.65 million (USD 545,337) in each month (BBS, 2014).

3 Investment in ICT Infrastructure Development and Pricing of Internet

Significant investments in ICT infrastructure development have been made over the last ten years. The key areas of investments include (i) improving internet connectivity through several submarine cables; (ii) investments in 3G/4G by MNOs; (iii) enhancing the data connectivity (Worldwide Interoperability for Microwave Access (Wi-Max), National Data Network (NDN), etc.); and (iv) establishment of hi-tech parks. However, these investments are long-term in nature, and there is a minimum investment size in most cases.

The government's investment in ICT infrastructure development was less than 1% of the annual development program (ADP) until the FY2013–FY2014. Afterward, except in FY2015–FY2016, the government allocated budgets over 8% of ADP, giving greater importance to this sector, mainly to realize the digital Bangladesh vision. A colossal increase in investment in the ICT sector was seen for three years in a row since FY 2012–2013 (Table 1). Such an enormous increase in the government budget allocated for the ICT division indicated a strong determination toward the development of the ICT sector of the country.

So far, Bangladesh has been providing internet services with two submarine cables: SEA-ME-WE-4 and SEA-ME-WE-5, which started their commercial operation in 2005 and 2017, respectively. Connectivity through another submarine cable network is in progress. It also has six International Terrestrial Cable (ITC) operators linked to India. Besides this, two National Internet Exchanges (NIX) are in operation to provide local peering. The government issued the Nationwide Telecommunication Transmission Network (NTTN) license in 2009 to put in place

Table 1 Public investments in the ICT sector

Fiscal year	*Total projects*	*Total amount (Tk. in billions)*	*% of total RADP*	*% change in the amount*
2008–09	29	1.4043	0.61	
2009–10	28	1.6502	0.57	17.51
2010–11	31	1.5196	0.43	−7.91
2011–12	30	1.3974	0.34	−8.04
2012–13	26	2.992	0.57	114.11
2013–14	32	15.5903	2.6	421.07
2014–15	26	46.3282	5.95	197.16
2015–16	27	18.0838	1.93	−60.97
2016–17	31	133.9693	8.17	640.82
2017–18	45	125.9318	7.99	−6.00
2018–19	55	133.5363	7.56	6.04
2019–20	58	167.9043	8.35	25.74
2020–21	50	181.9506	8.47	8.37

Source Annual Development Program, various years, Planning Commission, Bangladesh Government

optical fiber cables throughout the country to allow impeccable telecommunication services. So far, 79,000 km optical fiber cables have been installed.

Five mobile phone operators, which are now providing mobile phone services in Bangladesh, made substantial investments in developing mobile phone networks. As a result, one can observe that in Bangladesh, telecommunication FDI (Foreign Direct Investment) increased by 197% in the period 2015–2016, which is just lower than that of India's investments (ITU, 2018). Bangladesh's investment in the 3G/4G network is significantly impacting the growth of mobile broadband users, and the country is looking forward to introducing long-term evolution (LTE) technology.[4] However, fixed Internet penetration increases every day as several initiatives and policies have been formulated and implemented.

[4] Long-Term Evolution (LTE) is a standard wireless broadband communication for mobile devices and data terminals based on the Global System for Mobile Communications (GSM)/Enhanced Data for Global Evolution (EDGE) and Universal Mode Telecommunications System (UMTS)/High-speed Packet Access (HSPA) technologies. It increases the capacity and speed using a different radio interface together with core network improvements.

Bangladesh made substantial investments as a percentage of telecommunication revenue over 2014–2016 (over 30%). In 2015, Bangladesh's investment in telecommunication (as % of revenue) was higher than India, Pakistan, and Malaysia's. In 2016, Bangladesh's investment in this sector lagged behind India's one but was higher than many other countries (Table 1). With these impressive investments, Bangladesh achieved 100% mobile cellular subscription in 2017, though it accounts for a certain proportion of duplicate mobile phone connections (Table 2). According to a recent GSMA report released in 2021 (GSMA, 2021), the number of unique subscribers grew from 47 million in 2010 to 90 million in 2020, an increase of over 90%. At the end of 2020, Bangladesh had a unique-subscriber penetration of 54% and a total connections penetration of 101%, with some users owning multiple connections. However, despite the expansion of mobile coverage, about half of Bangladesh's population (46%) remains unconnected to a mobile network (GSMA, 2021). While Bangladesh has one of the highest levels of 4G coverage by population (95%) in South Asia, about 67% of the population do not use mobile broadband, that is, 28% of the population could not get access to the benefits of 4G coverage, which may be due to unaffordability, lack of digital literacy, and on top of these, the poor internet connectivity provided by the mobile broadband networks (GSMA, 2021).

Table 2 Telecommunication investments and its share in Telco. Revenue in selected countries, 2014–2016

Country	*Telecommunication capital expenditures (USD million)*			*Capital expenditures as a share of telecommunication revenue (%)*		
	2014	*2015*	*2016*	*2014*	*2015*	*2016*
Bangladesh	958	1488	1342	29.3	41.7	36.5
India	7,384	12,658	27,891	23.2	41.0	76.4
Pakistan	1,815	907	666	39.3	21.2	14.9
Malaysia	2,365	2,313	2,285	18.6	18.8	19.3

Source International Telecommunication Union (ITU) (2018) (Measuring the Information Society Report Volume-2)

3.1 *Pricing of Internet and Accessibility*

The pricing of the internet and other ICT products is an important determinant of digital transformation. According to ITU, Bangladesh, China, and India have achieved the threshold of mobile cellular baskets under US$3 per month and were featured among the top 20 countries with the lowest prices (ITU, 2018). Regarding handset-based mobile broadband prices below PPP$20 per month, Bangladesh is among the top 10 countries with the least expensive handset-based mobile broadband baskets. Moreover, Bangladesh, along with China, India, Indonesia, Japan, Pakistan, and the Philippines, offers handset-based mobile broadband prices below the 2% threshold, suggesting that 500 Mb per month of mobile broadband access is affordable to large segments of the population (ITU, 2018). Computer-based mobile broadband plans, including 1 Gb per month, were slightly above the 2% threshold in some of these countries, such as Bangladesh, India, and Pakistan.

Keeping the prices of the internet and other ICT devices affordable is essential for easy access of digital services to the mass population. Despite having the lowest threshold of internet pricing in Bangladesh, stakeholders often argue that the internet prices are not affordable to the majority of the low and middle-income users. 15% VAT (Value-Added Tax) and other supplementary duties (SD) on internet contribute to higher prices of the internet use and, therefore, impedes greater access to the internet. Furthermore, various taxes, such as SIM tax, Custom Duty, Minimum Turnover tax, VAT, supplementary duty, and surcharge, are imposed on MNOs that affect mobile phone operators and end-users.[5] A wide range of taxes creates obstacles for greater access to digital services through mobile broadband networks. Therefore, these taxes and duties need to be rationalized to make them consistent with the overall objective of digital transformation.

Table 3 shows that while the fixed broadband internet is relatively cheaper in Bangladesh, mobile broadband internet is relatively costlier than neighboring South Asian countries. Speedy internet access entails high cost, which refrains many from using high-speed internet, particularly freelancer programmers. The speed problem affects internet use greatly at the rural level.

[5] Bangladesh has the highest level of consumer taxes as share of the total cost of mobile ownership (TCMO, 35%) in the Asia region (GSMA, 2021).

Table 3 Broadband internet prices in South Asia, 2012–2017

Fixed broadband					*Mobile broadband (handset-based, 500 MB)*			
Country	*As % of GNI p.c.*		*USD*		*As % of GNI p.c.*		*USD*	
	2012	*2017*	*2012*	*2017*	*2012*	*2017*	*2012*	*2017*
Sri Lanka	2.1	1.40	4.5	4.51	0.8	0.60	1.8	1.77
India	5.1	4.80	6.0	6.40	2.9	1.90	3.4	1.59
Bhutan	6.2	3.90	10.7	7.80	1.9	0.80	3.2	2.53
Bangladesh	7.3	4.40	4.7	4.40	12.6	2.30	8.1	2.30
Nepal	15.5	10.30	14.5	6.25	n.a	9.50	n.a	5.78
Afghanistan	17.8	29.00	8	14.73	n.a	10.10	n.a	5.16

Source ITU (2017) (Measuring the Information Society Report Volume-2)

Establishing last-mile connectivity with fiber-optic is a solution to low-cost internet, and uniform bandwidth pricing across the country is desirable. BTCL (Bangladesh Telecommunication Company Limited) has upgraded its copper network to optical fiber through the Telecommunication Network Development Project, which began in 2009. The effect of such up-gradation on entry-level prices in the country has drastically dropped down from USD 50 in 2009 to USD 8.3 in 2010 and decreased further until reaching an outstanding low value of USD 4.3 in 2017. According to ITU, this is probably the lowest price level possible for entry-level fixed broadband plans without direct government intervention.

As a large section of the population is still out of internet connectivity because of affordability and accessibility. More reforms in sector-specific taxation and fees and policies like infrastructure sharing could be desirable as a mechanism for reducing the cost-of-service provision (Alliance for Affordable Internet, 2017). Further investments are required from the part of the government as well as MNOs (Mobile Network Operator) and ISPABs (Internet Service Provider Association Bangladesh) to increase internet speed, and ensure the reliability of connectivity.

4 The Current State of Digitalization

The investments in ICTs over the last decade have made a significant stride in improving the digital ecosystem of the country. The following four indicators are central to understand the current state of digital transformation in the economy: (i) Connectivity: mobile and broadband internet connectivity; (ii) e-services: e-governance, e-commerce, digital finance; (iii) ICT industry: MNO, IT, and ITES (Information Technology Enabled Service) industry; and (iv) Human resource development. A brief description in the light of the above four indicators is given below.

4.1 *Internet Connectivity and Access*

Mobile cellular subscription, fixed broadband subscription, secure internet servers, and internet penetration are crucial indicators that paint the picture of the digital scenario of a country. Bangladesh has come a long way in the last ten years. Internet access has increased exponentially since 2010. High mobile phone penetration rate (about 100%), the availability of smartphones, and 4G internet have contributed a lot to the meteoric rise in internet access and usage among the country's people. Smart mobile phones may be instrumental for mass internet usage by individuals. As of December 2018, in Bangladesh, over 90% are mobile-based internet users. However, according to a GSMA estimate based on unique mobile phone subscriptions, compared to the South Asia average (34%), Bangladesh has a low proportion of the population connected to mobile broadband services (28%). Other countries like Pakistan, India, and Sri Lanka have higher proportions of internet users: 53%, 63%, and 44%, respectively (GSMA, 2021).

Though fixed broadband internet provides a more reliable connection, its accessibility and affordability are the causes of concern. In recent times, though the government has attempted to establish broadband connectivity at the Union level (the lowest tier of the local government), its access depends on the affordability of the rural people. Fixed broadband price has come down substantially in the last decade (the decrease was over 100%), from BDT 18,000/Mbps in 2009 to BDT 180/Mbps in 2019. In big cities, broadband operators can provide shared bandwidth for which the prices of broadband internet have gone down. Still, at rural and district levels, the opportunity of sharing bandwidth is meager, leaving the cost of internet higher in those areas.

Despite the growing demand for the internet, relatively higher internet costs refrain mass people from broader use of the internet. Though the price of bandwidth has fallen significantly, connection in remote areas is dearer than in the capital city—about 7–10 times higher due to unchanged or increased transmission. Only 15% of the subscription cost is associated with bandwidth price, and the rest is for other operational expenses and transmission costs (Shamsuddin, 2018). The government has recently attempted to impose unified broadband bandwidth prices to reduce discrimination in internet pricing, which is a good move for the end-users but unsatisfactory to the operators.

Bangladesh uses two submarine cables to connect to the international gateway and buys bandwidth from India as a contingency. The introduction of 5G to the cellular network and connecting to a new submarine cable, which is now underway, is expected to improve vastly in the coming years. Table 4 portrays how various indicators of internet access had changed during 2010–2019. With more than a 100% increase in mobile cellular subscription and teledensity in the last ten years, internet users have increased to 300% or more. The most conspicuous change is observed in cases of fixed broadband subscription (1826%) at a compound annual growth rate (CAGR) of 31% and secured internet servers (70,000%) at a CAGR of 81%. Internet users have increased by over 300% in the last 10 years, it is about 25% of the total population. However, Bangladesh Telecommunication Regulatory Commission (BTRC) provides much higher estimates of internet subscribers including mobile and fixed broadband subscribers. According to BTRC, in 2020, there were 111.87 million internet subscribers of which 102 million were mobile phone-based and 9.5 million were fixed broadband subscribers. Though there are overlaps in fixed broadband and mobile phone-based internet users, according to BTRC estimate, individual internet users were 67.9% of the total population, which is apparently an overestimate compared to our survey results and ITU estimates. Again, the number of fixed broadband internet subscribers increased to 10.5 million in 2021 in the face of the Covid-19 pandemic (BTRC Website; The Daily Star Business Report, 2021). Since substantial investments have been made in internet infrastructures, it is now high time to focus on how to increase access to the internet.

A comparison of Bangladesh with Asia and Pacific countries and the world level can be seen in Table 5 for 2016 and 2017. Bangladesh has so far made commendable progress in terms of mobile cellular subscription, 3G/4G coverage and LTE (Long-Term Evolution)/WiMAX (Worldwide Interoperability for Microwave Access X) coverage, internet use as Bangladesh's achievement is almost at par with Asia and Pacific and ahead of the world average in some cases. However, Bangladesh has not made good progress in some other indicators, such as households with a computer, which has a consequential impact on households with the

Table 4 ICT parameters of Bangladesh through the last decade

Indicator	*2010*	*2011*	*2012*	*2013*	*2014*	*2015*	*2016*	*2017*	*2018*	*2019*	*2020*	*CAGR (%)*	*Change over ten years (%)*
Fixed broadband subscriptions (per 100 people)[a]	0.3	0.31	0.39	0.99	2.00	3.13	4.17	4.57	4.99	4.95	5.78	30.85	1826.00
Fixed telephone subscriptions (per 100 people)[b]	0.9	0.65	0.63	0.70	0.63	0.55	0.48	0.44	0.89	0.89	0.88	-0.20	−2.22
Mobile cellular subscriptions (per 100 people)[c]	46	56.52	64.36	76.30	82.10	84.07	86.08	94.53	100.24	101.54	103.31	7.63	124.56
Individuals using the Internet (% of the population)[d]	–	–	5.0	6.6	11.9	12.9	18.1	19.8	21.8	23.8	24.8	19.5	396
Secure Internet servers (per 1 million people)[e]	0.2	0.48	0.73	0.955	1.30	2.009	23.61	65.21	115.96	100.18	140.17	81.42	69,985.00
Teledensity(overall)[f]	44.6	47.8	61	64.64	77.81	79.3	81.48	87.32	96.36	97.10	99.68[6]	7.58	123.50
Mobile phone subscribers (in a million)[g]	67.92	84.37	97.18	116.55	126.87	131.37	135.98	150.94	161.77	165.57	170.14	8.70	150.50

Sources ITU[a, b, c]; Notes: ITU estimates the internet users by looking at individuals who have used the Internet (from any location) in the last 3 months. The Internet can be used via a computer, mobile phone, personal digital assistant, games machine, digital TV etc.[d]; World Development Indicators[e, f]; "Progress Towards Digital Bangladesh," 2017, Ministry of Finance, Bangladesh; CAGR: Compound Annual Growth Rate; Sajid (2020)[g]

Table 5 Selected indicators of connectivity, 2016–2017

Key indicators	*2017*			*2016*		
	Bangladesh	*Asia & Pacific*	*World*	*Bangladesh*	*Asia & Pacific*	*World*
Mobile cellular subscription per 100 inhabitants	88.1	104	103.6	83.8	98.9	101.5
Active mobile broadband subscription per 100 inhabitants	30	60.3	61.9	27.2	47.4	52.2
3G coverage (% of the population)	92.6	91.3	87.9	91.4	87.6	85
LTE/WiMAX coverage (% of population)	65	86.9	76.3	65	73.6	66.5
Individuals using the internet (%)	19.8	44.3	48.6	18.1	41.5	45.9
Household with a computer (%)	11.1[b]	38.9	47.1	9.6	37.8	46.6
Household with internet access (%)	19.4[a]	49	54.7	14.5	45.5	51.5
International bandwidth per internet user (kbit/s)	15.3	61.7	76.6	9.2	48	74.5
Fixed broadband sub. per 100 inhabitants	4.57	13	13.6	4.17	11.3	12.4

Source ITU (2017, 2018) (Measuring the Information Society Report Volume-2:);[a]World Development Indicators database; and [b]survey results from Bangladesh

internet, international bandwidth per user, and fixed broadband subscription per 100 people. Since the access to the internet and computer at the household level is somewhat dependent on household income above the poverty level, improving on this indicator will take a relatively long time. Since mobile-phone-based internet accessibility has increased substantially, Bangladesh should focus on this aspect of internet access and its beneficial usage. It is essential to increase free Wi-Fi hotspots in marketplaces, growth centers, educational institutions, etc., to increase access to the internet. Accessibility of smartphones is another obstacle for relatively poor people for better and broader use of the internet. Making low-cost smartphone handsets available (imported or manufactured at home) by reducing taxes could be an important policy agenda in enhancing internet accessibility and quality use.

Figure 2 provides the types of devices used to connect to the internet,

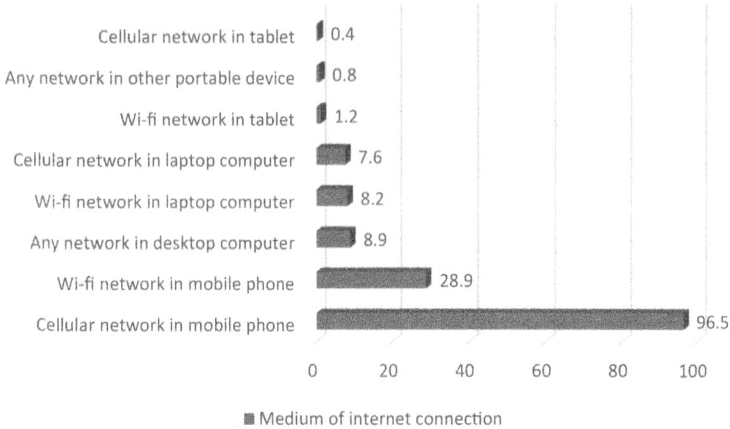

Fig. 2 Medium of internet connection (*Source* A2I Bangladesh National ICT Household Survey [2019a])

which shows mobile phones are the most frequently used devices for internet connection, followed by PC, laptops, and tablets. Less than 10% of people have a Wi-Fi network on their laptops or desktops, while about 25% use the internet on their mobile phones, particularly smartphones. Greater accessibility to the internet should be the critical policy option for achieving a digital society.

4.2 E-Governance Activities

So far, Bangladesh has made a significant improvement in the areas of e-governance[6] over the last ten years. To ensure e-governance, the government creates infrastructure to support the administration in digitizing their services as early as 2010, including communication networks, a centralized data center, a network of sub-district level digital centers, and digital architecture. A snapshot of a few such e-government projects is given in the box 1.

[6] According to UN e-government survey in media (2019), *"E-government can thus be defined as the use of ICTs to more effectively and efficiently deliver government services to citizens and businesses"*.

Box 1: E-government projects

Two electronic filing systems, such as e-Nothi (see Box 1 for details) and e-GP (e-procurement), have been introduced to expedite the digitalization of government activities and services.[7] From April 2010 to June 2014, a public network connecting all government organizations was created under the BanglaGovNet project. It joined the National Data Center with 43 ministries, 128 organizations, 64 districts, and one Upazila under each district. Another project, InfoSarkar, which began in July 2011 and ended in June 2016, was undertaken to increase the network capacity of the National Data Center. The network was established among the 64 districts connected to the backbone network and 488 Upazilas. Also, 800 video conferencing systems and a disaster recovery center were deployed. A training center for developing ICT capabilities was established at BCC. Further InfoSarkar was extended to the existing network to connect to even the lowest tier administrative wings. The project has been implemented to provide Internet access to 2600 Union Parishads, 488 Upazila Parishad (out of 495 Upazilas), and 1000 police stations nationwide.

As part of implementing e-governance projects, the government has established two national data centers (NDC) to host all government e-portals. The first one was built in 2009 and later upgraded to become a tier 3 facility in 2015, which now hosts about 90% of the public websites and around 40,000 email accounts. The second NDC, a tier-4 data center, is built in the Kaliakoir Hi-Tech Park to backup the first. The National Data Centre is expected to provide many services in the future, such as cloud computing, cloud desk, and cloud storage (ICT Division, 2019). Both centers are managed and run by Bangladesh Computer Council (BCC). A disaster recovery data center was built in Jashore to secure the recovery of public data.[7]

[7] The e-government procurement system, namely *e-GP* system, was launched in order to bring transparency and accountability in public procurements. It consists of the following components: Centralized Registration, Workflow Management System, e-Tendering (e-Publishing/e-Advertisement, e-Lodgement, e-Evaluation, e-Contract award), e-Contract Management System (e-CMS), e-Payments, Procurement Management Information System (PROMIS), System and Security Administration, Handling Errors and Exceptions, and Application Usability and Help.

[7] The Bangladesh National Digital Architecture (BNDA) is a strategic planning system developed by the LICT (Leveraging ICT) project to develop strategies for efficient provision of digital services in terms of both cost and quality. The key components of BNDA

Box 2: e-Nothi (e-filing system)

e-Nothi is a digital filing system to expedite the delivery of public services and deal with civil affairs and complaints faster to provide services more efficiently. It was launched in 2016 under the cabinet division. Nothi connects the central and local governments. The system uses a digital guard file (a file security component), unique user ID, official seal, soft signature, and digital signature. The supporting mobile app is available on both Android and iOS smartphones. Its main features include multiple searching options, SMS and email notification, single sign-on, multi-role access, citizen's corner as well as a combined view of note and Potro, note writing and editing, flagging, and linking references, guard file, and attachment.

Nothi was first introduced as a part of integrating ICT in the administration, aiming to move toward a paperless government slowly. It was expected to ensure transparency, accountability, and dynamism in work and reduce bureaucratic backlogging. As of February 2019, the total number of users of "e-filing" was 69,290. Besides the "e-filing" server, the mobile application for mid to top officials currently has 133,330 as of December 2018. Among 19,000 government offices, more than five thousand offices are using e-Nothi.

During lockdown and limited lockdown periods in Covid-19 pandemic, most of the government offices run through an *e-nothi* system allowing officials to "work from home" that provides efficient delivery of services as well as ensures the safety of the government officials from infections of the viruses by reducing human contacts in official file movements.

Source An evaluation of the "e-nothi" system in government office management (2019b)

Though a substantial investment has been made regarding infrastructure development for facilitating e-governance, the pertinent question is how accessible and usable the services are. The main concern is to make all the public services digitally accessible, which might increase the public services' efficiency and transparency. A study points out that about 92% of the respondents (the sample consists of 63 officials from 30 government offices) are regular and frequent users of the e-Nothi system, and about

are: (i) deploying a national enterprise architecture portal and data storage, (ii) building a shared network for national Digital Services and achieving data standardization, (iii) implementing a public service platform, and (iv) developing a governance system for the national enterprise architecture.

95% of the respondents are using both manual and "*e-Nothi*" for office management concurrently (Access to Information, 2019a). The study found that, on average, 72% of the total work is being done through *e-Nothi*. Some of the limitations of the *e-Nothi* (e-filing system) highlighted by the respondents are valid and need further action to reap the benefits of the e-filing system. The reported problems of *e-Nothi* include the low capacity of the server system; file size limitation; lack of backup and security in the server; lack of digital literacy, especially among older officers; lack of uninterrupted and fast internet; and bugs in the system such as, not displaying attached files.

However, according to the e-Government Development Index, Bangladesh ranked 115th out of 193 countries and scored 0.4862, pushing itself down to the middle-lower group. It scored lowest in the telecommunication infrastructure index, showing where Bangladesh needs to improve the most. Bangladesh ranked 51 out of 193 countries in the e-Participation index. Further investments in e-governance infrastructure and ICT upgrades are required, and the culture of paperless governance must be nurtured to digitalize the government. Table 6 portrays a comparison between Bangladesh and a few other countries in the Asia Pacific regarding e-government development on a national level and e-participation. Corresponding to the data for 2010, the e-participation index signifies a more fluid transmission of information and public services between the government and the citizens through ICT for all countries alike, including Bangladesh. However, the index fell in 2018, implying a much-needed improvement in the efficacy of online government services to the rest of the population. Similarly, the e-government development index too decreased in 2018 as opposed to 2010, creating the need for a closer inspection to improve the online engagement between the public and the government employing the applications of ICTs.

Various other efforts have been made to improve the e-governance system. A platform called "*Eksheba*" (one-stop service)[8] has been created to apply for online government services easily. In this platform, offices can easily create service application forms through the service builder, and applicants can apply online, which can be disposed of through "Electronic filing." This platform has the opportunity to create a profile of the service

[8] https://www.mygov.bd/.

Table 6 Rankings in E-Government development index, 2018

Country	*E-Government development index, 2018*	*E-Government development index, 2010*	*E-Participation Index (EPI), 2018*	*E-Participation Index (EPI), 2010*
Bangladesh	115	134	51	102
India	96	119	15	58
Sri Lanka	94	111	86	82
Pakistan	148	146	115	68
Bhutan	126	152	111	117
Nepal	117	153	55	127

Source UN, E-Government Survey (2018)

provider, and once the information and documents are uploaded, they can be used for further application.

"Bangladesh National Information Portal" is another website-based information providing service that has been initiated to make information and official forms/documents easily accessible. The website offers all related papers, e-books (textbooks for school-level students), and other necessary details. Digitalized service delivery mechanisms are now in place at the central and local governments levels. Such a mechanism is expected to reduce transaction costs and time of the service, making it beneficial for the clients. Notwithstanding those various initiatives undertaken in the last ten years to develop the e-governance system to improve public service delivery mechanisms, ensuring good governance depends on the effective use of digital platforms, which mainly depends on the integrity and efficiency of the government officials. A note of caution is that digitalization is not the panacea of all problems. Therefore, improving overall governance by reducing corruption and bringing corrupt people into justice should be the ultimate goal to get the maximum benefit from the e-governance system.

4.3 E-commerce Growth

About 52% of the IT firms appear to serve e-commerce firms (BIDS survey, 2019). During the COVID-19 pandemic, the e-commerce industry has reached an evolutionary state. About 2500 e-commerce firms have been trading goods and services valued over $2 billion, making

Bangladesh the 46th country in the largest e-commerce markets (Sahoo et al., 2020). The growing sales through online platforms have escalated to around 70–80%. Grocery produce is an integral contributor to such an increase in revenues. For example, Chaldal.com secured around 16,000 orders per day during the pandemic as opposed to 2500 orders in March 2020. Of those who purchase from online platforms, about 80% are residents of the main cities like Dhaka, Gazipur, Chattogram, Narayanganj, and Sylhet.

On the other hand, as individuals began to stockpile necessities, the sales for medicinal and healthcare products also expanded. Gradually, popularity increased for non-essential commodities such as apparel, accessories, crafted products, and many more. This is primarily due to the emergence of f-commerce in Bangladesh, where shops direct their modes of operation through Facebook pages. Such growth can catapult the fintech industry, enabling the perennial usage of electronic payments (Sahoo et al., 2020).

Despite huge potential of e-commerce in Bangladesh, a few fraudulent incidences posed a significant threat to the existence of the industry. For example, by offering huge discounts (even over 50% in some cases) below the cost of production of the items, they embezzled millions of taka of the customers by not delivering the products or repaying the money taken from the customers in the stipulated time. These companies, to some extent, introduce a kind of "Ponzi" scheme. As a result, most of the fraud owners now have landed in jail. These cases, however, reflect the lackluster in the regulatory framework of e/f-commerce in terms of monitoring and supervision of e/f-commerce in Bangladesh. What is important is to strengthen the regulatory and supervisory activities, identify the fraudulent cases and bring them to justice, but not create any obstacle to the potential of e-commerce.

4.4 *Software Industry*

The development of the IT industry is an essential prerequisite for widespread digitalization and leapfrogging to the next level of development. The prospects for the development of the IT industry in Bangladesh are thought to be quite promising given the government's favorable policy diffusions and demographic dividend in place. Excluding telecommunications and hardware, the market size of the IT sector ranges between US$1–2 billion in Bangladesh, of which export earnings are about US$1 billion (BASIS, 2018; ADB, 2019). The industry sets an export target of US$5 billion to be achieved by 2025, which has been disrupted due to the Covid-19 pandemic and also does not seem to be very realistic given the current growth of the industry. Most IT firms are small, and about 70% are domestic-market oriented. The industry started growing after 2000 when the government started liberalizing the telecommunications market to a greater extent. Currently, the industry employs over 0.3 million people, of which roughly 50% are IT professionals. The IT and ITES (Information Technology Enabled Service) exports registered growth at a compound annual growth rate of 17% during 2013–2018 (BCC, 2019).

Nevertheless, the software industry in Bangladesh is still at its nascent stage of development in terms of its market size, firm capabilities, and export market penetration, as discussed in Chapter 5. To move up the value chain of firms, in addition to policy supports, firm capabilities need to be strengthened (Hossain et al., 2012). At the firm level, the maturity and awareness and the management readiness of the organizations are key elements for demand generation. The "Digital Bangladesh" initiative has been instrumental in creating more demand for IT applications and software in the public/government sector. For greater international market access, the linkage is a critical factor rather than a potential market, which has been weak in Bangladesh. Without attracting FDIs in this sector and creating a favorable environment for offshore firms, it may not be possible for the Bangladeshi IT/software industry to achieve its target of earning export receipts worth US dollar several billion.

5 IT Human Capital for Leveraging Digital Bangladesh

The ICT sector currently employs about 0.3 million IT professionals, of which roughly 30% belong to software industries, 30% to freelance software service, 40% to IT jobs in different NGOs (Non-government Organizations), and other sectors. Apart from IT and ITES, about 80,000IT professionals are engaged in ISPs, 50,000 in call centers, and about 5000 in the hardware sector (Hossain, 2016; 2018). It is to be noted that the information on employment is gathered from industry leaders' assumptions as accurate information on IT professionals engaged in the sector is hard to obtain. Similarly, the supply of IT graduates is not well estimated. It is estimated that more than 95 universities and

200 polytechnic/technical institutes in Bangladesh have been producing around 10,000 IT/computer science graduates every year (Hossain, 2016; Ministry of Finance, 2015). More importantly, this number of graduates does not appear to be well acquainted with catering to the sector's needs given higher growth prospects. Capacity building of IT institutes to produce more qualified IT graduates could be an important agenda for further development of this service sector.

Both skill shortage and skill gap have been a perineal problem for the IT sector (Hossain, 2016). Though a good amount of IT related graduates enter into the job market, employers face difficulties in recruiting fresh graduates as the skill level acquired by these graduates does not seem to meet the required skills expected by the employers (Lahiri, 2019). On the other hand, the skill gap becomes an obvious challenge when an employer finds that the newly recruited graduates cannot execute their assigned job despite the training provided after recruitment. In the current context, graphic design and android programming are two areas where companies outsource foreign employees as the indigenous labor force does not have the advanced skill. Conversely, skilled professionals are inadequate to work for artificial intelligence (AI) big data analytics. The skill and skills gap issues have been analyzed in detail in Chapter 9.

Targeting the fourth industrial revolution (4IR) by focusing on artificial intelligence (AI), the internet of things (IoT), Robotics, Big data, skilled workforce has become a dire necessity. Lack of R&D facilities and linkage between academia and industry are the primary reasons for this skill gap. Active Network Unit (ANU) used in networking and ANU manufacturing has a lot of demand, but in Bangladesh, a workforce with the required skill is unavailable.

6 ICT Development Indicators: Comparison with South Asian Countries

Several global governing bodies have been developing ICT indices to measure the status of ICT development and rank the countries based on their scores. NRI (Network Readiness Index), ICT Development Index (IDI), ICT Price Basket (IPB) are some of the most commonly used ICT indexes. Comparing Bangladesh's rank with other SAARC (South Asian Association for Regional Cooperation) countries, one may get a better idea of where digital Bangladesh stands in the international context.

Bangladesh has been lagging far behind the comparator countries on several ICT indicators, such as readiness index, knowledge index, and IT development index.

6.1 Networked Readiness Index (NRI)

NRI measures the propensity for countries to exploit the opportunities offered by ICTs. The World Economic Forum develops it. The NRI includes four sub-indices: Technology Pillar, People Pillar, Governance Pillar, and Impact Pillar The first three accounts for the drivers of ICT development, and the last one looks at the impact on public life.

According to Table 7, in NRI, Bangladesh has moved to 105 in 2020 from 113 in 2010 and placed in just ahead of Pakistan and Nepal. Though Bangladesh made good progress in the government pillar (e-governance), people and impact remain a concern. Usage of the internet by the people must be enhanced, for which internet needs to be made cheaper and affordable to a large section of the population. The concerned authority should thus focus on the weaknesses in accessing and using the internet to enhance Bangladesh's position in NRI.

6.2 ICT Development Index (IDI)

The ICT Development Index is developed and measured by the International Telecommunication Union. This index is designed to reflect changes taking place in countries at different levels of ICT development. IDI comprises three sub-indices which are calculated from a total of 11 indicators. The sub-indices are (1) Access sub-index: This sub-index captures ICT readiness and includes five infrastructure and access indicators such as fixed telephone subscriptions, mobile cellular telephone subscriptions, international Internet bandwidth per Internet user, households with a computer, and households with internet access; (2) Use sub-index: This sub-index captures ICT intensity and includes individuals using the Internet, fixed broadband *subscriptions*, and mobile broadband subscriptions; (3) Skills sub-index: This sub-index seeks to capture skills which are important for ICTs. It includes three proxy indicators such as mean years of schooling, gross secondary enrollment, and gross tertiary enrollment.

As already discussed, the extent of fixed telephone subscriptions, *households' ownership* of computers, and internet access are poor in Bangladesh, which has downgraded Bangladesh's ICT development indicators. *Fixed telephone* subscription is now almost irrelevant with the

Table 7 Rankings in Network Readiness Index (NRI) in South Asia over the decade

Country	*NRI index*			*Technology pillar*			*People pillar*			*Governance pillar*			*Impact pillar*	
	2020	*2016*	*2010*	*2020*	*2016*	*2010*	*2020*	*2016*	*2010*	*2020*	*2016*	*2010*	*2020*	*2016*
Bangladesh	105	112	113	107	130	123	115	98	103	94	111	108	107	107
India	88	91	69	76	99	78	84	88	64	84	103	78	108	73
Nepal	113	118	128	111	110	125	113	106	111	114	121	135	113	128
Pakistan	111	110	102	98	115	112	106	104	97	115	118	107	110	105
Sri Lanka	83	63	71	84	73	71	94	63	67	81	67	71	74	49

Source Portulans Institute (2020) (The Global Information Technology Report [2016] & The Network Readiness Index [2020]: Accelerating Digital Transformation in a postCOVID Global Economy), World Economic Forum (2016) (The Global Information Technology Report)

Table 8 Rankings in the ICT Development Index (IDI) in 2017

Country	*IDI score*	*IDI rank*
Bangladesh	2.53	147
India	3.03	134
Nepal	2.88	140
Pakistan	2.42	148
Sri Lanka	3.91	117
Bhutan	3.69	121

Source ITU Website (2017)

emergence of mobile phones. Therefore, this indicator should not be included in the IDI index; it should get much less weight even if necessary. However, the other two indicators are important, and there are scopes of increasing/enhancing other access with proper policies. With suitable investments in connectivity, the government should now focus more on growing households' access to computers and the internet. This issue, though is related to household income, the government may provide laptops/tablets/smartphones, etc., at an affordable price and arrange stimulus loans for purchasing devices. It is also essential for the government to conduct a regular survey on households' access to computers and the internet to represent Bangladesh in the index correctly. Table 8 portrays that Bangladesh ranked higher at an IDI score of 2.53 than any relevant Asia Pacific country, except Pakistan in 2017. This puts into perspective that in terms of accessibility, frequency of usage, and skills required in the field of ICT, Bangladesh is performing relatively well yet leaving more room for improvement.

In the country's Five-year plans and Perspective Plan 2041, the government has emphasized growth acceleration by digital transformation to convert the economy into an innovation economy. Perspective Plan 2041 devoted a single chapter highlighting its importance in the government's policy agenda. The growth momentum can be accelerated by taking advantage of already-created connectivity, institution building, and policy formulation. The "2041 Perspective Plan" envisions making a substantial improvement in all ICT indicators so that Bangladesh can find its rank within the top 40 countries in the world (General Economic Division, Ministry of Planning, 2020).

7 Concluding Remarks

Bangladesh's position to achieve its Digital Bangladesh vision faster than other similar developing countries depends much on the effective utilization of the facilities already created and some bold policies to reduce the digital divide. Undoubtedly the country made substantial reforms and investments in various sectors related to ICTs. However, many other policy reforms are needed to attain the intended outcomes. Continued investments in maintaining and developing ICT infrastructures, keeping internet prices at an affordable level, creating the ICT human capital, and attracting FDIs in the ICT service sector are some of the key policies to be pursued.

So far, over the last decade, the country has made a good progress in achieving digitalization targets. However, a high rate of access to the internet and computer by households is still a far-reaching objective given the low affordability of the people, particularly in rural areas. The current level of access can be increased if the government could complete last-mile fixed broadband connectivity and provide incentives for the poor on internet access. The incentives may be given in the forms of free access to the internet through creating free hot spots in the marketplaces and educational institutions, and subsidized loan for purchasing computers and smart devices. It is also important to provide tax incentives to keep the prices of smart devices at an affordable level. On the other hand, there is ample scope for the IT industry sector to grow and flourish if businesses and the manufacturing sector are encouraged to go for large-scale automation. A large segment of the industry and service sector (Education, Agriculture, Health, and Fintech) is yet to be automated. For example, the present rate of automation in the RMG (Readymade Garments) sector is meager, and a large number of banks are yet to introduce core-banking software. New technologies, such as blockchain, AI, IoT, big data analytics, etc. have a high demand though Bangladesh could not capture these segments of ICTs due to the lack of appropriate human capital for these emerging areas. Therefore, devising appropriate incentive structures for automation of the business and manufacturing firms might boost the IT sector and contribute positively to the economy's growth.

It is to be noted that the rapid emergence of ICTs could also pave the way for further development of the electronics and computer hardware industries, which will lead to export diversification in the country. With a roughly 40% growth of the personal computer (PC) market (Hossain,

2018), the sector is intensely amalgamated with assembling and repairing services having strong potential to enter hardware manufacturing. In 2021, the market share of desktop computers and mobile phones in Bangladesh was 33.31% and 65.93%, respectively (see Statcounter, 2021). Proper incentives and policy support on taxes and subsidized credit are crucial for developing the hardware manufacturing sector.

Though substantial progress has been made toward digitalization, the challenges and missing links between digitalization and economic development deter the expected outcome of digitalization. Low-level digital literacy, poverty, and inequality are some of the factors impeding the expected pace of digitalization. Prioritizing the digitalization targets to achieve better economic outcomes could improve Bangladesh's position in the digital ecosystems.

References

ADB. (2019). *Tracer study Bangladesh: Computer and software engineering tertiary education in 2018*. Asian Development Bank.

Alliance for Affordable Internet. (2017). *Affordability report*.

A2I. (2019a). *Bangladesh national ICT household survey, report and overview of main result 2018–2019*. (2020). Alliance Affordable Internet and Access to Information (a2i) Program.

A2I. (2019b). *An evaluation of 'e-Nothi' system in government office management* (pp. 11–17). a2i.

Bangladesh Association of Software and Information Services (BASIS). (2018). *IT and ITES industry overview*.

Bangladesh Bureau of Statistics (BBS). (2014). *Census report on union information and service centers*. Bangladesh Bureau of Statistics, Ministry of Planning.

Bangladesh Computer Council (BCC). (2019). *IT-ITES industry statistics of Bangladesh*. Leveraging ICT.

Bangladesh Hi-Tech Park Authority. (2018). *All project information*.

Bangladesh Institute of Development Studies (BIDS). (2019). *Survey on labor market and skills gap in the ICT sector in Bangladesh*.

Department of Finance. (2018). *Progress towards digital Bangladesh 2017*. Government of the People's Republic of Bangladesh.

Duke Offshoring Research Network and Booz and Co. (2006). Offshoring research network 2006 Survey.Everest Group. (2017). *Betting on the future-The Bangladesh IT-ITeS industry is poised for growth*. Everest Group Research.

General Economics Division. (2020). *Making vision 2041 a reality: Perspective plan of Bangladesh 2021–2041*. Bangladesh Planning Commission. Ministry of Planning.

Grand View Research. (2017). *Knowledge Process Outsourcing (KPO) market analysis by service, by application (BFSI, Healthcare, IT & Telecom, Manufacturing, Pharmaceutical, Retail), by region and segment forecasts, 2014–2025*. https://www.grandviewresearch.com/industry-analysis/knowledge-process-outsourcing-kpo-market

GSMA. (2021). *Accelerating digital transformation in Bangladesh: recommendations for mobil-sector taxation reform*. GSMA.

Hossain, M. (2016). Labor market and skills gap in the ICT sectorin Bangladesh. In *BIDS study report: Labour market and skill gap in Bangladesh (Macro and Micro Level Study)*. Skills Employment Investment Program, Ministry of Finance, Government of Bangladesh.

Hossain, M. (2018). Labor market and skills gap in the ICT sector in Bangladesh: An exploratory study. *Asian Think Tanks Network Conference*, 22–23 August, 2018, Australian National University, Canberra. Also available: https://events.development.asia/materials/20180822/labor-market-and-skills-gap-ict-sector-bangladesh-exploratory-study

Hossain, M. (2020). Trade liberalization policies and trade performances in Bangladesh: An empirical evaluation. In *Bangladesh's macroeconomic policy* (pp. 241–265). Palgrave Macmillan.

Hossain, M., & Samad, H. (2020). Mobile phones, household welfare, and women's empowerment: Evidence from rural off-grid regions of Bangladesh. *Information Technology for Development, 27*(2), 191–207.

Hossain, M., Shinkai, N., Yunus, M., & Bakht, Z. (2012). *Integration of ICT industries and its impact on market access and trade: The case of Bangladesh and India*. Regional Integration and Economic Development in South Asia. Edward Elgar Publishing.

ICT Division. (2018). *Bangladesh national ICT policy*. Bangladesh ICT Division, Government of Bangladesh.

ICT Division. (2019). *e-Government master plan for digital Bangladesh*.

International Telecommunication Union. (2017). *Measuring the Information Society Report Volume 2*. ICT Country Profiles.

International Telecommunication Union. (2018). *Measuring the information society report volume 1 & 2*. ICT Country Profiles.

Internet World Stats. (2021). *Internet usage and population statistics*. https://www.internetworldstats.com/asia/bd.htm

Khan, M. R., & Taher, F. (2017, February 23). ICT opens up new prospects for Bangladesh. *The Daily Star*. https://www.thedailystar.net/drivers-economy/ict-opens-new-prospects-bangladesh-1364893

Lahiri, A. (2019). *Inputs for improving quality of CSE education in Bangladesh*. Mimeo.

Lopez-Acevedo, G., & Robertson, R. (Eds.). (2016). *Stitches to riches? Apparel employment, trade, and economic development in South Asia*. The World Bank.

Ministry of Finance. (2015). *Digital Bangladesh vision report, 2015*. Ministry of Finance, Finance Division, Government of Bangladesh.

OECD. (2003). *Information, Communication Technology (ICT) goods*. Organization of Economic Cooperation and Development. https://stats.oecd.org/glossary/detail.asp?ID=6274

Panko, R. (2019, June 19). *Small business outsourcing statistics in 2019*. Clutch.

Portulans Institute. (2020). *The network readiness index 2020: Accelerating digital transformation in a post-covid global economy*.

Raman, R. I. (2017). Labour market and skills gap in Bangladesh: Macro level analysis. BIDS Study Report. *Skills for Employment Investment Program*. Ministry of Finance, Government of Bangladesh.

Sahoo, S., Hossain, M. N. A., & Hassan, K. S. (2020, December 3). A boon for online commerce: How COVID-19 is rtansforming the industry in Bangladesh. *NextBillion*. https://nextbillion.net/online-commerce-covid19-industry-bangladesh/

Sajid, E. (2021, June 11). Bangabandhu satellite's two-thirds capacity remains unutilized. *The Business Standard*. https://www.tbsnews.net/tech/bangabandhu-satellites-two-thirds-capacity-remains-unutilised-259036

Sajid, E. (2020, December 17). Teledensity nearing 100% in Bangladesh. *The Business Standard*. https://www.tbsnews.net/bangladesh/telecom/teledensity-nearing-100-bangladesh-173080

Shamsuddin, A. K. (2018, July 27). The real scenario of internet access. *The Daily Star*. https://www.thedailystar.net/opinion/perspective/the-real-scenario-internet-access-1611499

Star Business Report. (2021, October 11). Broadband internet providers eye growth. *The Daily Star*. https://www.thedailystar.net/business/economy/news/broadband-internet-users-drop-2195641

Statcounter. (2021). *Global stats, 2021*. https://gs.statcounter.com/platform-market-share/desktop-mobile-tablet/bangladesh

Statista. (2021a). *The global market size of outsourced services from 2000 to 2019*. https://www.statista.com/statistics/189788/global-outsourcing-market-size/

Statista. (2021b). *Total contract value of the information technology outsourcing (ITO) market worldwide from 2000–2019*. https://www.statista.com/statistics/190122/total-gloabl-contract-va.

United Nations. (2018). *E-Government survey*. Department of Economic and Social Affairs.

World Economic Forum. (2016). *The global information technology report*.

Zaman, H., & Rokunuzzaman. (2020). *Achieving digital Bangladesh by 2021 and beyond: Background paper for the 7th Five Year Plan (7FYP)*. Ministry of Planning, The Government of Bangladesh.

CHAPTER 4

ICT Policy, Regulations, and Institutions

1 Introduction

The development of the Information and Communication Technology (ICT) sector started in Bangladesh in the mid-1990s with some key policy reforms. Bangladesh government has formally identified the ICT sector as one of the "Thrust sectors" in the 1990s.[1] In that pursuit, initiatives taken are exemptions of income tax, value-added tax, and customs duty for computer hardware and software, allowed the private sector to operate as internet service provider (ISP) using VSAT (Very Small Aperture Terminal) in 1996, and increased the number of mobile phone operators in the late 1990s. These policy reforms brought down the prices of computers and software, and played a critical role in promoting the ICT sector. Formulation of the National ICT Policy, the creation of the IT National Taskforce (chaired by the Prime Minister), the establishment of IT incubation center, enactment of Copyright Law (Trademark Act, 2009), and ICT Act, 2009 are some of the notable policy and regulatory reforms. Furthermore, an increase in IT budget allocation by the government (targeting at least 2% of annual development expenditure: ICT Policy 2006), to improve ICT infrastructure is aligned with the policy

[1] A committee headed by late Professor Jamilur Reza Chowdhury of Bangladesh University of Engineering and Technology (BUET) was appointed by the government in June 1997 to critically review the policy barriers of the ICT sector, which is thought to be the stepping stone toward the development of the ICT sector.

M. Hossain, *Digital Transformation and Economic Development in Bangladesh*, https://doi.org/10.1007/978-981-19-2753-9_4

of the development of the ICT sector with the highest priority. With the favorable policy support of the government, the software industry in Bangladesh started growing in the 2000s and the digital transformations started taking place.

The government has adopted the Development Vision 2041 giving the Digital Bangladesh agenda utmost importance. The focus of vision 2041 is to create a knowledge-based society to facilitate economic development—a digital economy is just the stepping stone for creating a knowledge-based economy. The prerequisite of a knowledge-based economy is to create a knowledge-intensive production system, which calls for a highly skilled labor force and an education/training system that produce such talent pool, innovative technologies and industries with high R&D (Research and Development) allocation, and lastly ICT infrastructures at every level of the economy starting from the root to the macro level to facilitate all these. Therefore, coherence in all types of IT-related policies with the government's various development policies is necessary to achieve digital transformation at a reasonable level consistent with leapfrogging into a developed nation status by 2041.

This chapter is organized as follows. Section 2 provides a brief chronology of significant IT policies, and Sect. 3 discusses ICT policy diffusions over time. Section 4 highlights the interface of development policies with ICT policies, and Sect. 5 highlights the key institutions responsible for implementing digitalization policies. Section 6 concludes the chapter.

2 A Brief Chronology of Significant ICT Policies

The ICT sector is the only sector in the country that receives adequate policies, regulations, and institutions. Some significant policies were undertaken to take the sector forward. Table 1 provides a chronological overview of the policies and acts associated with the ICT sector.

Table 1 Chronology of ICT related policies

Sector	*Policy*	*Key aspects*
Telecommunication	The National Telecom Policy (NTP) Bangladesh 1998, 2018 Telecommunication Regulation Act 2001, 2010 International Long-Distance Telecommunications Services (ILDTS) Policy 2010	Significant changes in the number of fixed and mobile services deployed and the numbers of services in operation have subsequently grown exponentially in the past years after the Policy and enactment of the Bangladesh Telecommunication Act 2001
	The BTRC Act 2001	Bangladesh Telecommunication Regulatory Commission (BTRC) is an autonomous Regulatory Commission established on January 31st, 2002, under the Bangladesh Telecommunication Regulatory Act 2001. The responsibilities bestowed upon the Commission include functioning, monitoring, and sustaining telecommunication institutions. This is also responsible for providing various telecommunication services across the country. The BTRC also monitors the activities of the telecom service providers to ensure the interests of the customers
ICTs	Bangladesh Computer Council Act, 1990	The Bangladesh Computer Council Act 1990 was enacted on 27th December 1989 to monitor and regulate Bangladesh's ICT sector and associated activities. The council's activities include promoting the use of computers, developing the application of computers, and providing assistance in education and training relevant to the use of computers
	National ICT Policy; 2002, 2009, 2015, 2018	Though ICT policy 2002 was not adequate, subsequently policies were formulated highlighting the emerging needs and actions regarding ICT sector development and expediting digitalization. The ICT Act has given confidence and a legal basis for ICTs and digitalization activities

(continued)

Table 1 (continued)

Sector	*Policy*	*Key aspects*
	The ICT Act, 2006, 2009	
	National Digital Commerce Policy, 2018	The National Digital Commerce Policy was structured to facilitate the progression of digital commerce. This policy was established to mitigate fraudulence, provide entrepreneurship and employment opportunities, and increase productivity by drawing in the pool of individuals from rural areas to be involved in the economic activity. The policy advocates for ensuring a secure stream of digital transactions encouraging banks to implement interbank mobile financial services or digital financial services, alongside providing much importance to cash on the delivery system to protect consumer rights
	Digital Security ACT, 2018	The Digital Security Act (DSA) was enacted in 2018 to ensure safety against digital misappropriation and cyber security. However, later the Act was criticized as it purportedly replaced the controversial Section 57 of the ICT Act 2006 (as amended in 2013). However, this new law has shown a more restrictive approach toward freedom of expression than the former in its wordings and application. The risk of unsupervised/unprotected use of DSA needs to be reviewed for its wider acceptance
Internet connectivity	Broadband Policy 2009	The policy was formulated to define the level of connectivity. The National Broadband Policy, 2009 has defined broadband as Internet connections with a minimum of 128 kbps of speed. Later, in 2016, the government upgraded it to a minimum of 5 Mbps of connectivity

Sector	*Policy*	*Key aspects*
Email	Email Policy 2018	The email policy was established to enable the government to fulfill its responsibilities by ensuring a secure electronic communication channel and instituting a durable email service. This also implicates quicker deliverance of government services to recipients enabling the efficacy of e-governance
ICT Institutions	Hi-Tech Park Authority Act 2010	The establishment is a priority agenda to help IT firms grow faster, taking lessons from Silicon Valley, Bangalore IT Parks, etc. However, it is also important to take the demerits of agglomeration economies from this policy perspective
	Establishment of ICT Division, 2014	This essential institution has been established to focus on the ICT aspects solely
	Intellectual property Rights Act 2006	Striking a balance between technology diffusion and incentives for innovation, enactment, and enforcement of IPR (Intellectual Property Rights) is necessary. Bangladesh has an IPR, but lack of enforcement somewhat impedes innovations in this sector
	A2I Program 2007	This program, located in PMO (Prime Minister Office), is an important component for implementing the Digital Bangladesh vision. This can be considered a research wing for supporting the Digital Bangladesh Vision of the government
	Union Digital Center 2009	Union Digital Center (UDC) is another innovation that delivers digital services in rural areas. With broadband connectivity, UDC could play an important role in digital transformation in the country

3 Key Information and Communication Technology Policy Diffusions

Five key areas of ICT policy diffusions can be traced that are instrumental for the development and growth of the ICT sector and the digital transformation. These are (i) Reforms and policies in the telecommunication sector; (ii) ICT policy and regulations; (iii) Policies regarding connectivity through IIG (International Internet Gateway); (iv) Policies for the establishment of Software Park to facilitate ICT industry; and (v) Policies for development of ICT human capital and innovations. These five thematic areas of policies are briefly discussed below.

3.1 Reforms in Telecom Sector Laid the Foundation for Digitalization

Widespread adoption of mobile telephones, easy access to a fixed-line telephone, and PSTNs (Public Switched Telephone Network) is thought to be instrumental for accelerating the growth and development and digitalization of the country. However, in some instances, the right policies were not undertaken at the right time. The liberalization of the telecommunications sector in 1989 began when City Cell, a private cellular mobile phone operator, was given the license to compete against the Bangladesh Telegraph and Telephone Board (BTTB), the previous monopoly provider of telecommunication facilities. However, it created another monopoly in mobile cellular services. Only one mobile phone company dominated the whole decade of 1990 that had restricted the access to mobile phones to a large section of the population due to monopoly structure. Significant changes in the number of fixed and mobile phone services occurred in the late 1990s, thanks to the adoption of the National Telecom Policy 1999 and the subsequent enactment of the National Telecommunication Act 2001. These policies and acts laid the foundation for more significant reforms in the telecommunication sector that make the sector more efficient and competitive.

The government monopolized the telecommunication industry by a few private sector enterprises until the 1990s. At that period, the telecommunication sector was characterized by a low penetration rate, limited capacity, low level of investment, and old, outdated systems. Liberalization in the telecommunication sector mainly started in the late

1990s, which has brought a paradigm shift from monopoly to competition through comprehensive regulatory interventions. The telecommunications and pricing regulations were critical in transitioning from a monopoly to a competitive market. A well-functioning regulatory regime with the enactment of the Act provided investors safety and security by creating a level-playing field free from anti-competitive practices. Such a regulatory regime paved the way for the development of sound telecommunication infrastructure to support the economy and welfare of the country by providing telecommunication facilities on demand, assuring the satisfactory quality of service, and ensuring value to the customers. Later, telecommunication policies and acts were amended several times (Begum et al., 2014).

Another critical policy, the International Long-Distance Telecommunications Services (ILDTS) Policy 2010, was formulated to regulate long-distance calls, primarily through Voice over Internet Protocol Services (VoIP). Though VoIP has been very popular among users because of its low-cost voice communication over the internet worldwide, the issue was not addressed in the previous telecom policy of 1998 and the Bangladesh Telecommunications Act 2001. As a result, the government incurred revenue losses through many secret operations of VoIP services mushroomed in the country. The new policy allowed the government to regulate long-distance international calls through approved technologies, including VoIP.

3.2 National ICT Policy and Regulations

3.2.1 A Brief Overview of Key ICT Policies

The National ICT policy was first initiated in 2002 and later has been revised and amended in 2009, 2015, and 2018 keeping the sector in focus since 2009. These policies and strategies have encountered issues related to developing ICTs and digitalization in the country. Nonetheless, policy coherence and the adoption of critical aspects and regulations are important for successful strategies. It appears, however, that strategies related to ICTs have been revised and restructured in a regular interval acknowledging specific weaknesses of previous strategies. Keeping track with rapidly changing technologies, revisions and amendments in policies reflects policy coherence and dynamism; however, Ad-hocism in policies as appeared in earlier versions is not expected for sustainable development of the sector.

The National ICT Policy 2002 was initially established to enhance the ICT sector of Bangladesh. The rationale was to transform the economy into a knowledge-based society driven by ICTs. However, without articulating action plans and political commitment, the policy was thought to be a failure as several objectives were not achieved by the intended year, 2006. Consequently, the policy was amended seven years later as National ICT Policy 2009 at the advent of the government's Digital Bangladesh vision. The policy had a well-defined structure with a comprehensive list of action plans that aided the specific strategies to achieve particular objectives.

A significant improvement in ICT policies was made in 2009. The policy introduced the 3G network service, and in 2015 the policy included the introduction of 4G network. As the country is embarking on a new era of ICTs and digitalization, the government devised a much more reformed policy in 2018 to support the 5G network. The National ICT Policy 2009 and 2015 were, to some extent, similar. However, the National ICT Policy 2018 was designed from an alternate perspective of entirely realizing the vision of Digital Bangladesh through the introduction of digital government, digital security, affordability, and accessibility to assist the advent of the 5G network. The hierarchal pyramid constituting the policies after 2009 was the same apart from the number of objectives, strategic themes, and action plans.

Additionally, there were action plans in the ICT policy 2009 to introduce a special tribunal to manage cybercrime and IPR (Intellectual Property Rights) violations and establish an internet exchange, all of which were not applied until the amendment of the policy in 2015. A supplementary policy was added in 2015 to ensure cyber security to create a Cyber Emergency Response Team (CER). The extension of the optical fiber network up to the Upazila level was deemed in the National ICT policy 2015. This enabled many people to be connected while increasing the demand for software and technology in rural areas. Regarding developing connectivity infrastructure, the government aimed to attain two more submarine cables in 2009s Policy to establish an efficient and economical internet supply. This policy was further refined in 2015 when the action plan was changed to establish terrestrial fiber connections. As stated before, comparatively, the action plans included in National ICT Policy 2015 were more specific, with instructions directing toward attaining one specific goal. While Digital Governance and Digital Security received greater importance with a set of curated action plans and strategies, most of the other objectives in the National ICT policy 2018 were an amalgamation of the goals harbored in the previous ICT policies.

In sum, the policies have been formulated with adequate revisions and amendments to bring dynamism into the ICT sector. The critical issue is that the strategies that are included in the policy must be amenable to mid-line and end-line evaluation. The strategy must be coherent with actionable plans that are implementable with predictable outcomes. The current ICT Policies, despite having merits in their right, need to be evaluated to test their sustainability and predictability. To some extent, the discussions and analyses in this book are expected to provide some shed into the suitability and applicability of the policies.

3.2.2 National Digital Commerce Policy 2018

With the scope and popularity of digital commerce[2] (e/f/m-commerce) being on the rise in Bangladesh due to the progress in digitalization, a policy framework for regulating the service was necessary. Coherently the utilization of the internet, social media, and mobile applications have been significantly facilitating IT-enabled businesses. The surge of e-commerce in the Covid-19 pandemic and some fraudulence cases in this sector made a strong case for better regulation of e/f/m-commerce. Given that digital commerce helps create entrepreneurship and employment opportunities and increase productivity, the National Digital Commerce Policy was formulated in 2018. The Policy deals with issues about building trust between buyers and sellers, taking steps to protect the interest of buyers and sellers, helping safeguard consumer rights, and avoiding risks during a digital transaction. In addition, the Policy addresses issues relating to the required infrastructure needed to manage digital commerce, provide necessary coordination and policy support in transportation and supply of goods, build a favorable environment for cross-border digital commerce

[2] E-commerce (electronic commerce) is the buying and selling of goods and services, or transmitting funds or data, over an electronic network, primarily the internet. These business transactions occur either as business-to-business (B2B), business-to-consumer (B2C), consumer-to-consumer (C2C), or consumer-to-business (C2B). F-commerce refers to conducting online business activities on a Facebook page or application. The principle of F-commerce is creating a new mode of consumption on the web: social shopping. Mobile commerce or m-Commerce corresponds to the use of wireless technologies and mobile phones for business purposes in particular (definitions are taken from various online sources).

management, and so on. However, some fraudulent e-commerce cases revealed in the Covid-19 pandemic reflect the weaknesses of the existing policy to address the fraud and forgeries in this sector and, therefore, needs some readjustments in the policy and regulatory frameworks.

With the emergence of digital commerce, the related digital finance and mobile financial service (MFS) policies are crucial to establishing secure, quick, and efficient tools for digital transactions. Mobile payment or other digital finance should be made safe to develop a cashless society. The policy also advises banks to take the initiative to implement inter-bank mobile financial service (MFS) or digital financial service (DFS) to adapt the existing payment system related to digital commerce and formulate specific guidelines for the digital commerce-related transaction and product delivery.

Much importance has been given to the cash-on-delivery system to protect consumer rights to relieve grievances of both consumers and traders. The bottom line is that with the vast potential of digital commerce in Bangladesh, continuous updating of the policies and regulations is a prerequisite to making digital commerce stronger.

Box 1. Email Policy 2018

As part of fulfilling the mandates of e-governance under the Digital Bangladesh Vision, the government initiated an email policy in 2018 to provide and host email services for government entities. The email policy was established to enable the government to fulfill its responsibilities by ensuring a secure electronic communication channel, ensuring accountability and efficacy, and instituting a durable email service. The government email services are designated to be used by all government officers and employees for official government purposes. According to the policy, government email service would be initiated by Bangladesh Computer Council under the ICT Division. The email facilities could also be used by constitutional institutions, national security institutions, law enforcement agencies, financial institutions, embassies, and government offices outside Bangladesh. Four objectives are outlined in the email policy:: ensuring the proper use of the email services by all government agencies and users alike: providing a standard and unique naming of government email services, safeguarding secure access and use of government email services for users, and maintaining an effective as well as the lawful and ethical electronic communication with citizens, service recipients, and partners.

If properly implemented, this service can even be extended to private sectors too, which will reduce the dependency on third-party email hosts, such as Yahoo, Gmail, etc.

Source Ministry of Posts, Telecommunications and Information Technology (2018)

3.2.3 *ICT Acts and Regulations*

The ICT Act, 2006 was designed to supply the necessary legal recognition and security of ICT and associated sectors. The Act mandates: (i) the recognition of digital signatures and electronic records, (ii) attribution, acknowledgment, and dispatch of electronic records (iii) security of electronic records and digital signatures, (iv) control and certifies authorities, (v) duties of subscribers, and (vi) penalties for breaching the rules. Confidential information must be protected regardless of the medium used for transmission, including a communication network. The objective of this Act was to ensure the security of documentation on a communication network shared between individuals, institutions, or the government. The Act is monitored by the Ministry of Information and Communication Technology.

Later, the ICT Act was amended in 2009 to incorporate some alterations and create the Controller of Certifying Authority (CCA). This was to ensure a secured online transaction, which will assist e-commerce in Bangladesh. The Act also introduced and expanded the idea of cybercrime and the implications behind the offense. Yet the Act still needs to safeguard data privacy and facilitate tighter security while persuading the government to accept electronic deeds (Hasan, 2014).

3.2.4 *Digital Security ACT, 2018*

The Digital Security Act was passed in the parliament on 19th September 2018. The bill includes provisions regarding defamation and human rights violations using electronic media. Providing cyber security to a rapidly digitizing nation and citizen is one of the objectives of this Act. This act calls for the following institutions: (i) Digital Security Agency: The Digital Security Agency to prevent cybercrimes using computers and digital devices. One or more digital forensic labs will be set up under its jurisdiction; and (ii) National Digital Security Council: A National Digital Security Council to be headed by the prime minister to discuss digital security issues. The key focuses of the Act include offenses against essential information, any forgery or fraudulence using a computer; commitment of cyber-terrorist activities; and any pornography and child pornography offenses.

However, the act already drew criticism for replacing the controversial Section 57 of the ICT Act, 2006 (as amended in 2013). However, this new law has shown a more restrictive approach toward freedom of expression than the former in its wordings and application. The risk of unsupervised and unprotected use of DSA needs to be reviewed and revised for its beneficial use.

3.3 *Intellectual Property Rights (IPR) Act, 2006*

Though the IPR Act is related to all products and services sectors, this has important implications for the ICT sector. An important threat for the firms' development is the lack of enforcement of intellectual property rights (IPR). Although the Bangladesh government enacted an IPR in 2006, lack of implementation and enforcement has become a significant threat to the company's potential.

The copyright amendment Act 2000 and 2002 can also be enforced to address IPR of the ICT sectors. According to the Act, the authors or the owners of Intellectual Property can effectively protect their body of published work and control its utilization by unauthorized individuals. The breach of this act may subjugate the individual in question to copyright infringement. However, the copyright ownership is limited to a certain period, between an average of 50 and 70 years, after which the right may expire, dissolving any claims of ownership. However, Bangladesh struggles to implement effective copyright laws primarily due to a lack of knowledge regarding the protection of Intellectual Property. Most individuals in the country are unaware of the laws of intrusions to rights. Additionally, there is a need for a proper set of legal guidelines devoted to safeguarding the copyrights and an effective and efficient Judicial System.

3.4 *Internet Connectivity Policy*

The government established the Bangladesh Submarine Cable Company Limited (BSCCL) in 2008 as a public limited company under the Posts and Telecommunication Division of Posts, Telecommunications, and

Information Technology Ministry to operate as the leading Telecommunication service provider and International Submarine Cable Operator of the country while also being an International Internet Gateway (IIG). It enables access to communication between Bangladesh and the rest of the world. The BSCCL shares SMW-4 (South East Asia-Middle East-Western Europe 4), introduced in 2006, and SMW-5 (South East Asia-Middle East-Western Europe 5), introduced in 2017, contributing to a greater dimension in Submarine Cables for Bangladesh. The main agenda that the company is conformed around is to enable individuals availing of broadband internet at a reasonable price with a quality service and to develop the tele-network and high-speed broadband internet in Bangladesh. The submarine cable is expected to be the main telecommunications framework to achieve the vision of "Digital Bangladesh" by supplying high-graded fiber-optic submarine cable bandwidth and skilled internet transit facilities.

The government has devised the National Broadband Policy initially in 2009 and later revised in 2016 and 2018. Broadband is defined as Internet connections with a minimum of 128 kbps of speed in 2009; seven years later, in 2016, the government upgraded it to a minimum of 5 Mbps of connectivity. Two years later, in 2018, the authorities doubled that speed to 10 Mbps. The frequent change in definitions within a short period indicated a weakness in policy formulation and a low capacity to undertake proper decisions with proper foresight. An associated policy is the International Long-Distance Telecommunication Service (ILDTS) Policy, which was formulated in 2007 and later revised in 2010. This policy allows licenses for wholesale service but effectively forbids foreign investments.

The ILDTS has been criticized for prohibiting sharing and deploying of optical fiber among mobile operators and internet service providers since July 7, 2011. According to industry insiders, this policy creates a mobile broadband divide—operators serving higher subscribers have lesser mobile towers plugged with optical fiber, resulting in slow internet speed. Bangladesh was ranked 135 among 140 countries for mobile internet, while its position was 98 among 177 countries for fixed internet (Ookla, 2021).[3] Nonetheless, the National Telecommunication Policy (NTP), 1998, was revised after two decades of procrastination in 2018,

[3] https://www.speedtest.net/global-index.

and it supersedes all preceding policies, including the controversial ILDTS Policy.

The NTP 2018 has set broadband penetration targets as follows. Fixed and mobile broadband penetration will be 30% in the short term by 2020, 70% in the mid-term (by 2023), and 100% in the long term (by 2027). Given countervailing regulatory measures, the targets appear ambitious (Khan, 2021).

Assigning radiofrequency for access and transmission networks was required to launch 2G (1997) and 3G (2013) mobile services. But the extensive deployment of optical fiber is essential to achieving 4G mobile broadband targets. And it is impossible to imagine the launch of 5G networks without a highly ubiquitous optical fiber transmission system. Massive optical fiber transmission through the "open access" principle is needed immediately to be applied across the broadband supply chain. Considering optical fiber as the artery of the digital world, predictable regulation is the best option to support the universal deployment of such capital-intensive infrastructure (ITU, 2012).[4]

3.5 *Policy on Software Technology Parks (STPs)*

Bangladesh's government has placed utmost importance on developing IT/software technology parks in various parts of the country to promote and encourage IT entrepreneurs and achieve last-mile digitization. A Bangladesh Hi-Tech Park Authority (BHTPA) has been established under the Bangladesh Hi-Tech Park Authority Act, 2010, to implement and manage the high-tech parks. The BHTPA is responsible for building Hi-Tech Parks or Software Technology Park and IT Training and Incubation Centers. So far, the BHTPA has undertaken projects to build 28 Hi-Tech Parks across the country. By now, the construction of 4 parks has already been completed, with business activities being in operation.

The BHTPA is mandated to monitor all operations relevant to all Hi-Tech Parks across the country, attract foreign investment by creating an investment-friendly environment in the Hi-Tech Parks, ensure a stable supply of skilled human resources well-versed in IT, and encourage the development of private STP. BHTPA also functions to propose rules including fiscal and non-fiscal incentives to invest in the country's STP

[4] According to the ITU, the payback period of an optical fiber project is 15 years (check out https://unesdoc.unesco.org/ark:/48223/pf0000218226).

(Software Technology Parks), develop new infrastructure and systems, and design infrastructure to support a star-tup. However, given the bureaucratic structure of the BHTP and the lack of an appropriate workforce, the mandates of the BHTPA may not be realistic. The BHTPA needs to be equipped with technical and qualified personnel hired outside government functionaries.

Moreover, a proper analysis is needed on the impact of ICT parks in terms of entrepreneurs' willingness to start IT firms outside Dhaka and the potential benefits of agglomeration/cluster-based industrialization before embarking on massive investments in ICT parks. Though many countries and cities followed the successful paths of Silicon Valley of the USA or India's Bangalore IT Park to develop the ICT industry, they have not been successful to that extent. Given the importance of this policy, a separate chapter on this topic has thus been developed in this book.

Being a bureaucratic organization, it is unrealistic that this authority could fulfill the mandates. However, if BHTPA is given more autonomy and strengthened capacities in the workforce and logistics, this authority could deliver its mandated activities to a reasonable level.

3.6 Policies for Human Capital Development and Innovations

Some of the government's policies and programs to improve ICT skills for human resources are noteworthy. In general, there are three types of policies in place for human capital development: (i) providing fellowships and scholarships for short-term training as well as higher studies in ICT-related subjects; (ii) funds for ICT innovation projects; and (iii) promoting industry-academia linkages by engaging selected University departments.

To provide special grants to the ICT sector from the ICT department, "Policies on Fellowships and Scholarships for Research in the Information and Communication Technology Sector, Grants for innovative Work (Revised)—2016" were devised. The policy has three parts. The first part is about providing fellowships and scholarships for research, the second part is related to providing for innovative work, and the third part is about giving special grants to individuals, educational institutions, public–private institutions for activities or projects capable of contributing to the socio-economic development and public service. The ICT Fellowship and Scholarship Awards activities have been vested upon the ICT Division of the government. Apart from Research Fellowships and Scholarships, the policy implicates the provision of Master's Fellowship, MPhil or equivalent Fellowship, Doctoral Fellowship, and Post Doctoral Fellowship. However, only a few grants have been awarded under the policies.

Learning and Earning Development Project (LEDP)[5] is a project under the ICT division of the government that provides professional outsourcing courses and other ICT skills such as digital marketing, graphics design, web design, development, etc. at free of cost. It has already provided services to over 166,320 individuals with its digital caravan bus. The minimum requirement for admission is a higher secondary certificate or equivalent educational qualification. They conducted training programs in 5 districts: Dhaka, Rajbari, Shariyatpur, Madaripur, and Netrokona. It is 200 h of training where over 900 people can participate. Moreover, mentoring centers were opened in all five districts to provide post-training support for trainees.

Skills for Employment Investment Program (SEIP) is an important project on ICT human capital development launched in 2014, co-financed by the Asian Development Bank (ADB) and Swiss Agency for Development and Cooperation (SDC) under the Finance Division of the Finance Ministry. The project aims to create a steady supply of skilled labor to tackle market demand. The project will support training providers to meet industry skill requirements; finance skills training of 260,000 trainees with 182,000 job placements; implement a vocational trainer development program; and implement a skills assessment, certification, and quality assurance system. The project activities cover the whole of Bangladesh through both public and private sector training providers. The project's commencement date was July 2014, and the duration of the program has been extended till 2024, though the initial completion date was December 2017.

So far, the Skills for Employment Investment Program (SEIP) has trained and certified 49,694 candidates for the ICT sector, including 13,134 (26% of total) females (SEIP, 2021). Among the trained candidates, 11,614 (from BACCO) and 17,717 (from BASIS) got jobs at a 59% job placement rate. The SEIP has conducted studies to assess the skills gap and labor market outcomes on critical industries and sectors. Bangladesh Institute of Development Studies (BIDS) has assessed the

[5] https://mcc.com.bd/learning-and-earning-development-project-ledp/.

labor market and skills gap for ten thrust sectors including the ICT sector in two rounds in 2016 and 2020. Apart from that, ADB also conducted employer and employee surveys, particularly for the ICT sector, in 2018 to understand the skills and job market prospects. The assessment identified some loopholes in the design and implementation of the training programs. The concerns were expressed on issues regarding short training duration, eligibility criteria (one cannot enroll twice), problems in scaling up the program, etc., that need to be addressed to make the training programs more effective. It is also important to note that these short-term duration training programs are not the substitutes for graduate-level degrees necessary for producing IT professionals. The training programs need to be tailor-made to fill the skills gap in various occupations of the IT sector.

3.6.1 Access to Information (A2I) Program

Access to Information Program, established in 2007, was later renamed **Aspire to Innovate (a2i)**. This program works under the Prime Minister's Office and provides research and other technical support toward implementing the Digital Bangladesh vision. UNDP (United Nations Development Program), USAID (United States Agency of International Development), and other development partners have supported this program to enable its mandates, notably supporting its research and development activities. A2I program works on innovation, digital finance, empathy training, formulating SDG tracker, skills development, etc.

A few examples of a2i-funded innovations projects supporting ICT4D are (i) Department of Environment's online-based service enhancement (Implementing Agency: Department of Environment) (ii) Development of a Bangla Optical Character Recognizer (OCR) (Implementing Agency: United International University); (iii) Online Fertilizer Recommendation: Automation of data processing and data updating (Implementing Agency: Soil Resource Development Institute); (iv) Production of Multimedia Digital Talking Book (Implementing Agency: Young Power in Social Action—YPSA); (v) Jibon Bima Corporation's Cell Phone Insurance Claim Payment (Implementing Agency: Jiban Bima Corporation); (vi) Development of multimodal transport web portal with mobile interactivity (Implementing Agency: Road Transport and Highways Division (RTHD) of the Ministry of Road Transport and Bridges); and (vii) Service Delivery of Department of Livestock Services through SMS (Implementing Agency: Department of Livestock Services).

4 Interface of ICT Policies with Development Plans

The government places utmost importance on developing the ICT and ICT for development (ICT4D) sectors in various Planning documents highlighting the widespread adoption of ICTs as a critical development strategy. Starting from the 6th Five-Year Plan (2011–2015) and subsequent 7th Five-Year Plan (2016–2020), and 8th Five-Year Plan (2021–2025), and the Perspective Plans 2021 and 2041, strategies and actions in regard to ICTs have been aligned with overall development vision. The Plans have emphasized the development of ICT and set strategic objectives to implement the Government's commitments in the medium to long term.

As already argued, digitalization has become a buzzword of development considering digitalization a key development strategy in various development plans. To achieve a knowledge economy, it is important to embed the strategy in the national policies so that Bangladesh can become both a consumer of technologies and a producer of them. The national strategies are devised to ensure technology transfer between academia and industry, non-resident Bangladeshis and domestic counterparts, and foreign companies and local partners. The perspective plan 2041 emphasizes that ICTs can play an essential role in knowledge management, collaboration on research and development, technology transfer, and marketing of non-ICT technologies. Specific policies and action plans are needed to mainstreaming ICTs in development plans and realize the objectives of the Perspective Plan.

Box 2. Vision 2041 on ICT Targets
The Vision highlighted the following objectives to be achieved by 2041.

- Emergence of more internationally recognized scientists from Bangladesh by establishing more institutes of higher learning in science and technology.
- Allocation of a higher share of GDP (Gross Domestic Product) to research and development.
- Productivity increases in all spheres of the economy, including Micro, Small, and Medium Enterprises.
- Inclusion of ICT in education and research to expand the scope and standard of knowledge on ICT throughout the country, to

ensure computer literacy at all levels of education and government, to encourage creativity through research and development, and to help in the creation of talent and absorption of ICT in all spheres of life.

- Availing employment opportunities at national and international levels through education and training of ICT professionals to international standards.
- Establishment of the prosperous software industry to offer services based on ICT, ecommerce/e-business and to ensure growth in the ICT industry to meet the demand in domestic and international markets, to increase income from external trade, to attract Foreign Direct Investment (FDI), and to reduce dependence on imports.
- Quality health care will be provided to all citizens through the innovative application of ICT.
- Ensuring universal access to internet/telecom connection as a part of public welfare.
- Improve management of climate change, the environment, and disaster management through ICT application. Develop and absorb environmentally friendly green technology and dispose of polluted waste, including e-waste generated by increased use of ICT products.
- Reduce the time taken to respond to disasters and ensure effective steps in the overall management of climate change.

Source Ministry of Planning (2020)

5 Institutions

Three vital institutions oversee, monitor, and supervise the digitalization process and other related activities of the ICT sector. The institutions are: (i) the ICT Division of the Ministry of Post, Telecommunications and Information Technology (MoPTI), (ii) Bangladesh Computer Council (BCC), and (iii) Bangladesh Telecommunication Regulatory Commission (BTRC). Though their roles are overlapping and cross-cutting in some cases, BTRC is mainly responsible for telecom regulations. The ICT division of the MoPTI is responsible for ICT-related policy formulations and regulations. A brief overview of these institutions' activities, roles, and responsibilities is given below.

The Ministry of Post, Telecommunications, and Information Technology (MoPTI) is the main regulatory body of the government to oversee all the issues related to the development of science and technology to contribute to the socio-economic development of Bangladesh. The Ministry mainly revise existing policies about science and technology, collaborate with various ministries to integrate National Science and Technology Policy, implement the propositions suggested by the National Council for Science and Technology (NCST), individuals and institutions in the science and technology sector.

With an exclusive focus on attaining Digital Bangladesh's Vision, *the Information and Communication Technology (ICT) Division* was established on 14 February 2014 under MoPTI. It is an important policy decision for upscaling the status of digitalization in Bangladesh with a sole focus on ICTs. The key functions of the division include the design and formulation of national policies and regulations associated with information and technology while adding the adaptation of said information and technology in various ministries, departments, and agencies. This division's mandate includes a wide array of activities, such as the implementation of the National Task Force in ICT, piloting R&D in this sector, increasing integrity in various countries associated with ICT, assisting the integration of e-governance, e-infrastructure, e-health, e-commerce, and many more, and ensuring accessibility of ICTs to individuals through commercial practices, creation of skilled workforce, increasing public awareness, and so on. The division also provides the legal validity of electronic records and all data repositories. The division, however, suffers from the lack of a skilled workforce, mainly due to the low wage structure of the government. This limitation is often overcome by hiring consultants under various donor-supported projects and the A2I program of the government. A2I program may be aligned to the need of the ICT division as a sustainable solution to provide technical support to the Division.

Bangladesh Computer Council (BCC) is another institution established under the MoPTI with the Bangladesh Computer Council Act 1990 to monitor and regulate Bangladesh's ICT sector and associated activities. The council's function entails promoting the use of computers, developing the applications, and providing assistance in education and training on computer applications. Building an efficient infrastructure to support IT is also one of the objectives of BCC. The BCC, technically playing the role of ICT laboratory, comprises three computer labs with supercomputers in place with computer training centers in 5 divisions. It hosts the National Data Center, the only TIER-3 certified Government

Data Center in Bangladesh that allows the hosting of all the government websites, email services, and web applications. These labs enable the government and other institutions access to knowledge about information technology and associated activities.

On the other hand, BTRC is mandated to promote the expansion of the Telecommunication System that improves the collective wellbeing, provide Telecommunication services and the internet at reasonable prices, and safeguard the competency of the Telecommunication System. It also refrains from discernment while promoting the application of new and emerging services to create a secure environment for foreign investors seeking to invest in the Telecommunication Sector of Bangladesh.

However, like other institutions, BTRC also suffers from appropriate staffing, particularly in its technology-related divisions. Currently, few workforces are responsible for the Information Technology (IT) branch of the admiration department of BTRC. Though the IT branch has been growing concurrently, integrating technologies with increasing demand for the internet, there is added demand for an appropriate workforce in the Commission. With emerging issues related to cybercrime, technology up-gradation, and so on, BTRC must be equipped with proper human capital and incentives to serve digital Bangladesh.

5.1 ICT Associations

Four business associations are associated with different segments of ICT businesses/sectors. The associations are: (i) Bangladesh Association of Software and Information Services (BASIS), the leading association of the IT and ITES industry; (ii) Bangladesh Computer Samity (BCS), an association of computer hardware and accessories traders and software firms though there are overlaps in membership between BASIS and BCS; (iii) Bangladesh Association of Call Center and Outsourcing (BACCO) is an association of call centers and BPO (Business Process Outsourcing) firms and (iv) Internet Service Providers Association Bangladesh (ISPAB), is an association of broadband internet service providers.

Bangladesh Association of Software and Information Services (BASIS): BASIS is the national trade body for Bangladesh's Software and IT-enabled Service industry. Established in 1997, the association has become the prime association of the country's software and IT service industry. Today the membership stands more than two thousand. BASIS members account for the lion's share of the country's total software and IT services revenue. As a vibrant industry association, BASIS organizes BASIS SOFTEXPO, the most significant software and ITES exposition in the country, every year. It periodically publishes software and IT service catalog/directory for promoting local solution providers to potential business clients. BASIS has been playing a commendable role by working closely with different concerned Ministries and agencies of government to deal with various policy matters and secure the interests of the members. It also conducts some research activities and collaborates with donor agencies to enhance capacity building process of the Association and its members. BASIS institute of technology (BIT), with support from ADB-funded SEIP programs, offers training and skills development programs.

BASIS represents the industry in different national level committees, including the Digital Bangladesh Task Force (headed by PM), High-Tech Park Development Authority, and Executive Committee of Bangladesh Computer Council (BCC). The BASIS has played a role in securing the best interests of the ICT industry with its active role, which makes it the main ICT business body.

Bangladesh Computer Samity (BCS) is the apex ICT business and trade industry association of Bangladesh. It represents the industry comprising distributors, dealers, resellers of computer, and allied products, locally assembled computer vendors, software developers and exporters, internet service providers, ICT-based educational institutions and training houses, and other ICT-enabled services providers. Established in 1987 with 11 founding members, the total number of members now stands at 2173. A 7-number executive committee runs the body elected every two years. BCS looks into the interest of ICT entrepreneurs, promotes the effective use of ICT, renders expert business advice on ICT to the concerned authorities, and so on. It mainly represents the hardware sector of the ICTs. However, this association appears to be relatively weaker in its activities, such as developing hardware skills development, market access, effective communications with the government and donor agencies, promoting research and development, etc. However, BCS should focus on transforming the computer and other ICT hardware assembling sectors into manufacturing by pushing the government to formulate appropriate policies and incentive mechanisms. Also, BCS should focus on providing cheaper access to computers and accessories to all, mainly rural poor people, in materializing the Digital Bangladesh vision by working closely with the National Board of Revenue (NBR).

Bangladesh Association of Call Center and Outsourcing (BACCO) represents the Business Process Outsourcing (BPO) and Call Centre industry in Bangladesh. This vibrant association works with all stakeholders to create the right ecosystem and employment in this sector. The association contributes to formulating an appropriate policy, rules, and regulations for the sector to get greater market access both at local and international levels. They also oversee the industry needs and ensure appropriate education and training to create the workforce to support its growth. The industry has been enjoying a very high growth of its workforce and greater diversification of its work portfolio. In the next five years, BACCO has a target to outsource a sizable workforce for the government to citizen (G2C) services and banking and insurance services. However, the association should prioritize registering all unregistered members under the Association to provide better services to the customers by ensuring transparency and accountability of the firms.

Internet Service Providers Association of Bangladesh (ISPAB) is an association of internet service providers in Bangladesh. It was formed to seek Govt.'s help/attention, defining a legal framework to protect the industry, expanding the domestic internet connectivity market, providing education on websites, internet usage, etc. Though the ISPAB has been fulfilling its mandated activities successfully in liaising with the government on the interests of the ISPs, subscribers are still not fully satisfied with broadband internet services provided by many ISPs for their unreliable internet connections. The ISPAB must work seriously to bring all ISPs under the Association's membership to make them accountable and ensure better internet service. Also, internet pricing and cabling issues (underground cabling) of ISPs are major concerns on which the ISPAB needs to work efficiently with the respective agencies of the government (Table 2).

6 Concluding Remarks

Bangladesh has already formulated some important ICT sector-related policies, which provide strategic guidance to the sector and contribute to the country's digitalization. The evolution of the ICT sector policies can be divided into three phases, consistent with the phases of digitalization.

Firstly, deregulatory measures in the telecom sector, including reductions of import duty and VAT on computers and accessories in the 1990s coupled with financial and trade liberalization policies, set the foundation for developing the ICT sector. Secondly, during 2000–2008,

Table 2 Registered general members of different associations, 2016–2022

Name	*Members in 2016*	*Members in 2021*
Bangladesh Association of Software and Information Services (BASIS)	997	1891
Bangladesh Association of Call Center and Outsourcing (BACCO)	76	238
Internet Service Providers Association Bangladesh (ISPAB)	64	225
Bangladesh Computer Samity (BCS)	1452	2371

Source Association Websites

drastic reforms in the telecom sector allowed fixed and mobile telephones in the private sectors, considerable investments in the telecom sector, and connectivity with IIG through submarine cable network significantly reduced internet and mobile telephone call rates. Such improvements in ICT infrastructures and regulatory frameworks have kicked off the software industry since 2000 (Shinkai & Hossain, 2011). Thirdly, the government's Digital Bangladesh vision in 2009 made truly a flying start of the ICT sector through various policy and regulatory frameworks, digitalization measures, and infrastructure development reflected in productivity enhancements of the software firms by the end of 2020.

However, as discussed in this chapter, policies in some cases were premature in terms of lack of the proper conceptualization of ICT-related emerging issues, unrealistic implementation targets, and to some extent, un-implementable due to the lack of coordination among the government ministries and agencies, etc. Furthermore, policies related to foreign exchange regulation, licensing fees, VAT and Tax regulations, delay in the full implementation of ICT parks, hassles in getting a license and work permits for foreign IT experts, etc., are some of the issues that require further attention. Tax and tariff policies need to be rationalized to create a conducive environment for promoting the manufacturing of ICT hardware (computers, laptops, smartphones, semiconductors, etc.) by removing anti-export biases. Policies regarding ICT4D for specific sectors, such as health, education, agriculture, industry, etc., need a kick-off in fostering the development of the sectors. Thus, the critical task is to identify the policy-related impediments that hinder the potential growth and development of the ICT sector, in general, and trade and investment, in particular. Appropriate policies and incentives are needed to be devised to reduce digital inequality across regions, ethnicities, and income groups.

Finally, proper coordination between various stakeholders and government agencies is expected for the effective digital transformation of the country and to achieve a knowledge-based economy. More investments in R&D in the ICT sector are needed to accelerate the digital transformation of the economy.

References

Begum, A. M. A., Murad, M. H., & Hoque, K. A. (2014). Telecommunication regulation in Bangladesh: An overview. *IIUC Studies, 10 & 11*, 157–172.

Finance Division. (2015). *Digital Bangladesh vision report, 2015*. Ministry of Finance, Government of Bangladesh.

Hasan, S. (2014). ICT Policies and their role in governance: The case of Bangladesh. *Science, Technology and Society, 19*(3), 363–381.

International Telecommunication Union (ITU). (2012). *The state of broadband 2012: Achieving digital inclusion for all*.

Khan, A. S. (2021, July 17). Broadband landscaping in post-Covid-19 Bangladesh. *The Daily Star*. https://www.thedailystar.net/opinion/news/broadband-landscaping-post-covid-19-bangladesh-1903195

Ministry of Planning. (2020). *Making vision 2041 a reality: Perspective plan of Bangladesh 2021–2041*. General Economics Division. Ministry of Planning.

Ministry of Posts, Telecommunications and Information Technology. (2018). E-mail Policy. Department of Information and Communication Technology. Government of the People's Republic of Bangladesh

Multimedia Content and Communication Ltd (MCC). (n.d.). *Learning and Earning Development Project (LEDP)*. https://mcc.com.bd/learning-and-earning-development-project-ledp/

Shinkai, N., & Hossain, M. (2011). Productivity and performance of the IT sector in Bnagladesh: Evidence from firm-level data. *Bangladesh Development Studies, 34*(2).

Skills for Employment Investment Program (SEIP). (2021). *Training statistics*. https://seip-fd.gov.bd/

Speedtest by Ookla. (2021). *Bangladesh's mobile and fixed broadband internet speeds*. Speedtest by Ookla—The Global Broadband Speed Test. https://www.speedtest.net/global-index/bangladesh

Trademark Act. (2009). Department of Legislative and Parliamentary Affairs. Ministry of Law, Justice and Parliamentary Affairs.

CHAPTER 5

IT and IT Enabled Service (ITeS) Sector in Bangladesh: Current Status and Future Potentials

1 Introduction

A widely argued proposition is that the ICT sector may provide a developing country an opportunity to "leapfrog" into the industrialized economy status (Perez & Soete, 1988) through their comparative advantages in human capital and low wage structure. The ICT industry may contribute to the economic development in two ways: one, the development of the ICT industry will lead to more export and employment, and two, the adoption of ICTs in different sectors of the economy will enhance productivity in addition to many other spillover benefits. For example, there are huge opportunities for developing countries to take advantage of the US$700 billion markets for global offshore and outsourcing IT services, mostly belonging to developed countries. The emerging and ever-expanding global offshore and IT outsourcing industry could lead to phenomenal growth in export earnings and employment generation in developing countries due to low wages and declining costs of the internet, telecommunications, and computers. The rapid decline in the cost of ICTs helps the emergence of the offshore/outsourcing industry in developing countries too. Therefore, one of the objectives of developing the IT industry should be to grab a certain share of the highly growing (at a CAGR of over 7.7%) global outsourcing and offshore service sectors with a market size of about US$175–180 billion and US$ 520.74 billion, respectively (Everest

M. Hossain, *Digital Transformation and Economic Development in Bangladesh*, https://doi.org/10.1007/978-981-19-2753-9_5

Group, 2017; Grand View Research, 2017).[1] The global offshore and outsourcing service markets are dominated by the IT outsourcing market (ITO), followed by Business Process Outsourcing (BPO) and Knowledge Process Outsourcing (KPO). If properly harnessed, developing countries can exploit this opportunity of the phenomenal growth of the outsourcing industry in their favor in creating employment and enhancing service exports.

The importance of developing the ICT industry can be seen not only by its contribution to the economy but also by its spillover benefits to other sectors. For example, ICTs could pave the way for other industries, such as electronics, automobiles, electric goods, servitization of manufacturing, digital finance, etc. ICTs, in most cases, create backward linkages for these industries by supplying software, microchips, etc. Therefore, the skills in the ICTs may complement the other hi-tech industries. This argument is consistent with the Product Space Theory of diversification (Hidalgo et al., 2007) because countries find it easier to diversify into products that require skills that are broadly similar to skills already present in the country and embodied in existing products. Let's look at the East Asian development model. Japan, the ASEAN 4 (Indonesia, Malaysia, Philippines, and Thailand), and other latecomers followed the flying geese development model whereby they start with manufacturing non-durable consumer goods like apparel and then progress to durable consumer goods, and afterward to capital goods of higher value (Lopez-Acevedo & Robertson, 2016). The export-led growth in these countries was initially supported by the labor-intensive apparel sector and then progressed towards capital-intense sectors like electronics and ICTs.

The cost escalation in developed countries leads to the rapid growth of the outsourcing industry in developing countries. India and other emerging countries have already captured a substantial portion of outsourcing and offshore businesses. However, Bangladesh has not been able to gain a considerable market share of global offshore and outsourcing business.[2] With a population of over 170 million and the

[1] There are differences in estimates of global outsourcing market size. For example, Statista estimated that the global IT outsourcing market size was US$92.5 billion in 2019 (Statista, 2021a, b).

[2] Although multinational corporations (MNCs) and large firms receive the most significant proportion of ICT business services, the participation of small and medium-sized enterprises (SMEs) is gradually increasing in offshore services. In 2006, about 30% of

demographic dividend in place, the prospect of IT outsourcing is bright in Bangladesh, if the country can exploit the potential of the youths properly. The number of registered IT (Information Technology) firms (with BASIS) grew at over 40% during 2010–2020 with annual revenue growth of the ICT industry (excluding telecom) of 15% or so, and annual profitability rate in between 15% and 20%. The phenomenal growth of the mobile phone service and the "Digital Bangladesh" initiative of the government contributed to the present growth of the industry. With various government initiatives and the private sector, the usability of ICT-enabled services by the people has been growing steadily over time. The number of internet, mobile, and fixed telephone users and the amount of investments in ICTs have been expanding gradually. However, to reap the benefits of ICTs at their full potential, it is necessary to put appropriate policies for human capital development in place.

This chapter attempts to provide an overview of the ICT industry in Bangladesh in terms of its market size and potential, important ICT policies of the government toward various sub-sectors with performances, and challenges of the ICT industry. To do so, the chapter is organized as follows. After the introduction, Sect. 2 discusses the comparative advantages for Bangladesh to develop the IT sector and Sect. 3 gives an overview of the ICT service sector of Bangladesh. Section 4 discusses the various aspect of the ICT sub-sectors in Bangladesh, and Sect. 5 highlights multiple challenges that the ICT sector has been facing. Section 5 concludes the chapter.

2 Overview of IT Service Industry

Excluding the telecom sector, the ICT sector in Bangladesh consists of four sub-sectors: IT (Information Technology) enabled services (ITES), internet service providers (ISPs), call centers, and the ICT hardware sector. In 2020, there are about 2000 registered software and IT-enabled service (ITES) firms, about 129 internet service providers (ISPs), and

the small firms contributed to outsourcing processes, while in 2000, only about 10% of small companies offshored services (Duke Offshoring Research Network and Booz and Co., 2006). In comparison, 37% of small businesses opted to outsource in 2019 (Panko, 2019). The opportunity for ICT SMEs in offshore services is increasing over time as venture capital firms are increasingly initiating offshoring in their business models.

297 licensed call centers,[3]—most of them are based in Dhaka. The size of the ICT market in Bangladesh, excluding telecom, is estimated to be around $120 million in 2010, which has increased to about US$1.1 billion in 2017 (BASIS, 2018). The sector expects to increase its exports to US$5 billion by 2025. Currently, the industry employs roughly about 0.3 million IT professionals and other support staff. According to Oxford Internet Institute, Bangladesh has the second-largest pool of freelancers globally. According to BACCO, over 40,000 individuals are employed in the outsourcing industry, earning over $300 million annually (Ahmed, 2019).[4]

Most of the IT firms are small and medium in size; however, a few large firms capture a significant market share. In addition, six mobile phone operators, 37 IIG (International Internet gateway Service), 6 NTTNs (Nationwide Telecommunication Transmission Network) firms, 12 PSTN (Public Switched Telephone Network) operators, 44 VSAT (Very Small Aperture Terminal) users, 26 Interconnection Exchange (ICX) Services, and 2500 hardware sales and servicing centers have been supporting IT, ISP, and call center firms (Bangladesh Telecommunication Regulatory Commission).[5]

The exports of IT & ITeS services grew from 319 million US dollars in 2013 to 802 million US dollars in 2018 at a compound annual growth rate (CAGR) of 17%, and at a similar rate, domestic sales grew from 93 million US dollars to 232 million US dollars during the same period (Fig. 3). However, there is no reliable estimate of aggregate revenue generated by the industry. The market segment ratio of IT (software) and ITeS is 55:45. The maturity level of the IT companies is reflected in their standard certifications obtained from internationally accredited organizations. However, there is no concrete information on IT companies' certifications. Though a good number of companies have obtained ISO (International Organization for Standardization) certification, only

[3] The figures mentioned here are taken from the websites of the industry associations. The number of registered firms with an industry association or BTRC is lower than the mentioned figures.

[4] One of the weaknesses in the development of the ICT industry is the lack of official statistics on market size, employment, revenue, etc. The information given here is based on piecemeal studies and scattered documents, which may not reflect the actual scenario of the ICT industry.

[5] The numbers are taken from the official website of BTRC.

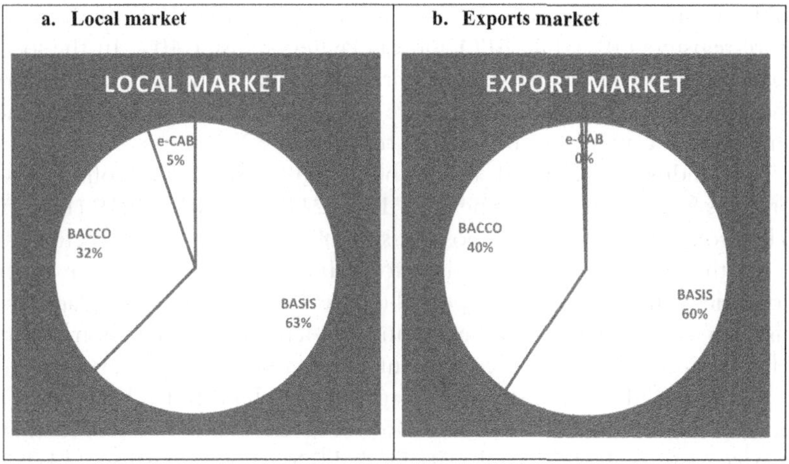

Fig. 1 Market share of sales revenue, 2018 (*Source* Bangladesh Computer Council [2019])

a few companies have achieved CMMI (Capability Maturity Model Integration)[6] Level 3 (Bangladesh Hi-Tech Park Authority).[7] To gain clients ' confidence, firms need to achieve CMMI certification level 3 or more. Numerous Indian software firms are equipped with CMMI Level 4 or 5, which shows a sign of maturity in the industry (Parthasarathy, 2015).[8]

Figure 1 shows the market share (local and export) of the firms registered with BASIS (mainly software), BACCO (call centers and BPO),

[6] CMMI is a process improvement approach that provides organizations with the essential elements of effective processes that ultimately improve their performance. CMMI can be used to guide process improvement across a project, a division, or an entire organization. It helps integrate traditionally separate organizational functions, set process improvement goals and priorities, provide guidance for quality processes, and provide a point of reference for appraising current processes. There are five levels, of which the first two are elementary, that most firms can achieve. However, reaching level 3 and above is particularly important to be internationally competitive.

[7] The numbers are taken from the official website of BHTPA.

[8] Indian software industry was developed with the infrastructure, technology, quality process, productivity tools, and methodologies of the customer workplace. By June 2002, 85 Indian software firms were certified with CMMi 5 Level compared with 42 in the rest of the world (Parthasarathy, 2015).

and e-CAB (e-commerce). In the export market, the share of the software registers 60% while BPO and call centers register 40%. In the local market, the share of the software firms is similar to that of the export market, only e-commerce firms have a 5% share here and therefore the share of call centers and BPOs have reduced to 32%.

The industry registered a slow but steady increase in profit (Gross profit as % of revenue) ranging from 16 to 21% over 2015–2019 (Fig. 2). The profitability rates cast a positive sign of the growth of the sector.

In the context of South Asia, except India, the ICT sector in other countries is not growing as expected (Table 1). The case of Bangladesh is also not very promising as the country has fetched only 1 billion dollars of ICT service exports, which is about 17% of its total service exports and 0.3% of its GDP (2019 estimates). Lagging far behind India, Pakistan's IT & ITeS exports constitute about 0.45% of its GDP and 4.55% of its total service exports. For Sri Lanka, its IT & ITeS exports constitute 14.29% of total service exports, and its share in GDP is negligible. In the case of India, its IT & ITeS service exports constitute 36% of total service exports and 8% of GDP. Bangladesh's position is second in South Asia in terms of service exports. However, Bangladesh has yet to reap the sector's full potential given its comparative advantages in policy support and abundance of human resources. The constraints are discussed in the latter part of this chapter.

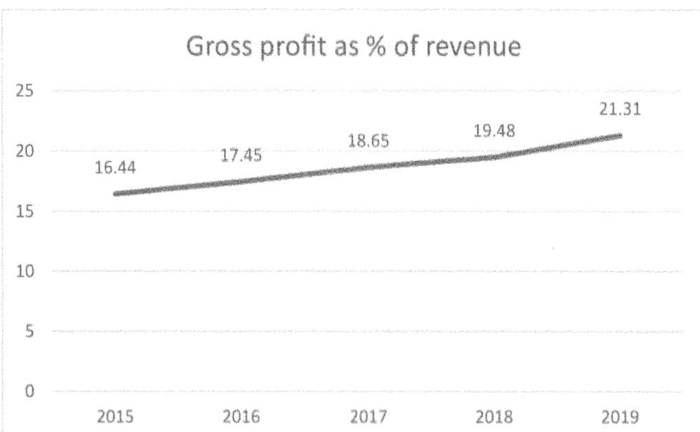

Fig. 2 Gross profit as a percentage of revenue

Table 1 IT & ITeS exports in South Asia

	Bangladesh	*India*	*Pakistan*	*Sri Lanka*	*Nepal*	*Bhutan*
Export (IT & ITES)	$802 million (2018)	US$ 79 billion (2020)	$1.23 billion (2019–2020)	US$ 925.7 thousand (2017)	US$ 287.7 thousand (2017)	US$ 411.6 thousand (2017)
IT & ITeS export as % of total service exports	16.67	38.58	4.55	14.29	–	–
IT & ITeS Exports as % of GDP	0.3 (2018)	8 (2020)	0.45	0.001	0.001	0.02

Sources Worldstopexports.com; Bangladesh Computer Council (2019)

3 ICT Sub-Sectors

3.1 Software/IT Industry

The IT industry has been growing steadily from both quantitative and qualitative aspects. The current employment in the sector is estimated at over 0.3 million in 2020, of which IT professionals dominate. Bangladeshi IT sector registers a phenomenal growth of software and ITES exports, with an estimated annual compound growth rate (CAGR) at 16.67% during 2013–2018 (Fig. 3a). However, export earnings from freelancing and some IT-enabled services remain unreported due to online payment-related obstacles.[9] It is to be noted that a 40% growth of the complementary personal computer and electronics market provides support to the development of the ICT industry (Hossain, 2016). On the other hand, the local market revenue from the IT and ITeS sector is estimated at US$232 million in 2018 at a CAGR of 16.5% over the period 2013–2018, according to the BCC study (Fig. 3b).[10]

The main activities of the IT firms are related to web development, e-commerce, ERP (Enterprise Resource Planning), and Graphics. Over the

[9] According to Export Promotion Bureau (EPR), Bangladesh earned only around $276.45 million by exporting software and ITES in 2018–2019 (Ovi, 2020).

[10] The local market revenue earned by the IT and ITeS sector is grossly underestimated due to problems in reporting as well as tax evasion motives of the firms.

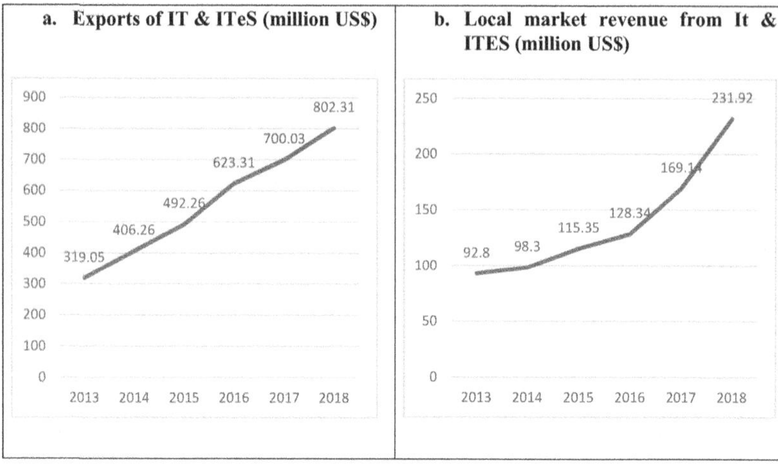

Fig. 3 Exports and local market revenue of IT and IT-enabled services, 2013–2019 (Million US dollars) (*Source* Bangladesh Computer Council [BCC] [2019])

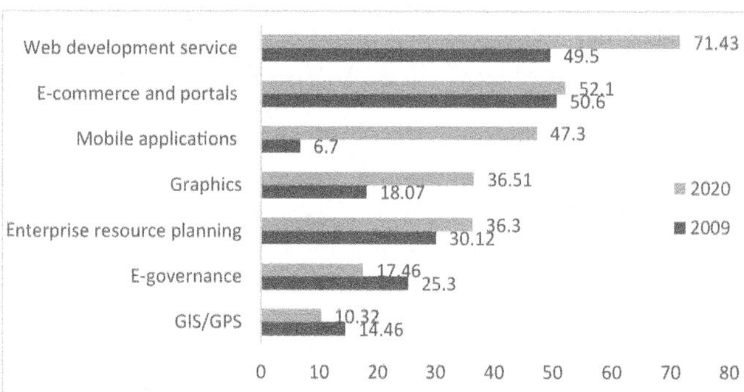

Fig. 4 Major areas of activities of software industries, 2009–2020 (%) [$N = 82$ (2010)/124] (2020) (*Source* BIDS Survey, 2009; BIDS-SEIP Survey, 2020)

last ten years, a significant increase in the proportion of firms involved in web development, graphics, and mobile applications is observed; however, in other services, the proportion of firms has not increased, indicating stagnation in their business (Fig. 4). This reflects that Bangladeshi software firms heavily rely on low-value adding web development and application-related software development. To achieve the target of 5 billion or more export earnings from the software industry, the industry will need to focus more on high-value-added consulting and packaged software with gaining share of offshore services in software exports. Compared to India, Bangladeshi software firms suffer from low value-added products and services, and therefore, there is a high prospect for Bangladeshi IT firms to establish a production network with Indian firms (Hossain et al., 2012). Further development requires investment in R&D services with emphasis on embedded system including the production of semiconductor.[11]

IT Freelancing: IT freelancing came up as a boon for Bangladesh. The freelancers capture about 20% of the freelancing market share, which is significant for an individual country context. Freelance services and earnings largely remain unnoticed due to the official hassle of money transfer and, therefore, are not accounted for export statistics. These unreported freelance service exports undermine the country's overall exports and sector potential. The absence of an international payment gateway, such as PayPal, is an important hindrance to the development of the freelance industry. Even incentives for buying computers/laptops and necessary training programs for freelancing would create enormous growth in this sector.

Box 1: Freelancers in Bangladesh
Freelancing has been increasing significantly in Bangladesh, especially among young individuals. According to a study conducted by the Oxford Internet Institute (OII), Bangladesh facilitates the second-largest pool of online IT workers, after India, which provides 24% of the global freelancers. Around 650,000 certified freelancers have been working in Bangladesh, representing about 16% of the global freelancers. The freelancers have been earning about USD100 million every year. Meanwhile, the USA is a close contender, facilitating only about 12% of the global freelancers.

[11] India's experience of shifting from body-shopping to offshore turnkey contracts made a significant leap to Indian software industry since the 1990s, leading to the emergence of software technology parks (STPs). Further shift in Indian software industry was seen from turnkey contracts to R&D services with embedded system (Parthasarathy, 2015).

About 40% of the freelancers in Bangladesh belong to marketing and sales, which makes up about 6.8% of the aggregate number of freelancers operating around the globe. Twenty-two percent are adept in software development and technology, and around 25% work with media management. Yet, only 10% of freelancers are employed in jobs requiring soft skills such as writing, translating, or data entry. Meanwhile, the software development and technology market is overpowered by Indian freelancers obtaining 55% of the market share. The freelancers from the UK domineer over the professional service market segment hold 22% of the share. This includes jobs relating to accounting, the law, and business consultancy.

Sources LightCastle Partner (2020).

3.2 *Internet Service Providers (ISPs)*

Currently, around 2,000 ISPs (most unregistered) provide broadband internet services to over 10 million subscribers across Bangladesh. However, most ISP firms operate informally as only 550 ISPs are registered in 2020 with the BTRC (Bangladesh Telecommunication Regulatory Commission). With a significant increase in internet usage, particularly broadband internet usage, the growth of ISPs in terms of numbers and bandwidth delivery has been very rapid, according to the Internet Service Provider Association of Bangladesh (ISPAB). About 50,000 people are engaged in the ISPs, of whom 30–50% are IT professionals, and the rest are from non-IT backgrounds. About 10 to 12 medium to large-sized ISPs has been operating in the country with employees of more than 400. Given the increased demand for the internet, the ISP sector has been growing rapidly. However, the sustainability of the growth of ISPs depends on the continuous increase in bandwidth supply and investments in last-mile connectivity to reach out to rural areas. The primary activities of the ISP firms are internet and web support (77%) and networking (66%), as indicated in Table 2.

A recent estimate shows that the size of bandwidth is now about 1600 Gbps per month from two submarine cables, and 400 Gbps is imported from India, which was 300 Gbps in 2016, of which ISP subscribers consume 75% of bandwidth and the rest 25% are by mobile phone subscribers. The broadband internet market is now worth around Tk. 800 million, and according to industry insiders, about 0.8 million customers

Table 2 Major activities of ISPs

	Percent of cases
Internet/Web support	76.62
Networking	66.23
Others (specify)	1.3
N	35

Source BIDS-SEIP Survey (2020)

are added every year to the broadband customer base. The cabling (transmission) services to ISPs, almost being monopolized by two NTTNs (National Telecommunication Transmission Networks), disrupting efficient services of the ISPs through their inefficiencies. Providing licenses to more NTTNs and bringing all ISPs under the registration process would thus be the potential policy options to increase competition and service quality of ISPs.

3.3 *Call Centre and BPO Services*

The importance of call centers has been growing in the country with a growing corporate sector and demand for value-added services. About 80 call centers are now operational, creating employment for about 40,000 people. Most call centers are domestic-market focused as lack of adequate English proficiency professionals deters their access to the international market. The majority of call centers, about 80–85%, provide voice, and the rest, 15–20%, provide non-voice outsourcing services. Non-voice service includes some of the knowledge process outsourcing (KPO) services, such as Accounting, Human Resource Management, and Legal Services. The market size of the BPO industry is about $300 million, as estimated in 2018 (BACCO, 2019). The BPO/call center service industry has a high potential for creating employment opportunities for less-educated youths (Table 3). However, the potentials are partly tamed down due to the absence of skilled people.

Despite the limitations, the current growth of the BPO industry is noteworthy (Fig. 5). The industry's market size has increased from US$4 million in 2008–2009 to over US$150 million in 2015 and further to US$300million in 2018. This is considered one of the most profitable sectors. The growth prospects of the BPO industry underline the importance of having appropriate policies and incentive mechanisms in

Table 3 Major activities of call centers

	Percent of valid cases
Call center services	45.45
Business process outsourcing (BPO)	77.27
Data entry and processing	27.27
Graphic Design & Image processing	18.18
Total valid cases	21

Note Multiple Responses are considered; *Source* BIDS-SEIP survey (2020)

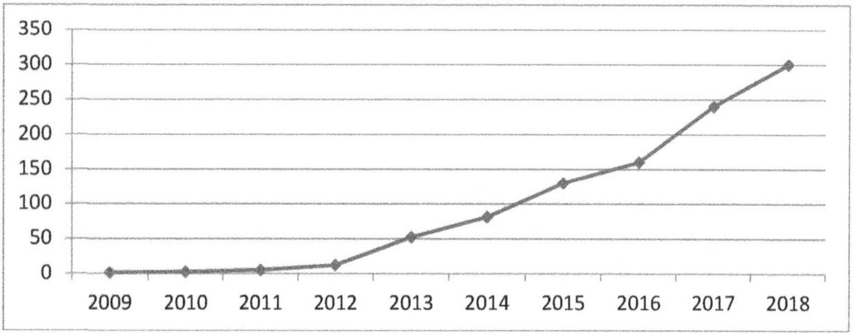

Fig. 5 Revenue from BPO service during 2009–2018 (million US$) (*Source* BACCO [2019])

place. For further growth of the sector, it must explore access to international markets. Bangladesh's BPO industry has the potential to get access to both English-speaking and Arabic-speaking countries. Since many students are studying in the Qowmi Madrasha (Arabic), who is proficient in Arabic, Middle-Eastern countries may be targeted by the BPO/call center firms. This will not only increase the market size of this sector; it also will create employment for Madrasha students.

3.4 *Hardware Sector*

The hardware sector consists of approximately 10,000 firms, but the industry mainly provides assembling and repairing services. Most of the firms sell computer and computer accessories. About 60,000 PCs and laptops are sold per month in Bangladesh, which is low for a country having over 160 million people.[12] About 2,500 hardware/system engineers are engaged in this sector with diplomas or training on computer hardware systems. Most of them either completed HSC exams or a diploma in engineering, except a few having higher degrees. They are primarily trained in BIOS editing, BGA installation, micro-chip, and basic computer knowledge, as indicated by the industry Association officials. As the manpower force is suitable for the hardware assembling sector, it may not be suitable for the hardware manufacturing one. New training and skills would be required for the manufacturing of ICT hardware. The hardware sector is relatively smaller at this moment given the lower demand arising out of the low purchasing capacity of the poorer people.

Bangladesh could not yet find its place in computer parts and accessories manufacturing. Mobile phone sets, LED TVs, and refrigerators are now being manufactured at a smaller scale by some Bangladeshi companies with joint venture initiatives. With an increasing demand for computers and laptops, the need for hardware engineers has also been increasing gradually.

4 Challenges of the Sector

Some of the critical challenges of the ICT sector that deter its expected growth and development are highlighted below.

Creating a brand value for knowledge-based industries: Creating a brand value for the knowledge-based industries is exceedingly essential to gain enormously from the ICT sector and use it as a base for development leap. Current demographic dividend and success in freelancing may be the starting point in addition to the country's impressive economic progress for creating a brand value for the ICT sector. Digital Bangladesh policy of the government and significant investments in the ICT sector could help uplift the country's image and improve the perception of foreign investors about this sector. Moreover, Bangladesh may be an important destination for offshore and outsourcing IT businesses. What is important for this is to communicate the positive changes that happened in the country to foreign investors.

[12] There is a lack of appropriate data on hardware demand and supply in the country.

Attract FDIs in the IT sector: The inflow of foreign direct investments (FDI) in the IT sector is still very low. Without having FDIs, it is tough to expand and gain significantly from the sector. Allowing multinational enterprises to set up their subsidiaries and joint ventures will lead the sector to move forward in value-added software activities and earn substantially from exports of e-services.

Turn hardware assembler into hardware manufacturer: Numerous hardware assembler firms operate in the country, mainly by importing parts and accessories from China. Proper incentives and policies are required to turn them into manufacturing units. Anti-protectionist policies need to be reviewed and revised to encourage local and foreign investors to invest in computer and telecommunications accessories.

Invest in R&D and innovations: Most Bangladesh IT firms do not have R&D labs, and they do not invest adequately in R & R&D. Investment in R&D in the IT sector is necessary to upgrade their products and services constantly. This will enable the firms to expand their export base through innovations. However, the government may provide incentives, such as easy access to bank credit to encourage private IT firms to establish R&D labs.

Move up the value chain by focusing on high-value-added consultancy and package software: Bangladeshi software firms are still engaged in low-value-added web development and applications software. These activities will not give them a competitive edge after a few years. Therefore the firms, at least the larger firms, should focus more on high-value-added consultancy services and package software. To create value for the industry, they also need to invest in new and emerging areas such as artificial intelligence, robotics, big data, etc. Though these activities are dependent on the availability of human capital, creating industry-academia linkages would be helpful in this matter.

Expand call centers and BPO in Arabic languages: Lack of English language proficiency deters the growth of the call center services from overseas. India has been the most preferred outsourcing location because call centers in India offer a wide variety of advantages due to good English proficient and IT-savvy workforce that many other countries do not provide. Since it is difficult in Bangladesh to develop an English-proficient workforce overnight to cater to the growing demand for overseas call center services, it may expand the call center services for the oil-rich middle-eastern countries using its Arabic language-proficient Madrasha students/graduates. Proper training, tapping the

Arabic outsource markets, and adequate incentives and policies might help expand the call center business.

Bring ISPs into the regulatory framework to provide efficient internet service: As discussed in the chapter, the majority of small but illegal ISPs have mushroomed in the country that is outside the regulatory framework, and therefore, clients have to compromise with the quality of internet services. BTRC needs to focus this issue seriously so that these small ISPs come into the regulatory framework and do their business properly. There should not have any entry barriers for these smaller ISPs.

Focus more on international quality accreditations and process maturity levels: International accreditations enhance international orientation and professionalism that will ultimately help the IT firms grow better. One criticism for the IT firms in Bangladesh is that they lack professionalism, and therefore, they are not competitive in getting even domestic IT projects. Only a few firms have received ISO 9000 certificates, and quite a few received CMMI level 3 and above, indicating that more efforts are required to get international accreditations to remain competitive in the sector.

Expand supply base of software firms by focusing on manufacturing sectors: The IT firms should focus more on developing industry-specific software. The manufacturing sectors in Bangladesh lack automation and investments in innovation, which is crucial for enhancing productivity and efficiency. There is a vast scope for automating the manufacturing sector. The IT sector may target both SMEs and larger firms to provide them with necessary IT services. The IT firms may create proprietary software for service and manufacturing sectors. IT and business associations should work closely to unlock the potential of automation and innovations in the manufacturing industry.

Meet the growing scarcity of a Skilled workforce: Most IT firms suffer from the shortage of qualified and skilled human resources and frequent mobility of skilled workers, which threatens the firm's position in the market niche. The majority of graduates do not have skills appropriate to the ICT industry. As a result, every firm has to provide them with on-the-job training. The skill gap is estimated at 40% regarding non-availability and lack of desired quality (Hossain, 2016). There is also evidence of skill mismatches. Appropriate policies for skills development and close coordination between academia and industry might reduce the skills gap situation.

Access to finance: Inadequate access to finance for IT companies is another hindrance to their growth and development. As IT companies lack tangible assets that can be collateralized (like traditional businesses) for getting a bank loan, their access to bank finance is limited. As a solution, an Equity Entrepreneurship Fund (EEF), an equity financing facility, was created in 2000 for the IT and other sectors with a particular preference to the IT sector. However, the outcome was unsatisfactory as many borrowers, including IT firms, embezzled the fund (Bakht & Hossain, 2013). Like other countries, alternative financing options for IT companies such as venture capital, angel capital, and other long-term equity finance could overcome their financing needs.

Intellectual Property Rights (IPR): Another threat to the development of the IT industry is the lack of enforcement of IPR acts. Although the Bangladesh Government enacted Trademark Act 2009 in this regard, lack of implementation and enforcement appears to be a significant threat to the development of this industry.

Foreign exchange regulation and online payment: IT/Software exporting firms can remit abroad up to US$40,000 in a calendar year for paying various fees, such as software registration fee, domain registration/hosting fee, server maintenance fee, account verification/remittance test fee, etc. However, the industry is demanding to increase the ceiling up to US$50,000. Another potential problem regarding international payment is that internationally reputed online payment gateways, such as PayPal and others, still are not interested in operating in Bangladesh. The problems in the online payment create an obstacle for remitting the appropriate amount quickly and cost-effectively, particularly for the smaller IT firms, which poses a threat to the sector's growth.

The Lack of data and statistics: The ICT sector in Bangladesh has been heavily suffering from accurate data and statistics, which is an impediment to the development of the sector. There are no reliable estimates on software and ITeS service exports as all the export proceeds are not realized through the official channels. Difficulties in money transfer for software purchases and other purposes undermine the actual figures of export earnings reported by the Export Promotion Bureau (EPB), including earnings from freelancing activities. Even ICT exports are reported in a category that combines other sectors too. Furthermore, employment, aggregate revenue, and market size of the sector are not accurately and authentically estimated. The lack of data, therefore, hampers research and development in this sector. A coordinated approach involving all relevant agencies and ministries should be taken to resolve the data problem.

5 Conclusions

The growth path of the ICT industry is complex and, to some extent, path-dependent. The country undertook digitalization efforts at a massive scale under its Digital Bangladesh agenda, and the development of infrastructure toward connectivity and digitalization are in progress. Despite the progress, private sector automation and access to the internet by households is still very low, impeding the benefits of the digitalization process. The analysis in this chapter highlights that incentives and motivations are needed to increase access to digital connectivity at a larger scale. Simultaneously, the development of the IT industry, which is important for the overall digital transformation of the economy, is still at its nascent stage, embarking on only human capital. The industry needs proper support and guidance to undertake productivity-enhancing innovations to capture a segment of global IT outsourcing/offshore industry services. The IT industry needs to enhance dynamic firm capability and specialize in emerging areas.

A handful of ICT firms export their products and services to over 60 countries. The primary export market is North America, followed by EU countries and East Asian countries, especially Japan (BASIS, 2018). However, Bangladeshi firms mainly export less sophisticated software services, including business process outsourcing services, web solutions, graphics, and GIS content, leaving a great potential to expand its export market on high-end IT services. The other software products of the industry are e-commerce, e-governance, enterprise resource planning (ERP). However, the demand for sophisticated software products like programming and R&D, IT consultancy, and KPO is insignificant in Bangladesh.

While manufacturing was the lowest of the ladder of value addition in 2010, with banking and financial services being the leader, manufacturing has been adopting ICTs slowly over time which will help the sector integrate into the global value chain. It is expected that further adoption of ICTs will add greater value to other sectors and the ICT sector itself. However, a proper analysis is needed to identify the IT applications and software for the manufacturing industry. With slow but steady adoption of ICT applications by the manufacturing industry, including the manufacturing SMEs, would be able to move up the value chain through more efficient production, which will provide the highest value addition to the ICT sector itself. Enhancement of productivity of the IT firms is crucial for achieving a competitive edge and moving up the value chain (Athreye, 2005).

Market expansion and linkages are critical to the development of the ICT industry. In Bangladesh, in the absence of institutional mechanisms for establishing market linkages, individual-level efforts, particularly from non-resident Bangladeshis (NRBs), some donor-funded projects and EPB supported overseas fair participation (every year Bangladesh takes part in 3–4 international fairs) are some of the notable market linkage programs that have played an important role for better market access, enhanced exports and brand value creation. A few foreign entrepreneurs who have established fully owned subsidiaries in Bangladesh also provide market linkages. However, direct marketing and setting up marketing and client servicing offices in vital overseas markets could have been very successful initiatives. Encouraging foreign direct investments in this sector could play a catalytic role in developing the IT industry to its next level through establishing international market linkages.

Given the enormous potential of the country with a population of over 160 million and adult literacy rate is close to 75%, the development of the ICT industry is thus essential to cater to the needs of digital transformation of the economy to leapfrog into a developed nation by 2041, as the government envisioned. It is thus necessary to transform a large number of educated and energetic youths having bright aptitude into the skilled human capital required for the ICT industry.

Rightly branding and arranging target market-specific business linkage programs are possible options that might help buyers to look at Bangladesh seriously as an outsourcing option. Bangladesh can take advantage of its low wage in the context of wage hikes in countries like India and China, along with its demographic dividend. If the youths are adequately groomed, Bangladesh can offer a unique combination of IT and English Language skills at a very competitive cost. This could be an attractive option for investment in IT and language skills development programs. For call center outsourcing services, apart from English, Arabic language-based call center services can be offered targeting Middle-Eastern Arab countries. More efforts are needed to reduce the digital divide in ICT infrastructure by improving access to the internet and other connectivity in the rural lagging regions to enhance IT services.

Appendix 1: Definitions of Activities of Software Firms

Activities	*Definition*
e-commerce	E-commerce is defined as any transaction that involves the buying and selling of products and services by businesses and consumers through an electronic medium. E-commerce includes three categories: business to business (B2B), e.g., Cisco, business to consumer (B2C), e.g., Amazon, consumer to consumer (C2C), e.g., eBay. It is also known as electronic commerce
e-governance	E-governance refers to the use, by government agencies, of information technologies (such as Wide Area Networks, the Internet, and mobile computing) that can transform relations with citizens, businesses, and other arms of government. These technologies can serve various quarters: better delivery of government services to citizens, improved interactions with business and industry, citizen empowerment through access to information, or more efficient government management. The resulting benefits can be less corruption, increased transparency, greater convenience, revenue growth, and cost reductions (World Bank)
Enterprise Resource Planning (ERP)	ERP is an integrated software solution used to manage a company's internal and external resources. It is also known as enterprise requirement planning
Business Process Outsourcing (BPO)	Business Process Outsourcing refers to contracting out the operations and responsibilities of specific business functions or processes to a third-party provider. BPO activities include enterprise resource management (ERM), comprehensive finance and accounting, procurement-logistic and supply chain management, content and document management, human resource management (HRM), payroll and benefits administration, customer relationship management (CRM), etc.
Knowledge Process Outsourcing (KPO)	KPO refers to relatively high-level tasks. Unlike BPO, where the focus is on process expertise, KPO focuses on knowledge expertise; hence, it is a high-level task. KPO includes research and advisory services, reference data management, engineering service, etc.
Graphics	Graphics are visual presentations on surfaces, such as a wall, canvas, computer screen, paper, or stone to brand, inform, illustrate, or entertain. Examples are photographs, drawings, line art, graphs, diagrams, typography, etc. Graphics often combine text, illustration, and color

References

Ahamed, M. (2014). *A report on Information Communication Technology (ICT) Sector of Bangladesh*. Japan Bangla Business Center.

Ahasan, N. (2017, October 30). When PayPal didn't come to town. *The Daily Star*. https://www.thedailystar.net/opinion/perspective/when-paypal-didnt-come-town-1483426

Ahmed, F. (2019, May 14). Bangladesh emerging as a new IT hub in South Asia. *Deutsche Welle*. https://www.dw.com/en/bangladesh-emerging-as-a-new-it-hub-in-south-asia/a-48728439

Asian Development Bank. (2019). *Bangladesh: computer and software engineering tertiary education in 2018-tracer study*.

Athreye, S. S. (2005). The Indian software industry. In A. Arora & A. Gambardella (Eds.), *From underdogs to tigers: The rise and the growth of the software industry in Brazil, China, India, Ireland, and Israel* (pp. 7–40). Oxford University Press.

BACCO. (2019). *Bangladesh BPO news*. The BACCO Newsletter.

Bakht, Z., & Hossain, M. (2013). Review of Equity Entrepreneurship Fund (EEF), Bangladesh Institute of Development Studies, unpublished

Bangladesh Computer Council. (2019). *IT-ITES industry statistics of Bangladesh*. Leveraging ICT.

Bangladesh Hi-Tech Park Authority. (2018). *All project information*.

Bangladesh Hi-Tech Park Authority. (2019). *Hi-Tech Park—Prospective gateway of investment & employment*.

Bangladesh Telecommunication Regulatory Commission. (n.d.). *List of licensees*. http://www.btrc.gov.bd/list-licensees

Bangladesh Telecommunication Regulatory Commission. (n.d.). *VSAT services*. http://www.btrc.gov.bd/vsat-service

BASIS. (2016). *ICT Journey of Bangladesh*.

BASIS. (2018). *IT and ITES industry overview*.

BIDS Survey. (2009). *Assessment of the impact of clustering on IT industries*. Bangladesh Institute of Development Studies (BIDS).

BIDS-SEIP Survey. (2020). *Labor market and skill gap in the ICT sector in Bangladesh*. Bangladesh Institute of Development Studies (BIDS) and Skills for Employment Investment Program (SEIP), Finance Division. Ministry of Finance.

Everest Group. (2017). *Betting on the future-The Bangladesh IT-ITeS Industry is Poised for Growth*. Everest Group Research.

Grand View Research. (2017). *Knowledge Process Outsourcing (KPO) market analysis by service, by application (BFSI, Healthcare, IT & telecom, manufacturing, pharmaceutical, retail), by region and segment forecasts, 2014–2025*. https://www.grandviewresearch.com/industry-analysis/knowledge-process-outsourcing-kpo-market

Grand View Research. (2020). *IT services outsourcing market size, share & trends analysis report by service (application, emerging technology), by location (on shore, odd-shore), by end-use, and segment forecasts, 2020–2027*. https://www.grandviewresearch.com/industry-analysis/it-services-outsourcing-market

Grand View Research. (2021). *Business process outsourcing market size, share & trends analysis report by service type (customer services, finance & accounting), by end-use (IT & telecommunication, BFSI), by region, and segment forecasts, 2021–2028*. https://www.grandviewresearch.com/industry-analysis/business-process-outsourcing-bpo-market

Hidalgo, C. A., Klinger, B., Barabási, A. L., & Hausmann, R. (2007). The product space conditions the development of nations. *Science, 317*(5837), 482–487.

Hossain, M. (2016). Labor Market and Skills Gap in the ICT Sector in Bangladesh. In BIDS Study Report: Labour Market and Skill Gap in Bangladesh (Macro and Micro Level Study). Dhaka. Skills Employment Investment Program, Ministry of Finance, Government of Bangladesh.

Hossain, M., & Shinkai, N. (2011). Productivity and performance of IT sector in Bangladesh: Evidence from the firm-level data. *Bangladesh Development Studies, 34*(2), 1–22.

Hossain, M., Shinkai, N., Yunus, M., & Bakht, Z. (2012). Integration of ICT industries and its impact on trade and market access: The case of Bangladesh and India. In Rahman, Brunner, & Khatri (Eds.), *Regional integration and economic development in South Asia*. Edward Elgar.

ICT Division. (2020). *11 years of ICT*. Ministry of Post, Telecommunications and Information Technology, The Government of Bangladesh.

International Telecommunication Union. (2017). *Measuring the information society report 2017—Volume 1*.

Lal, K. (2002). *E-business and export behaviour: Evidence from Indian firms* (Discussion Paper No. 2002/68). United Nations University/WIDER.

LightCastle Partner. (2020, January 17). *ICT outsourcing: Catering to the growing demand*. https://www.lightcastlebd.com/insights/2020/01/ict-outsourcing-catering-to-the-growing-demand#:~:text=The%20ICT%20sector%20in%20Bangladesh,the%20ICT%20industry%20in%20Bangladesh

Lopez-Acevedo, G., & Robertson, R. (2016). *Stitches to riches? Apparel employment, trade, and economic development in South Asia*. The World Bank.

Mahmud, F. (2017, October 3). *The evolution of ICT sector in Bangladesh*. Fintech. https://fintechbd.com/the-evolution-of-ict-sector-in-bangladesh/?amp=1

Market Research Reports. (2020). *BPO services global industry Almanac 2016–2025*.

Ovi, I. H. (2020, August 17). Exports from computer services jump 15.24% in FY20. *Dhaka Tribune*. https://www.dhakatribune.com/business/economy/2020/08/17/exports-from-computer-services-jump-15-24-in-fy20

Panko, R. (2019, June 19). Small business outsourcing statistics in 2019. *Clutch*. https://clutch.co/bpo/virtual-assistants/resources/small-business-outsourcing-statistics

Parthasarathy, B. (2015). The ICT service industry in Bangalore, India: Its changing structure and characteristics. In L. Hirakawa & N. Shinkai (Eds.), *Servitization, It-ization, and innovation models*. Routledge.

Perez, C., & Soete, L. (1988). Catching up in technology: Entry barriers and windows of opportunity. In C. Freeman, G. Silverberg, G. Dosi, L. Soete, & R. Nelson (Eds.), *Technical change and economic theory*. Pinter Publishers.

Statista. (2021a). *Global market size of outsourced services from 2000 to 2019*. https://www.statista.com/statistics/189788/global-outsourcing-market-size/

Statista. (2021b). *Total contract value of the information technology outsourcing (ITO) market worldwide from 2000–2019*. https://cutt.ly/2Rcy3dV

World Bank. (2020). *Literacy rate, youth total (% of people ages 15–24)—Bangladesh*. World Development Indicators. https://data.worldbank.org/indicator/SE.ADT.1524.LT.ZS?locations=BD

CHAPTER 6

Access, Awareness, and Perceived Demand for ICT Services in Rural Areas: Household Level Analysis

1 Introduction

Balanced economic development can be realized through digital transformation if information and communication technologies (ICTs) are used as a pro-poor tool for improving people's living standards, especially in rural areas. Access to internet connectivity with emphasis on the ICT for Development (ICT4D) sectors such as e-education, e-health, e-Agriculture, e-governance, e-payments, etc., could play a catalytic role in reducing poverty by leveraging the effects on earning opportunities, educational and health services, and good governance (Chapman & Slaymaker, 2002; Kelles-Viitanen, 2005).

The importance of improved access to ICTs in rural areas is well argued in many studies (Hossain & Samad, 2020; Minges, 2016). However, proper incentives for rural poor people to avail digital services are instrumental in minimizing the digital divide and improving living standards. The underlying view that exerts "everyone, everywhere should have the opportunity to participate, and no one should be excluded from the benefits the Information Society offers (WSIS, 2003)" is the crux of minimizing the digital divide. Another aspect of ICT is its strong network externalities. The value of being connected to the network increases exponentially with the number of users connected, implying that a lack of access leads to a lack of opportunities. Therefore, connectivity

M. Hossain, *Digital Transformation and Economic Development in Bangladesh*, https://doi.org/10.1007/978-981-19-2753-9_6

linking with ICT4D paves the way for economic and social development, particularly in rural areas.

E-governance and e-commerce are two critical areas of intervention that could provide the poor with greater opportunities to improve their livelihood. For example, e-governance (e–G) allows speedy transmittal of information that enhances transparency, voice to the citizens and makes the administration more accountable, lowering transaction costs (Rao, 2004). Reviewing e-governance projects, Malhotra et al. (2008) emphasized the importance of an integrated and participatory approach in implementing e-governance projects to achieve its sustainable impact. Note that e–G entails the possibility of multi-directional interactions allowing government to government, people to government, government to people, business to government, and government to business contact through the medium of ICT. On the other hand, *e-commerce* or electronic commerce is defined as any transaction that involves the buying and selling of products and services by businesses and consumers through an electronic medium without using any paper documents. It essentially reduces transaction costs drastically. E-commerce includes three categories: business to business (B2B), business to consumer (B2C), and consumer to consumer (C2C) interactions. By using an e-commerce platform, rural people can sell their products without an intermediary, ensuring a better and fair price through reducing transaction costs.

Connectivity of the people is thus a crucial step to bring mass people into the beneficial coverage of ICTs. The concern is to make the services accessible to all, particularly the poor. One possible way to make the internet and digital services available in rural areas are to create rural telecenters or digital centers, which is also evident in Latin America (Proenza et al., 2001). Bangladesh did the same thing by establishing Union Digital Center (UDC) at each Union Parishad (UP), which has opened up the possibility to make the digital services 'accessible to the poor' and a 'powerful instrument' to rural development and poverty reduction through improving rural connectivity, training, financial inclusion, income generation and access to e-services. The critical issue is to equip the UDCs with a proper workforce and make it a service-oriented place.

This chapter assesses connectivity in rural areas and ICT4D activities to enhance inclusive development.[1] Using various sources of household

[1] A baseline study on e-upazila initiatives of Katalyst (a project of the Swiss NGO, Swisscontact) was conducted during June–July, 2012 by the author as the leader of the

Table 1 Access to electricity and ICT devices in rural households, 2010–2019, %

ICT devices	*2010*	*2016*	*2019*
Electricity connection to households	55.26	75.92	92
Mobile phone ownership	63.74	92.50	94.20
Computer (desktop/laptop/tablet etc.)	3.04	3.01	3.32
Radio**	5.52	–	0.27
Television**	26.25	–	46.63

Note The information on 2010 and 2019 has been extracted from the BIDS/Institute of Microfinance (InM) Survey (2010, 2019) on Rural Poverty Dynamics. Data on 2016 has been taken from BIDS-IDCOL survey (2016) conducted in rural areas on renewable energy aspects

survey information over 2010–2020, the progress on mobile penetration, internet connectivity, and perceived demand for ICT4D services in rural Bangladesh have been assessed.

This chapter is organized as follows. Section 2 highlights the use of ICT devices in rural areas. Section 3 assesses the perceived demand for e-information in rural areas linking with ICT4D services. Section 4 highlights the functioning of Union Digital Center and assesses its capacity and service provisions. Section 5 concludes the chapter.

2 Use of ICT Devices in Rural Households

The proportion of mobile phone ownership by households has been increasing at a rate higher than electricity connectivity to households indicating that households use various commercial sources for charging their mobile phones (Table 1). While 64% of households had mobile phones

team in order to understand the access to digital services to the rural people. It has been revealed that the households have very limited access to computer and internet and most of them are not aware of the benefits of these services/technologies. However, more than 80 percent of the households use mobile phone, but mostly for talking with family and friends. They are not aware of some of the mobile phone value-added services like money transfer, online banking, health-line/telemedicine, agriculture support line, online shopping, e-ticketing, bill pay, etc. So, there are huge potentials to train the poor people about these services and make them interested to use these facilities in a cost-effective and affordable manner. Most of the respondents showed their willingness to take training by themselves or their children on computer education. They also want electronic information and services on health, education, agriculture, weather forecasting, financial services, etc.

in 2010, it increased to over 92% from 2016 onward, making Bangladesh the country with the highest mobile phone penetration. Fortunately, by 2019, about 92% of households got grid electricity connectivity, making it favorable to access digital devices and services. However, a sorry state of computer ownership in rural households has been depicted, as only about 3% of households had a computer in 2019 (Table 1). Though mobile broadband internet can allow people to avail various digital services, a computer might facilitate digital connectivity better with its multiple features and software use. As the price of a computer/laptop is still relatively high, most rural households cannot afford it. However, half of the rural households now have a television, which is expected with higher grid electricity access. The use of radio/transistors has been decreasing, mainly due to the availability of mobile phone-based radio options. Television ownership has increased twofold from 26.25% in 2010 to 46.63% in 2019, and as a communication device, this allows rural people much easier access to information and entertainment.

2.1 *Mobile Phone Penetration and Usage*

Access to mobile phones has been rapidly expanding in Bangladesh. As already mentioned, over 90% of the households own a mobile phone in Bangladesh, with limited network signals in some places, particularly in rural areas. About 40% of mobile phone owners reported that network signals are strong, and a similar proportion thought moderate (Figs. 1 and 2). None of the villages were found without having access to the

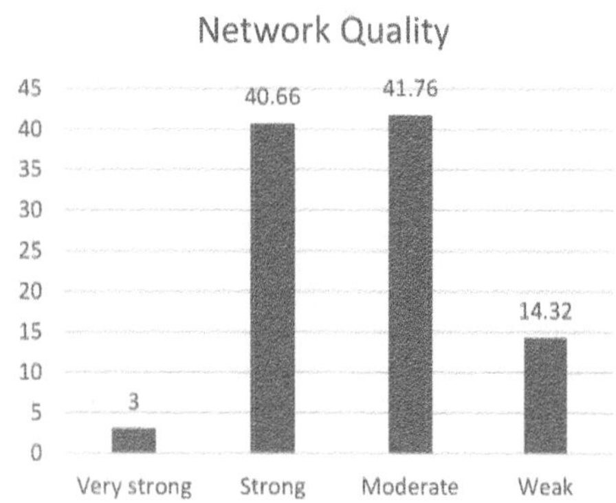

Fig. 1 Perception about mobile network quality (%) (*Source* BIDS-IDCOL survey, 2018)

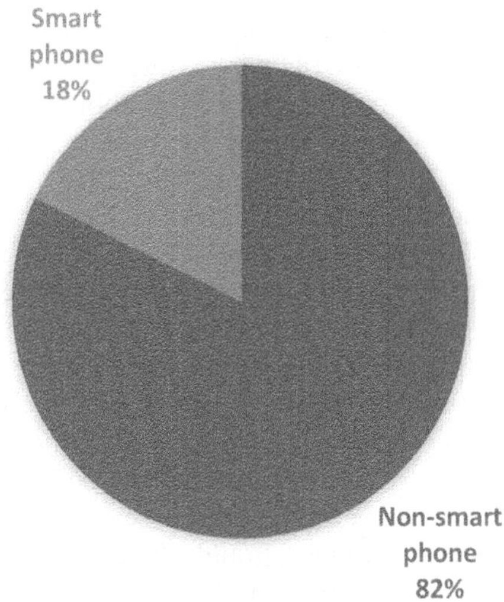

Fig. 2 Types of phones used by the household (*Source* BIDS-IDCOL Survey, 2018)

mobile phone network. However, the extent of network coverage and mobile phone penetration rates are different across locations. Village-level penetration rate ranges between 70% and 88%. Survey results suggest that about 77% of the households own at least one mobile phone (Table 1). Some households own more than one mobile phone. Of the mobile phone users, 82% of phone sets are typical basic feature phones, and 18% are smartphones (Fig. 2).

Interestingly, in 2016, about 16% of the non-electricity households owned mobile phones indicating the ubiquity of mobile phones that have brought a transformational change in the lives and livelihoods of rural people (Table 1). These mobile phone owners used to go to neighbors' houses (13%) or shops/markets (12%) for charging their mobile phones, and they pay in most cases Tk. 5 (approx. 6 cents) for one-time charging. Adding travel cost, the total costs for charging the mobile phone once ranges from Tk. 10 to Tk. 30 (12 cents to 40 cents) (BIDS-IDCOL survey, 2018).

2.1.1 Mobile Phone Usage

From multiple responses on the purpose of mobile phone use, apart from conversation/talking, which is almost 100% of the time, it is observed that mobile phone use for value-added services has been increasing over time.

Average talk-time has been estimated at 46 min/day in rural areas. The use of mobile phones for business purposes and MFS (Mobile Financial Services) has increased from about 3% in 2012 to 13% in 2018. The use of the internet among the mobile phone owners has increased from less than 1% in 2012 to 12% in 2018. News searching has increased from about 4% in 2016 to 20% in 2018.

Mobile phones can be used for multi-dimensional purposes with their new features. However, most respondents in rural areas are restricted to its traditional use such as for talking, gaming, video watching, listening to songs, and taking photos. Only a tiny proportion of the people is aware of sophisticated value-added services, such as health-line, agriculture market, mobile banking, bill pay, e-ticketing, e-education, etc. Thus, there are scopes for raising awareness of people on these services for optimal and better use of mobile phone services that might improve the livelihood of the poor people. Though the current state of households' increased usage of mobile phones and the internet for value-added services is encouraging, this is not sufficient for the widespread digital transformation of the economy. What is needed is to assess the demand for digital services among the rural population and ensure appropriate policies and incentive mechanisms are in place (Table 2).

Table 3 presents the basic socio-economic and demographic characteristics of the mobile phone owners and their corresponding households. As 2016 data reveals, relatively younger people (household head) own a mobile phone, and only about 8% of the women-headed households own a mobile phone. Relatively better-off families with lower poverty, better-educated households have a mobile phone. About 80% of households with

Table 2 Purpose of mobile phone use other than talking/conversation (%)

	2012	*2016*	*2018*
Business purpose	2.5	9.51	12.4
Newspaper reading/getting news/exam results	4.1	1.76	19.99
Internet browsing	0.7	3.71	12.3
Listening to songs/Watching video	44.3	42.42	–
Money transfer/MFS/bill pay	3.2	0.4	13.04
Sending picture messages and video	11.5	10.83	–
Number of observations	600	3540	1476

Note Information is obtained from rural area surveys in different locations; *Sources* BIDS-SDF Survey (2012); BIDS-IDCOL Surveys (2016 & 2018)

Table 3 Basic characteristics of mobile phone owners

Characteristics	*Overall*	*With Mobile phone*	*Without Mobile phone*	*Diff*	
	(1)	*(2)*	*(3)*	*(2) − (3)*	*p-value*
Average age of HH head (Years)	45.82	43.38	54.01	−10.63	0.00
Currently Married (%)	50.59	50.00	52.59	−0.03	0.20
Ever Married (%)	4.13	3.78	5.28	−0.01	0.06
Proportion of Female-Headed HH (%)	8.64	8.54	8.99	0.00	0.69
Household Size (average)	4.78	4.69	5.08	−0.39	0.00
Economic Dependency Ratio	45.72	43.73	52.44	−0.09	0.00
Average cropped landholding (decimal)	140.01	131.37	169.01	−37.63	0.00
Weekly mobile charging frequency	7.31	8.00	–	–	–
Never went to school (%)	53.22	48.04	70.50	−22.46	0.00
Years of schooling (average)	5.72	6.0	4.1	1.90	0.00
Poverty (Headcount) %	–	27.56	32.63	−5.07	
Income inequality (Gini coefficient)	0.383	0.382	0.379	–	–
Average distance to the district (Zila) headquarters (km)	41.10	40.92	41.68	−0.75	0.35
Average distance to sub-district (Upazila) headquarters (km)	20.56	20.50	20.82	−0.33	0.39
Access to solar electricity (%)	70.59	80.19	19.81		
Head has a mobile phone (%)	76.92				
Main women member has a mobile phone (%)	32.0				

Source BIDS-IDCOL Survey (2016); *Note* The data were collected from off-grid regions and therefore it may not represent the whole country's situation

solar electricity own a mobile phone in off-grid areas. In most cases, the difference between the household characteristics with or without mobile phones is statistically significant.

Occupation might determine mobile phone ownership (Table 4). More than 90% of salaried employment, transport owner, and business people have a mobile phone, which is higher than the average proportion of mobile phone ownership (77%) in the rural areas. Over 80% of the wage employed people in the non-farm sector have a mobile phone. Daily talk-time is also somewhat higher in these groups of people (about 50 min/day). The ownership of mobile phones of other occupations represents average mobile phone penetration rates in rural areas.

The estimated determinants of mobile phone possession using a probit model are shown in Table 5. All the variables except livestock and fisheries occupations show the expected signs and significance level. Age and education are significant variables for possessing a mobile phone,

Table 4 Mobile phone use by occupation in rural areas

Occupation	*% of occupation*	*% have a mobile phone*	*Average talk-time daily (minutes)*	*Respondents*
Wage employment in the farm sector	13.4	73.47	39.67	475
Wage employment in the non-farm sector	9.5	81.85	47.48	336
Salaried employment	5.03	93.26	47.19	178
Self-employment in the farm sector	26.53	69.86	41.02	939
Self-employment in the non-farm sector	1.95	78.26	40.61	69
Transport owner	2.97	90.48	49.95	105
Fisherman	8.05	76.49	52.28	285
Skilled traders	3.4	85	45.28	120
General business	12.74	90.69	54.81	451
Housewife	7.63	77.41	43.06	270
Disabled/Old age	4.3	40.52	32.68	153
Others (student/pensioner/hawker, etc.)	–	78.57	70.00	–
Total		76.92	45.67	3540

Source BIDS-IDCOL Survey (2016)

Table 5 Determinants of possessing a mobile phone

Determinants	*Coef*	*Robust Std. Err*	P-*values*
Access to electricity	0.50282	0.055	0.000
Sex	−0.22268	0.086	0.007
Age	0.04008	0.002	0.000
Years of schooling	0.0729	0.0091	0.000
Small farm holders in the village	0.004474	0.0018	0.018
Distance from district	−0.00201	0.0012	0.019
Occupation in livestock	−9.84E-07	6.84E-07	0.15
Occupation in fisheries	−7.01E-07	5.83E-07	0.23
Occupation in non-farm activities	1.59E-06	3.32E-07	0.000
Constant	3.75411	0.195765	0.000

Note $N = 3516$; Log pseudolikelihood = −1603.09; *Data source* BIDS-IDCOL Survey (2016)

indicating that relatively older and educated household heads have a higher probability of owning a mobile phone than younger and uneducated household heads. Incomes from different assets and occupations are considered proxies for wealth. Income from non-farm activities is significant, indicating that business people are more likely to afford a mobile phone.[2] Access to solar electric power has significant effects on mobile phone ownership because, in a remote area, people have short-lived batteries and therefore need frequent charging. The concentration of small farm holders in a village is significant, indicating that small farmers use mobile phones for marketing decisions and other types of communications. Distant to the district as a proxy for market access is an important determinant of mobile phone ownership. As the sign of the variable is negative, it indicates that people close to the market centers and administrative units have a higher probability of owning mobile phones than those far from these centers. Mobile phone networks and signals are better if closer to the districts or more prominent marketplaces. It is thus noteworthy that mobile phone use in rural, remote areas also contributes significantly to income generation at varying degrees depending on the occupations.

[2] The endogeneity aspect of mobile phone ownership is somewhat irrelevant as almost all the households own a mobile phone and selection bias is not a big concern (Hossain & Samad, 2020).

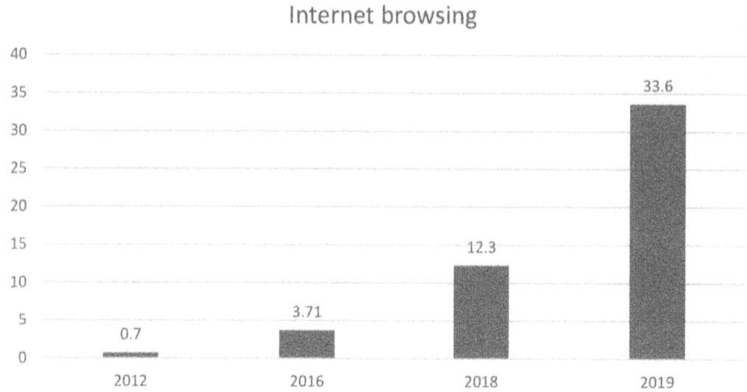

Fig. 3 Individual using mobile-based internet in rural areas (%) (*Sources* BIDS-SDF Survey, 2012; BIDS-IDCOL Surveys, 2016, 2018; BIDS Survey on poverty dynamics, 2019)[3]

2.2 *Internet Access and Usage*

In the absence of broadband internet connectivity at the rural level, mobile-based internet connectivity has been the primary source until recently as broadband connections have recently reached almost all the Union Parishad. As Fig. 3 shows, internet browsing at the household level has increased from less than 1% in 2010 to over 33.6% in 2019 at an annual compound growth rate of 62% in the last eight years.

Among the South Asian countries, Bangladesh's situation on individual's internet use has been improving over time, but not at a satisfactory level. Bangladesh's position is just better than Pakistan among the South Asian countries (Fig. 4). Note that the international organizations' data on internet use by individuals is lower than the survey results shown in Fig. 3. While South Asian average is about 30% of the total population having internet access (Fig. 5), some local surveys suggest that the percentage is higher than the South Asian average (A2I, 2019). However, a recent survey of a2i shows that the percentage is 43.1% (55% in urban and 35% in rural areas).[4] In Asia, the situation of China is much better,

[3] https://bigd.bracu.ac.bd/wp-content/uploads/2021/03/Understanding-the-First-and-Second-Digital-Divides-in-Rural-Bangladesh_working-paper.pdf.

[4] A proper survey covering rural and urban households on various aspects of digital connectivity is not available yet in Bangladesh, which deters truthful reporting of IT

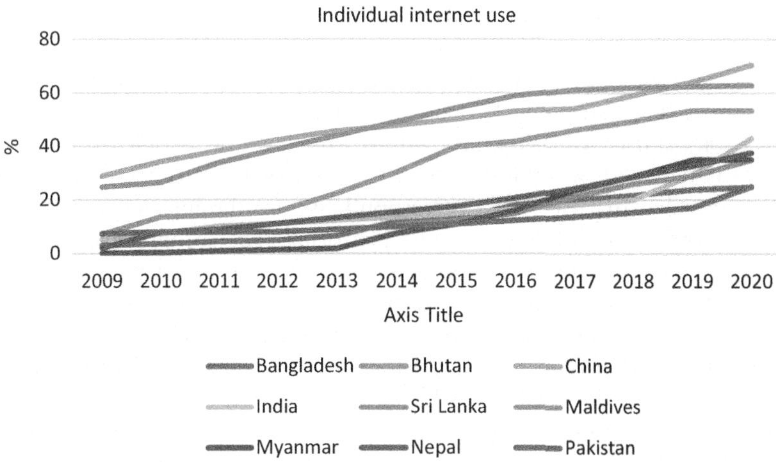

Fig. 4 Percentage of individuals using the internet in South Asia, 2012–2020 (*Source* International Telecommunication Union; World Development Indicators, various years)

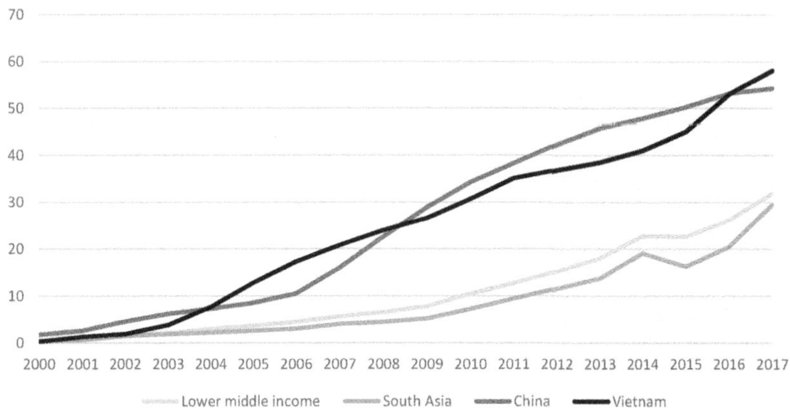

Fig. 5 A comparative scenario of the percentage of individuals using the internet, 2000–2017 (*Source* World Bank Development Indicators, various years)

having the proportions over 70% in 2020. The critical point is that policies and incentives are needed to increase access to the internet and its beneficial use. To improve the internet access, the prices of the internet and smart devices have to be made affordable to low-income people.

A comparative scenario on the internet usage by the people over 2010–2019 is depicted in Table 6. From the data of the 2019 survey, it has been revealed that over 91% of respondents use the internet mainly for being connected with social media platforms. The second most important purpose of internet connectivity is entertainment/watching video, etc. While about 28% use the internet for sending/receiving emails and the same percentage for reading online newspapers, about 23% use the internet for business purposes, 21% for job searching, and 17% for seeking government services. About 12% of the respondents use the internet for internet banking, and 10% for online shopping. Compared to 2012, except for social media, the proportion of people using the internet for various purposes has increased five to seven times more in 2019.

Table 6 Purpose of internet use (%)

Type of activities	*2012*	*2019*
Social media	–	91.8
To send or receive emails	5.3	28.9
Online shopping	0.2	10.2
Internet banking	0.0	12
For education and training	1.2	12.5
For entertainment (Watching movies/Listening to songs)	9.3	76
For business purpose	0.3	23
For job searching	3.8	21.3
For government form download/govt. services	1.7	17.4
For online news/newspaper	3.2	28
For watching TV	0.2	6.3
For sports news and picture	2.2	4.3

Sources A2I (Bangladesh National Household ICT Survey, 2019) and BIDS-SDF Survey (2012)

related statistics. The a2i program has done a household survey in 2019 with a coverage of 20 districts and 2000 households, which doesn't seem to be quite representative (a2i, 2019).

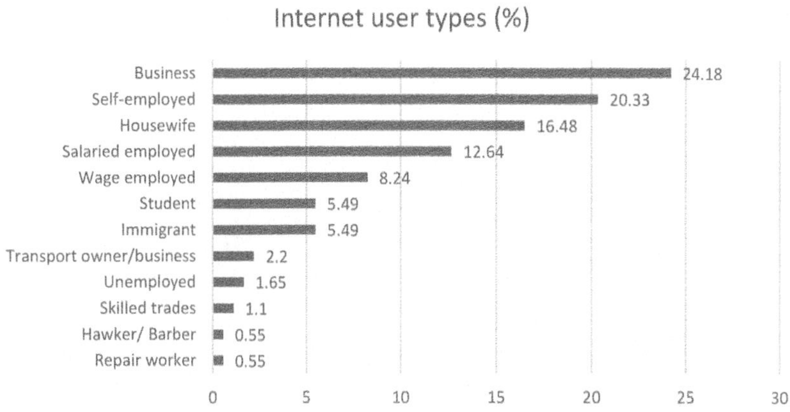

Fig. 6 Occupations of internet users in rural areas (*Source* BIDS-IDCOL survey, 2018)

From a survey conducted in 2018 (BIDS-IDCOL survey, 2018)[5] among rural households, as Fig. 6 demonstrates, business people have been using the internet at a higher proportion (about 24%) compared to others, including self-employed (20.33%), housewives (16.48%), salaried employed (12.64%), wage employed (8.24%), students (5.5%), and immigrants (5.5%). The proportion of internet users from other occupations is below 3%. Homemakers stand at third position in terms of internet use, which is a good indication for enhancing women's empowerment through the benefits of information networks. Moreover, apart from business people, employed people use the internet more often.

3 Perceived Demand for E-Information Services and Linking with ICT4D

To portray the perceived demand for e-information, we are constrained by the older survey results of 2012. Since the results are related to assessing the need for digital services, the context and people's eagerness might not have reduced, instead of increased over time with greater exposure

[5] A survey on Conducting Impact Assessment of Solar Irrigation, Solar Mini-Grid and ICS Projects of IDCOL, by BIDS in 2018.

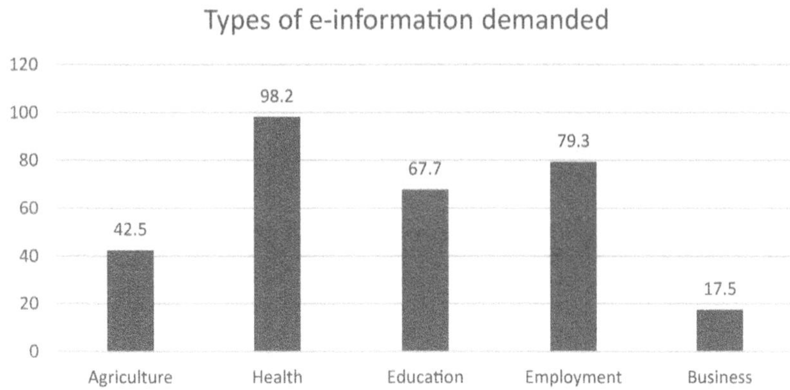

Fig. 7 Types of e-information needed by the respondents (*Source* BIDS-SDF survey [2012])

to internet connectivity. This section reports the perceived demand for various digital information services among the respondents in rural areas in Bangladesh. Figure 7 shows the broad category of digitalized information that the people in rural areas aspired to receive. The respondents mainly need e-information on health (about 98%) followed by employment (80%), education (67%), agriculture (43%), and business (18%). Though the results are somewhat outdated, the demand for such information might be more relevant in recent times with better internet connectivity in rural areas.

3.1 Agriculture Related Information

The survey results revealed that about farmers need information mainly on new crops/varieties, crop diseases, weather, and inputs/fertilizer (BIDS-SDF Survey, 2012). More than one-third of respondents request for information on inputs/fertilizer and new varieties of crops regarding agricultural information. About 30% of respondents mentioned that they need weather and disease-related information. About 23% need information on the price of commodities. However, less than 10% of respondents need information on markets, the wage of day laborer, government policy, etc. Agriculture technology-related information is required for about 15% of the respondents (Fig. 8). Though the survey was conducted in 2012, the results may indicate farmers' demand for e-information.

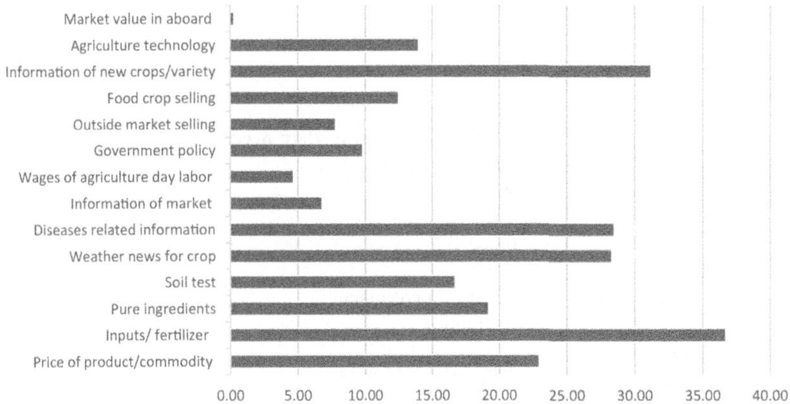

Fig. 8 Types of agricultural information needed (*Source* BIDS-SDF survey, 2012)

3.1.1 *Weather Information*

Being Bangladesh vulnerable to climate change and natural disasters, framers often face natural calamities like floods, rain, drought, cyclones, salinities, etc., that may cause considerable losses to crops and other products. It is more important for farmers to get accurate short to medium-term weather forecasts to mitigate climate change risks.

Only a little more than 40% of respondents gave their opinion on weather forecasting—the rest remained unanswered. They think that weather information is essential for good harvesting and cropping. When they were specially asked about types of weather information they need, more than 41% respondents mentioned of the information related to rain and flood, followed by sunshine (30%), fog (18%), wind (11%), and so on (Table 7).

3.2 *Education*

About 50% of the respondents want information on admission tests. Other notable responses regarding e-information related to education include exam results (43.8%), educational institutions (26.8%), distance

Table 7 Demand for weather forecasting

Need weather information?	*2012 (%)*
Yes	42.0
No	1.5
Types of forecasting they need	
Rain	41.0
Sunshine	30.2
Fog	18.3
Flood	40.5
Wind	11.0
Moisture percentage	6.7
Drought	7.8

Source BIDS-SDF survey (2012)

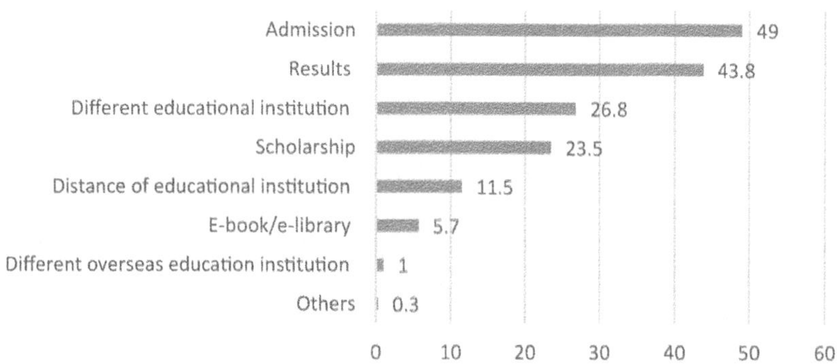

Fig. 9 Types of educational information needed (*Source* BIDS-SDF survey [2012])

to an educational institution (11.5%), scholarships (23.5%), and so on (Fig. 9).

3.3 *Health*

The perceived demand for health-related digitalized services was the highest among other services in rural areas. Among the people willing to receive e-information/services on health, most respondents mentioned that they would seek specialized doctor's advice from Dhaka (about 80%). In contrast, more than 75% of respondents wanted to know about clinics

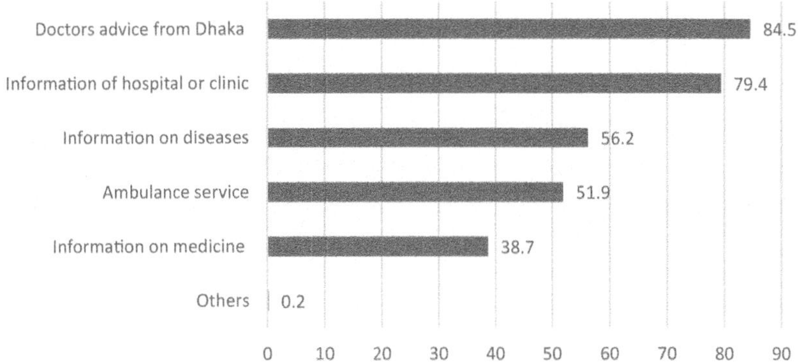

Fig. 10 Demand for types of e-health information (*Source* BIDS-SDF survey [2012])

and hospitals. About 50% of respondents need information on ambulance services and diseases, while 40% reportedly need information on the medicine (Fig. 10).

3.4 *Employment*

More than 50% of the respondents need information on job vacancies through an online platform. The other crucial online information that they want to know includes different types of jobs (47.7%) and potential areas of employment (62.8%). Only about 3% of respondents wish to get information on the overseas job. More than 60% of respondents want information on wage rates for day laborers and wage rates in different regions of the country (Table 8).

3.5 *Government Policy/Services*

About 55% of the respondents need information on citizen charter, while about 35% require information on government khas land and water bodies (Table 9). About 44% of respondents want local news, and 20% need information on land records. About 12% want to download various government forms, and about 18% of respondents wanted to know about the government's Right to Information (RTI) policy. About one-third of

Table 8 Types of employment-related information needed

	Percent
Job advertisement vacancies	54.0
Types of job	47.7
Overseas job	3.2
Passport or visa	4.3
Potential areas of job	62.8
Others	0.2
Wage	
Wages for the day laborer	58.5
Wages in the different regions in the country	63.7
Wages for construction laborer	8.0

Source BIDS-SDF survey (2012)

Table 9 Types of government information needed

	Percent
Government form	11.8
Government policy	4.8
RTI (Right to Information) Policy	16.3
Citizen charter	56.0
Activities of different govt. Department	22.0
VGD/VGF/TR/KBITA/KABIKHA	34.8
100-days employment program	32.7
National budget	2.8
Land record	21.3
Govt. Land and water bodies	33.7
Local news	43.5
Others	0.2

Source The information is drawn from an earlier survey conducted in 2012 to assess the impact of the e-Upazila initiative of Katalyst, Bangladesh, which was later discontinued. The survey was sponsored by Social Development Foundation (SDF) and conducted by BIDS

respondents need information on various social safety-net programs and 100-days employment program.

In sum, the demand for various e-information services revealed that almost 100% of respondents need health/medical information, followed by employment (80%), education (68%), and agriculture (43%). Regarding health, respondents want doctors' advice from Dhaka as most good doctors are based there and information on hospital/clinic, disease, and ambulance service. Telemedicine has been pointed out as an essential mechanism and technology to reach health services to the general masses. For employment, respondents need information on potential areas of the job, advertisements on job vacancies, wage rates for day laborers, and wage rates in different parts of the country. Respondents reportedly need information mainly on admission, exam results, scholarships, and other educational institutions for education.

For agriculture purposes, respondents mainly require information on the price of commodities, inputs, weather, and crop diseases. They need weather forecasting on rain, flood, and sunshine. About 40% of respondents think that weather information is essential for cropping and harvesting, and they are willing to subscribe information if available. The majority of the respondents want daily and monthly basis weather forecasts. Respondents also want information on different government policies and services, including social safety-net programs, citizen charter, khas land and water bodies, land record, government forms, etc. Thus the perceived demand for various e-information services is high among the respondents, which may be considered in designing digital value-added content targeting the beneficiaries in rural areas. The services providers, particularly those based in Union Digital Centers, should be given appropriate training on various available e-services to communicate to rural people on demand.

4 Service Provided by Union Digital Centre

The ICT facilities and equipment available at a UDC are not enough to cater to the need of the population of a Union, comprised of about 30–35 thousand. The addition of more computers, routers, and other devices could help in offering more and better services. Though more trained operators are needed, there is a shortage of supplies. It is better if operators for UDC can be hired from the local level school/college students to work on a part-time basis and earn from there.

Many types of services are demanded and obtained from the telecentres. Internet browsing, in general, is a standard service. Specific services include exam results, job advertisements, training in computer use, Compact Disk (CD) recording, composing, photocopy services, photography, and flexiloads (mobile phone recharge) for prepaid mobile telephony. Services are offered in quite a friendly atmosphere. But the regularity of service is not always maintained. Improving service quality is dependent on several types of additional facilities. Awarding certificates after training will make more people interested in such activity. On the other hand, the information base needs to be broadened to have all the necessary information.

UDCs are usually located at the Union Parishad office, which is considerably far from the majority of residents of the Union. Up to 2–3 km may have to be traveled to reach the center. It restricts the number of users, in particular, the children and women are more constrained than others. If every village has at least one digital center/telecentre, the situation might improve.

5 Conclusions and Recommendations

The Digital Bangladesh concept remains hazy to many rural people, which is not surprising given the lack of appropriate facilities, accessibility, and relevant information. There is a similarity of views on these synergies between current and prospective users of ICTs. There has been a demand for information related to education facilities, admissions, exams, exam results, various health services related information, agricultural inputs, supply problems and sources of non-adulterated inputs, raw materials for processing and business, information related to jobs and job availability, wages and salaries offered. Such services, if available widely, can help reduce rural–urban migration, create jobs, reduce poverty and lower-income inequality, and the digital divide, in general. But some services may help people in other ways and improve their life. The people understand the use of various ICT services for income, improvement of quality of life, etc.

ICT adoption in rural areas has started rolling on with better last-mile connectivity. People are getting certain services from UDCs, but these are actually from the normal functioning of computers and mobile phones. But the real essence of a digital Bangladesh, namely e-services, e-governance and e-citizenship, and participation and transparency, is yet to permeate.

The constraints are three types: technical, financial, and information availability. The technical restrictions pertain to power sources, lack of adequate and proper hardware, and lack of trained personnel. The financial constraints have to do with both costs of services due to high costs of equipment and organization and management as well affordability of clients. People would like to have at least a single digital center in each village to access digital services easily. This will resolve the constraint of having smart devices and computers at home, and also facilitate information access to women, the disabled, and the destitute.

However, the real problem is the availability of information and its ease of retrieval in the long run. While internet connectivity is essential, so is its speed; more importantly, the question is who provides the information, in what form and frequency, and their relevance. Information collection, processing and dissemination, and retrieval appear to be the real bottleneck to achieving a digital transformation in Bangladesh.

From a supply-side perspective, with the rapid development of wireless technologies and mobile telephony in Bangladesh, given poor access to the internet to households, rural digital centers have been instrumental in overcoming the access barriers to information technology to the people, particularly the poor (Rothenberg-Aalami & Pal, 2005). Though mobile telephone achieved almost 100% penetration even in rural areas, the most significant development in terms of internet connectivity has taken place by connecting the majority of Union Parishads (UPs) with broadband fixed internet connectivity. Some barriers that may hinder the prospects of rural telecenters or UDCs are distance, lack of trainers, proper awareness, and higher costs. Addressing these issues properly could turn a tele/digital center into a social network for development in rural areas. Mobile broadband services suffer from poor internet service quality, particularly in rural areas along with higher prices. The VAT and other taxes imposed on the internet have also been contributing to higher prices of the internet, thereby creating obstacles to greater access to the internet in rural areas.

In sum, three issues have thus emerged in our discussions in this chapter to meet the demand for e-services of the rural poor people that appear to be crucial to increase access to digital services and reduce the digital divide:

1. *Building awareness*: Building awareness about digital services and their utilities is pertinent for the effective utilization of e-services. Most rural people are not aware of the extensive use of mobile phone applications and services, the internet, and computer applications. Without proper awareness of these services, their benefits, and drawbacks, it will be difficult to attract people to receive digital services even at the telecenters. Involving NGOs (Non-government

Organizations) and other relevant organs of the government could be effective means to build awareness of various digital contents and their utility.

2. *Cost-effectiveness of services*: The second most crucial issue is the cost-effectiveness of e-services, which includes an optimal distance of telecenters from the locality and pricing of services. It appears that telecenters within 1–2 km may attract more people. Allowing free Wi-Fi/internet connectivity in some specific places (in schools/education institutions, marketplaces, UDCs etc.) could reduce services' costs, making it affordable to the poor.
3. *Proper training facilities*: People in rural areas appear to be very willing to get trained in computers and internet use, and they are also interested to train their children. However, the availability of skilled trainers is a concern, and therefore it is essential to design localized training programs to develop necessary ICT skills in the locality/Union. Trainers and operators must be aware of the needs of stakeholders and the respected/dedicated websites or e-services available to meet the demands. This is also necessary to improve digital literacy in rural areas.

References

A2I. (2019). *Bangladesh national ICT household survey, report, and overview of main result 2018–2019*. Alliance Affordable Internet and Access to Information (a2i) Program.

BIDS-IDCOL Survey. (2016). *Baseline survey for estimating socio-economic benefits of solar mini-grid in Bangladesh, 2016*. Bangladesh Institute of Development Studies (BIDS) and Infrastructure Development Company Limited (IDCOL).

BIDS-IDCOL Survey. (2018). *Assessing the impact of solar mini-grid projects in Bangladesh, 2018*. Bangladesh Institute of Development Studies (BIDS) and Infrastructure Development Company Limited (IDCOL).

BIDS-SDF Survey. (2012). *An assessment of e-Upazila initiative, 2012*. Bangladesh Institute of Development Studies (BIDS) and Social Development Foundation (SDF).

Chapman, R., & Slaymaker, T. (2002). *ICTs and rural development: Review of the literature, current interventions, and opportunities for* action (Working Paper No. 192). Overseas Development Institute.

Hossain, M., & Samad, H. (2020). Mobile phones, household welfare, and women's empowerment: evidence from rural off-grid regions of Bangladesh. *Information Technology for Development, 27*, 1–17.

Kelles-Viitanen, A. (2005). *The role of ICT in governing rural development* (pp. 11–14). IFAD Workshop on What are the Innovation Challenges for Rural Development.

Malhotra, C., Chariar, V. M., Das, L. K., & Ilavarasan, P. V. (2008). *ICT for rural development: An inclusive framework for e-governance.* Computer Society of India Special Interest Group on e-Governance.

Minges, M. (2016). *Exploring the relationship between broadband and economic growth.* World Development Report 2016: Digital Dividends (102955).

Proenza, F. J., Bastidas-Buch, R., & Montero, G. (2001). Telecenters for socioeconomic and rural development in Latin America and the Caribbean investment opportunities and design recommendations, with special reference to Central America.

Rao, T. P. R. (2004). *ICT and e-Governance for Rural Development.* Center for Electronic Governance. Ahmedabad: Indian Institute of Management.

Rothenberg-Aalami, J., & Pal, J. (2005). *Rural telecenter impact assessments and the political economy of ICT for Development (ICT4D).* (BRIE Working Paper 164). Berkeley Roundtable on the International Economy.

World Summit on the Information Society (WSIS). (2003). *Declaration of principles: Building the information society: A global challenge in the New Millennium.* https://www.itu.int/net/wsis/docs/geneva/official/dop.html

PART II

ICT Industry Development

CHAPTER 7

Dynamic Capability and Productivity of ICT Firms in Bangladesh

1 Introduction

Bangladeshi IT (Information Technology) firms started growing steadily since 2000 with various supportive measures of the government. The development of the IT industry is one of the prerequisite conditions in implementing the digital Bangladesh agenda. However, the growth of the software industry depends on factors, such as skills, market linkages, and productivity. Effective use of these factors depends on a firm's dynamic capabilities. Dynamic capabilities are the capabilities that enable firms to use changing opportunities to carve out a niche in the outsource markets and understand which product market or business model best utilizes the internal and external assets of the firm.[1] The analysis of dynamic capabilities of firms through productivity channels is thus important to understand the industry's maturity level. The main objective of this chapter is to assess the current status of dynamic capabilities of the ICT

[1] Dynamic capabilities resemble mechanisms that build, gain, integrate, reconfigure and release internal and external resources to address rapidly changing environments. Such capabilities not only have a direct effect on the output of the firm, but also indirect effects on the configuration of more basic operational resources (Eisenhardt & Martin, 2000; Helfat & Peteraf, 2003; Teece et al., 1997). To this end, a recent study by Gebreeyesus and Mohnen (2013) shows that network capability is an important channel of knowledge flows and innovation of cluster-based firms.

M. Hossain, *Digital Transformation and Economic Development in Bangladesh*, https://doi.org/10.1007/978-981-19-2753-9_7

firms in Bangladesh, which could be instrumental for further development of the industry and the digital Bangladesh vision.

As research on firm capabilities has focused primarily on the link between capabilities and performance-related outcomes (Clark & Fujimoto, 1991; Liberman et al., 1989), the analysis in this chapter thus attempts to explain differences in ICT (Information and Communication Technology) firm's competitive capabilities by analyzing the economic performance of firms embedded in their activities, size, labor productivity, skill intensity, collaboration with foreign firms, and innovation. Mainly descriptive statistics and OLS (Ordinary Least Square) regressions are used for the analysis. Further, Stochastic Frontier Production model analysis is used to assess variation in firms' technical efficiencies. To capture dynamism in capabilities, several composite indexes of dynamic capability of firms, such as "resource acquisition," "resource reconfiguration," "marketing networking," and "learning network" indicators, are created by applying the Principal Component Analysis (PCA), which later has been factored in the regression model to assess their effects on productivity. For the analysis, panel data of 85 firms for two-time periods, 2009 and 2020, has been used.

The chapter is organized as follows. After the introduction, Sect. 2 reviews the literature on firm growth and capabilities. Section 3 analyzes the productivity of the ICT firms, while Sect. 4 reports the determinants of firm capability indicators. Section 5 provides an analysis of the capabilities of firms. Section 6 shows the regression results that assess the impact of firm capability on productivity, and Sect. 7 concludes the paper.

2 A Brief Review of Literature on Firm Growth Theory and Capabilities

The capability of a firm, either static or dynamic, may be explained from the perspectives of firm growth theories. There are at least three views on firm growth: agency *view*, *social capital view*, and *resource-based view*. The *Principal-agent approach* to firm capability focuses solely on the functioning of corporate governance with managers' interests aligning with those of the owners. Various studies suggest that corporate governance has implications for enhancing a firm's capability in multiple ways (Chatterjee & Harrison, 2001). *The Social Capital approach* considers the significance of firm-level relationships (including interlocking directorates) with other entities as a social capital (Koka & Prescott, 2002;

Nahapiet & Ghoshal, 1998). Social capital facilitates firm-level actions by increasing its awareness of competitive opportunities in various forms. Dynamic relations between social capital and firm-level resource accumulation may signal, *albeit* partially, the overall feature of a firm's resource status as well as its pattern of resource flow (Gnywali & Madhavan, 2001). In this approach, the board of directors can supplement the firm with "board capability" based on directors' own social and human capital. It appears that the relevance of these theories to the growth of ICT firms is limited because of the simplified structure of corporate governance and the dynamic characteristics of ICT firms. Instead, the Resource-based view of firm growth may better explain the firm capability of ICT firms.

The *Resource-Based View* (RBV) of firm growth emphasizes the role of capabilities that may create new resources and restructure old resources of the firm into valuable resource configurations. The RBV literature signifies that it is not the resources that contribute to competitive advantage; instead, it is the capability of rearranging the resources into resource configuration (Grant, 1996). New market strategies, innovations, and many more are necessary for better configuration of specific resources—it may either be labor or activities or skills or market, or altogether (Brush et al., 2001; Mauri & Michaels, 1998). Therefore, the dynamic capability approach for the ICT firms appears to be associated with RBV to the firm growth.

In this framework, the dynamic capability of firms is nothing but innovative actions taken by firms to enhance their productivity and profitability, which is related to the firm's growth (Brush et al., 2001; Grant, 1996). Teece et al. (1997) explain dynamic capabilities aligned with the RBV in terms of three organizational and managerial key processes. These include (i) coordination/integration of both internal and external activities, (ii) learning through experimentation, which enables firms to perform better and quicker, and (iii) reconfiguration and transformation of resources based on the ability to scan the environment to evaluate the markets and competitors. Therefore, theoretically, the dynamic capability refers to mechanisms through which a firm takes actions to build, gain, integrate, reconfigure and release internal and external resources to address rapidly changing environments. The critical aspect of such capabilities is to make a network that helps a firm best utilize internal resources, create new products, improve present competence, and so on (Greene et al., 1999; Hitt et al., 2001; Eisenhardt & Martin, 2000; Pisano, 1994).

Within this framework, it can be argued that improving the dynamic capability of ICT firms is particularly important for their growth momentum as they are engaged in knowledge-based innovative activities.

3 Productivity Analysis

To understand IT firms' productivity, we rely mainly on the labor productivity of the firms considering that labor is the primary input for the IT firms. Productivity has been estimated across sizes of the firms, such as micro, small, and medium firms, to see if size matters. Further, productivity is examined for export-oriented (EO) (those that sell products in both domestic and overseas markets) and non-exporting (NEO) firms, assuming that firms having export orientation are more capable of adopting innovative strategies than those of the non-export-oriented firms.

Table 1 presents the productivity across the size of the firms in two periods, 2009 and 2020, for three different categories of firms: IT, ISP (Internet Service Provider), and call centers. It is observed that productivity is higher for relatively larger firms in 2020 for all three categories of firms. However, in 2009, productivity did not vary for small, medium, and large firms. The results indicate that labor productivity has increased in the ICT sector over time.

Figure 1 shows that productivity is driven by e-commerce, e-governance, and GIS (Geographic Information System); however, they vary substantially in 2020 compared to 2009. Though productivity is higher in 2020 for all types of activities, these three activities appear to be the main driving force of the IT industry in recent times.

In Table 2, first, we assess the productivity differences with a group over time. The results show that productivity is significantly higher within the group over time, 2009–2019, implying that both types of firms have improved their productivity progressively. We further investigate productivity across groups (EO vs. NEO) in Panel-II to assess whether they have improved productivity with time. The results show that the productivity of EO firms is significantly higher than non-export-oriented firms in 2019 though such difference did not exist in 2009.

The results suggest that firms undertake innovative strategies over time, and develop employees' skills, market linkages, etc., which might lead to improved productivity. This, in other words, indicates a certain

Table 1 Labor productivity across sectors and size

	2020				*2009*			
	Micro	*Small*	*Medium*	*Large*	*Micro*	*Small*	*Medium*	*Large*
IT	13.2	13.56	13.79	13.94	12.37	12.67	12.67	12.67
ISP		13.29	13.5	14.05	11.53	12.60	12.60	12.60
Call center		13.09	14.37	14.21	–	–	–	–

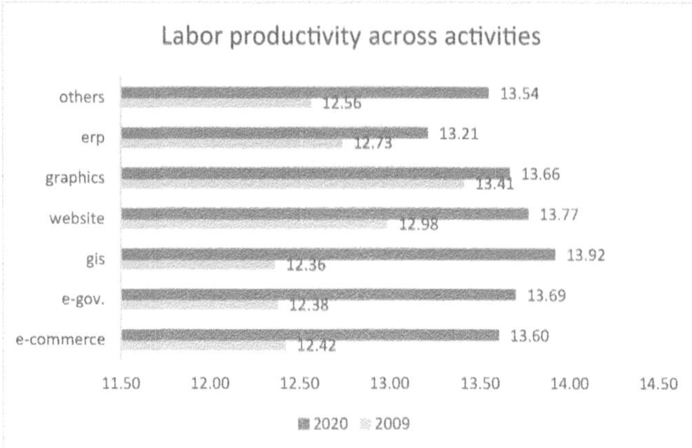

Fig. 1 Log of labor productivity across activities of software firms

Table 2 Differences in productivity, 2009–2019

Panel-1: Differences in between periods within the group				
	Export-oriented firms		Non-export-oriented firms	
	Obs	Average labor productivity in logarithm	Obs	Average labor productivity in logarithm
2009	37	12.89	44	12.77152
2019	31	13.93	52	13.68476
Difference		−1.03***		−0.91***
t-value		−4.71		−4.07
Panel-II: Differences between firm groups in a year				
Group	EO	NEO	Difference	*t*-value
	Average labor productivity in logarithm	Average labor productivity in logarithm		
2009	12.89	12.77	−0.128	−0.43
Obs	37	44		
2019	13.93	13.68	−0.254**	−1.9
Obs	31	52		

***indicates significance at 1% level

level of dynamic capabilities of IT firms that could be instrumental for the development of the IT industry.

3.1 Older Firms Are More Productive

Analyzing the productivity of IT firms, it is observed that older firms having age over 15 years are relatively more productive than newer firms. This indicates that firms established in the early 2000s are now more productive than newer firms. The reason behind this might be that after 2000 majority of the IT firms were established by Bangladeshi IT professionals returning from the North American countries, mainly from the USA as a result of the liberalization of the IT sector/market in Bangladesh. Using their market linkages in the USA and other countries and their professionalism helped them to be more productive (Table 3).

4 Determinants of Firm's Performances: Regression Results

In this section, we attempt to analyze the determinants of IT firm performances, in particular labor productivity, sales revenue, and profit. We have conducted a fixed effect regression analysis using panel data. The data consists of information from 85 IT firms for two-time points: 2009 and 2020. The logarithm of labor productivity and sales revenue has been used.

The results are reported in Table 4. The results show that age (older), gender (male), and public listed status of the companies contribute to

Table 3 Test of productivity differences with firm age, 2020

Firm age	*Obs*	*Mean*	*Std. Err*	*Std. Dev*	*[95% Conf. Interval]*	
Less than 15 years	86	13.53	0.08	0.72	13.38	13.69
More than 15 years	58	13.80	0.08	0.59	13.64	13.95
Combined	144	13.64	0.06	0.68	13.53	13.75
diff		−0.26	0.11		−0.49	– 0.04
t-value		−2.32***	df	142		

***indicates significance at 1% level

Table 4 Fixed effect panel regression estimates

Variables	*(1)* *Log (labor productivity)*	*(2)* *Log (revenue)*	*(3)* *Profit (as % of revenue)*
Gender of the owner (M = 1, F = 0)	1.273**	−4.719	57.045***
	(0.608)	(4.485)	(18.136)
Age of owner	0.035*	0.171	0.305
	(0.021)	(0.135)	(0.285)
2. Proprietorship: partnership (base: individual)	−0.595	2.286	20.745*
	(0.762)	(5.273)	(11.455)
3. Proprietorship: Private limited company (base: individual)	0.294	2.665	26.135***
	(0.453)	(3.496)	(9.417)
4. Proprietorship: public listed company (base: individual)	1.603**	8.161	79.328***
	(0.743)	(6.145)	(12.858)
Export (1 if exports)	−0.006	0.036	0.252***
	(0.008)	(0.045)	(0.093)
Skill intensity (ratio of engineers to total employee)	0.541	3.782	−16.954
	(0.633)	(5.377)	(15.337)
e-governance	−0.449	2.746	9.734**
	(0.404)	(2.248)	(3.875)
e-commerce	0.167	−2.576	7.410
	(0.383)	(2.250)	(4.573)
GIS	0.481	−0.960	14.298*
	(0.587)	(4.286)	(7.279)
Web development	0.303	0.301	−3.768
	(0.233)	(1.827)	(6.022)
Graphics	0.032	−2.917	−2.669
	(0.372)	(2.287)	(5.599)
ERP	−0.126	0.911	10.823
	(0.347)	(2.378)ara>	(8.416)
BPO	−0.813*	−1.572	10.021*

(continued)

Table 4 (continued)

Variables	*(1) Log (labor productivity)*	*(2) Log (revenue)*	*(3) Profit (as % of revenue)*
	(0.456)	(2.545)	(5.705)
Firm's age	0.015	0.140	−0.198
	(0.033)	(0.193)	(0.361)
Manager ratio (no. of managers to total employee)	1.997	−13.571	−55.933*
	(1.308)	(9.002)	(31.234)
2. Firm_size (Small)	0.323	−2.634	18.462**
	(0.584)	(3.839)	(7.188)
3. Firm_size (medium)	0.727	−8.606*	16.778**
	(0.786)	(4.716)	(8.055)
4. Firm_size (large)	0.775	−3.779	13.184
	(0.805)	(4.903)	(10.608)
Constant	9.111***	7.129	−82.107***
	(1.236)	(8.544)	(24.021)
Observations	154	154	114
R-squared	0.391	0.241	0.699
Number of qid	85	85	83

Notes Robust standard errors in parentheses; *, **, ***represent significance level at 10, 5 and 1% respectively

enhancing the firms' productivity and, to some extent, the firms' profitability. Apart from firm and management characteristics, some activities, such as e-governance, GIS, BPO, and firm size (small and medium), contribute to the higher profitability of the firms. However, none of the firm activities are associated with labor productivity; instead productivity hinges on the firm's dynamic capability reflected in the owner's experience and the firm's legal status (proprietorship). We have not found any significant effect of skill intensity on firm performances over time. The reason may be that only an engineering degree (academic degree) is not sufficient for enhancing firm productivity; rather, hands-on skills matter.

5 Analysis of Firm Capability

In this section, we provide an analysis of the dynamic capabilities of firms by assessing technical efficiency and dynamic capability indicators. Both the analyses are done with the data of 2009 for 100 IT firms. Though older data are used due to the lack of some relevant information in 2020 data, the analysis may provide a relevant direction for the ICT sector for the short to medium-term.

5.1 Technical Efficiency Analysis

A firm's capability can be judged by its ability to utilize all inputs more efficiently, which critically depends on the resources available and its allocation. There is a scale economy and additional insights to be gained by analyzing the technical efficiency of firms as well as the sources of inefficiencies. The degree of efficiency determines whether a firm might survive or stagnate and fail over time.

For this purpose, stochastic frontier production functions in Translog functional form are specified below:

$$\ln Y_i = \delta_0 + \sum_{j=1}^{3} \delta_j X_{ji} + V_i - U_i \qquad (1)$$

and

$$\ln Y_i = \delta_0 + \sum_{j=1}^{3} \delta_j X_{ji} + \sum_{j=1}^{3} \sum_{h=1}^{3} \delta X_{ji} X_{hi} + (V_i - U_i) \qquad (2)$$

where Y represents gross output (revenue) and X represents explanatory variables, such as skilled labor (L), capital (K), and electricity (E). V_i represents a random error term and assumes to be iid with $V_i \sim N(0, \sigma_v^2)$. U_i are technical efficiency errors and assumed to be iid with $U_i \sim N^+(0, \sigma_u^2)$, where N^+ represents a non-negative truncated normal distribution. If $\gamma = \sigma_u^2/\sigma^2$ lies between 0 and 1, it means a certain level of technical inefficiencies. If $\gamma = 0$, there is no inefficiency, and $\gamma = 1$ indicates highly technical inefficiency in the production process. Technical efficiency of firms in the context of the stochastic frontier production function can be expressed in terms of error as

$$TE_j = E\left[\exp(-U_i) | (V_i - U_i)\right] \qquad (3)$$

Stochastic frontier production functions are estimated based on Eqs. (1) and (2). Firms with a standard combination of production activities are used as sample units, e.g., export vs. non-export-oriented firms, cluster vs. non-cluster firms, small vs. medium-sized firms, and firms specialized in various sectors (e.g., financial sectors, telecommunications, etc.), so that a standard production function is applied to all sample firms. Results are presented in Table 5. As the gamma values are close to zero, it indicates a certain level of efficiencies of the IT firms though not significant.

As such, capital and skilled labor (engineers) are the key factors, as no other raw materials are required for software development. Therefore, we first estimate the Cobb–Douglas production function considering GVA (Gross Value Added), and the results are reported in Column 1 of Table 5. The results show that capital has a factor share of 0.25 and labor has a factor share of 0.78, indicating the greater importance of human capital in the ICT industry. Models are estimated with various characteristics of firms in a more flexible Translog functional form in columns 2–10 of Table 5. Results suggest that all three factors (capital, labor, and electricity) are positive and significant to software firms. For non-export-oriented firms, as L^2 is positive and significant, it indicates that employing more skilled labor can increase the productivity of firms. Electricity has been significant and positive for ICT firms. Given the challenges that the energy sector in Bangladesh faces, establishing more ICT Parks can be a solution for providing firms with uninterrupted electricity. The hypothesis of no technical inefficiency cannot be rejected for any type of firms. This indicates that IT firms in the early 2010s were not technically efficient in using its resources, particularly the human capital. The problem of human capital still persists, and therefore IT firms have been facing challenges from technical efficiency ground.

5.2 *Firm's Dynamic Capability Analysis*

The discussion in this chapter leads to the conjecture that dynamic capability indicators might positively impact the productivity of the ICT firms through innovations. In this section, three composite indexes of the dynamic capability of firms are generated through a set of related variables. Particularly, we look closer into capabilities that may contribute to entrepreneurial strategies enhancing productivity within ICT SMEs. Reviewing the SME literature, we consider four types of capabilities that appear to be most critical in facilitating innovative strategies for improved productivity and profitability (Borch & Madsen, 2007). In line with the

Table 5 Estimates from stochastic frontier production function, 2009

	All Firms (value added is the dep. Var.)	*All firms*	*Non-export-oriented firms (N = 52)*	*Export-oriented firms (n = 46)*	*Small-size firms (n = 68)*	*Medium-sized firms (n = 32)*	*Financial service-focused firms*	*Data entry firms*	*Telecommunication service-focused firms*
Capital (K)	0.25*** (0.06)	1.48* (0.88)	2.84** (1.24)	1.00 (1.24)	2.33* (1.36)	1.95 (2.91)	0.40 (2.25)	−18.62 (11.34)	0.66 (2.57)
K^2	…	−0.04 (0.03)	−0.08 (0.03) **	−0.02 (0.03)	−0.06 (0.04)	−0.05 (0.08)	−0.01 (0.08)	0.74* (0.39)	0.01 (0.09)
Labor (L)	0.78*** (0.11)	0.15 (0.34)	−0.05 (0.35)	0.53 (0.77)	0.14 (0.89)	−2.37 (2.93)	−1.11 (3.05)	26.59)** (13.90)	4.45 (4.66)
L^2	…	0.11* (0.06)	0.12* (0.06)	0.05 (0.12)	0.11 (0.18)	0.49 (0.49)	0.09 (0.20)	1.98* (1.09)	0.18 (0.59)
Electricity (E)	…	0.16** (0.08)	0.32*** (0.09)	−0.03 (0.13)	0.20** (0.09)	−0.14 (0.28)	0.22 (0.19)	0.91** (0.36)	0.23 (0.24)
LK	…	…	…	…	…	…	0.08 (0.23)	−2.26** (1.01)	−0.29 (0.39)
Constant	10.38*** (1.17)	−0.50 (7.32)	−12.30 (10.04)	4.56 (10.74)	−7.51 (10.87)	4.48 (26.62)	8.70 (16.62)	123.89 (80.70)	−2.67 (20.48)
/mu	…	−0.11 (20.24)	−0.07 (10.38)	−0.09 (23.10)	−0.09 (13.34)	−0.05 (13.43)	−0.08 (31.17)	−0.10 (28.23)	−0.07 (17.38)
/lnsigma2	…	−0.65*** (0.20)	−1.02***(0.28)	−0.53* (0.32)	−0.94***(0.23)	−0.40 (0.50)	0.10 (0.34)	−0.33 (0.61)	−0.45 (0.38)
/ilgtgamma	…	−7.27 (218.29)	−6.63 (162.66)	−6.94 (265.3)	−6.97 (169.5)	−5.88 (162.03)	−6.88 (287.35)	−6.32 (275.68)	−6.73 (243.72)
sigma2	0.54 (0.07)	0.52 (0.10)	0.35 (0.09)	0.58 (0.18)	0.39 (0.08)	0.66 (13.43)	1.10 (0.38)	0.71 (0.44)	0.63 (0.24)

	All Firms (value added is the dep. Var.)	*All firms*	*Non-export-oriented firms (N = 52)*	*Export-oriented firms (n = 46)*	*Small-size firms (n = 68)*	*Medium-sized firms (n = 32)*	*Financial service-focused firms*	*Data entry firms*	*Telecommunication service-focused firms*
gamma	…	0.0006 (0.15)	0.001 (0.21)	0.0009 (0.25)	0.0009 (0.15)	0.002 (0.44)	0.001 (0.32)	0.001 (0.49)	0.00118 (0.28)
sigma_u2	…	0.0003 (0.07)	0.0004 (0.07)	0.0005 (0.14)	0.0003 (0.06)	0.001 (0.29)	0.001 (0.32)	0.001 (0.35)	0.0007 (0.18)
sigma_v2	…	0.52 (0.07)	0.35 (0.69)	0.58 (0.12)	0.38 (0.06)	0.66 (0.21)	1.10 (0.21)	0.71 (0.29)	0.63 (0.17)
H0: No inefficiency component		Z = 2.87 Prob < = z = 0.99	Z = 0.96 Prob < = z = 0.83	Z = 1.611 Prob < = z = 0.94	Z = 2.63 Prob < = z = 0.99	Z = 0.34 Prob < = z = 0.63	Z = 1.54 Prob < = z = 0.93	Z = 0.78 Prob < = z = 0.78	Z = 0.54 Prob < = z = 0.70

(continued)

Table 5 (continued)

	All Firms (value added is the dep. Var.)	*All firms*	*Non-export-oriented firms* (N = 52)	*Export-oriented firms* (n = 46)	*Small-size firms* (n = 68)	*Medium-sized firms* (n = 32)	*Financial service-focused firms*	*Data entry firms*	*Telecommunication service-focused firms*
Mean TE		0.99	0.99	0.99	0.99	0.97	0.98	0.98	0.99

Note *, **, ***represent significance level at 10, 5 and 1% respectively

literature, some hypotheses are postulated to explain the growth and development of ICT SMEs in Bangladesh.

5.2.1 Resource Reconfiguration/Integration Capabilities

Resource reconfiguration or integration capabilities refer to the capability to patch or realign business concepts where resources are added, combined, or split (Eisenhardt & Brown, 1999). This is very important for a highly competitive sector like the ICT sector. ICT SMEs, in most cases, have a simple organizational structure where the manager (in most cases, the owner) is closely involved in daily operations. This gives the manager a unique overview of all available potential resources. For greater market access, and the competitive strategy to enter into the global value chain depends on managers' ability to build an external network, as most of them are educated from overseas. The firm has to identify new combinations of productive resources within the firm and extend the frontiers of capabilities. This can be facilitated by synergies between old resource combinations and new resources outside the firm (Venkataraman et al., 1992).

Effective linkage or networks improve overall innovation management, enable the firm to reconfigure its resources, and provide ways to experiment with new ideas (Dougherty, 1995). This linkage serves as a basis of a firm's capability to adjust to a changing and turbulent external environment and the firm's market-product portfolio (Shinkai & Hossain, 2011; Eisenhardt & Martin, 2000; Grant, 1996; Pisano, 1994).

5.2.2 Resource Acquisition Capabilities

The acquisition of new resources through the accumulation of own equity capital is not an issue of ICT SMEs. Instead, the development of business relations through person-to-person contacts and trust may give the ICT firms access to complementary resources and reduce the risk of opportunistic behavior, thereby transaction costs. Organizational networks are essentially concerned with human relations that transcend organizational structure requirements, commercial relationships, etc. (Hall, 1993). Hall (1993) argued that networks, reputation and culture, and employee know-how are the most valuable resources for business success for SMEs.

Building a network works as an instrument for market access that can help a firm acquire more resources. Such an effective network can support the firm in its early stages of development; moreover, it can help the firm process information. Factor mobility may reduce by linking internal resources with external networks and creating network systems at a higher complexity level (Black & Boal, 1994). The network structure of a firm is likely to influence its performance through knowledge transfer and use; hence, it is indicative of the firm's capability (Zaheer & Bell, 2005).

5.2.3 *Learning Network Capabilities*

Better capabilities in learning play an important role in creating a sustained competitive advantage for the ICT firms. In general, increasing skills serve as a source of continuous renewal of all the resources in the firm and not only the basic operational competence needed for efficient implementation of strategies (Zollo & Winter, 2002). Organizational learning effort is about the incremental improvement of existing and new knowledge, skills, and processes. (Cohen & Levinthal, 1990; Levinthal & March, 1993). Thus, a learning network demands broad channels of information exchange and cross-functional teams that bring together different sources of expertise. The learning process includes routines that exchange joint experience among the groups and functions; extensive communication links out of the firm increase the number of new impulses. The continuous process of skill development, innovation, and acquiring new technologies involves the learning process, which appears very crucial for the initial development of the ICT sector.

6 Regression Results

The analysis in the previous section indicates the importance of various firm capability indicators for the improvement of productivity. In this section, we empirically test the hypotheses postulated in Sect. 3 by generating some dynamic capability indicators from the sample and then assessing their effect on the productivity level of the firms.

Productivity is measured by total productivity (TP), defined as the Hicks neutral efficiency term in the production function

$$\text{In}\,\text{TP}_{it} = \text{In}\,\text{Y}_{\text{it}} - \text{LS}\,\text{In}\,\text{L}_{\text{it}} - \text{CS}\,\text{In}\,\text{K}_{it} \tag{4}$$

Where Y represents sales, L is labor; LS is labor share, CS is capital share, and K is capital, respectively. Here, *i* represents a firm, and *t* represents the year. Capital was constructed by reported capital in 2009 and investment each year. Capital share was calculated from the replacement cost and sales. Labor share was computed from wages and the number of employees and sales. Total productivity (TP) resembles total factor productivity (TFP). However, strictly speaking, value-added instead of sales/output should be used to calculate TFP. For IT firms, materials may not be significant production inputs—therefore, TP and TFP may not differ much. Nevertheless, to differentiate the method to lead the difference in results, here we call Total Productivity following Hulten et al. (2006). On the other hand, we consider gross profit (before tax and interest payment) as a percentage of sales revenue to measure ***profitability***.

Thus, the regression model is specified as:

$$\text{In}\,\text{TP}_{it} = \text{In}\alpha + \beta x_{\text{it}} + \gamma z_{\text{it}} \tag{5}$$

Where x_{it} is firm-specific factors and z_{it} is dynamic capability indicators. Firm-specific factors, such as revenue earned in 2009, size (in terms of employee numbers), and company age, are used as control variables. Four dynamic capability indicators are considered as mediating variables in the analysis. These indicators are developed through the factor analysis of a combination of relevant factors discussed in Sect. 3. For example, ***resource acquisition capability*** is measured through the factors related to foreign degrees of managers or owners and collaboration with domestic or foreign firms. ***Reconfiguration capability*** is drawn from product and process upgradation and expenditure-cut measures taken to minimize the risk of the global financial crisis in 2007 and 2008.

Learning network capability is measured through the factors like in-house skill development programs and the extent of usefulness for the skill development of employees. We also include one additional capability indicator, such as the marketing network of firms, which is mainly aligned with resource acquisition capability. ***Marketing network capability*** is measured by factors like mode of communication with customers and promotional activities undertaken.

It may be noted that several explanatory variables used for the estimation might be endogenous. Amount of output, activity, the status of the firm, age of firm, location, managers, and even capability indicators, particularly learning network capability, all are choice variables that are possibly dependent on the performance of sample firms, so does on productivity. Testing the endogeneity of so many variables poses a formidable task. As an experiment, the endogeneity test was conducted on the output level following Hausman (1978). As the results suggest, the output level, in this case, is endogenous. Hence, the 2SLS (Two-Stage Least Square) results are preferable. However, finding exogenous instruments is difficult and critically hinges on the orthogonal condition and error terms. As instruments for output level, participation in the market promotion and skill development programs are considered. As there was more than one instrument for the ***endogenous*** output level, Hansen's (1982) *J*-test of overidentifying restrictions was conducted to check the exogeneity of the instruments. As the results in the bottom panel show, the instruments satisfy the exogeneity condition.

None of these variables are perfect instruments. Participation in any promotion or skill development programs is a choice variable. Thus, the 2SLS regressions with GMM (Generalized Methods of Moments) estimators are considered to examine the robustness of the estimates, as presented for three regression specifications, such as for all firms, export-oriented units (EOUs), and non-export-oriented units (NEOU) in Table 6.

The first specification suggests that none of the dynamic capabilities are significant to firms' productivity; however, EOUs are relatively more productive than NEOUs. The second specification for EOUs suggests

Table 6 2SLS regression with GMM estimators

Log (Productivity)	*All* Coef. (Std. Err.)	*EOU* Coef. (Std. Err.)	*NEOU* Coef. (Std. Err.)
Log (size)	0.67 (0.61)	−0.40 (0.83)	−0.26 (0.43)
Log (company age)	0.40 (0.38)	−0.21 (0.51)	0.33* (0.20)
Marketing network (mnetwork)	−0.24 (0.35)	−0.12 (0.35)	0.09 (0.44)
Reconfiguration network (reconfig)	0.10 (0.15)	0.27** (0.13)	−0.07 (0.12)
Learning network (lnetwork)	−0.17 (0.33)	−0.01 (0.45)	0.04 (0.23)
Resource acquisition (acquisition)	−0.11 (0.20)	0.12 (0.16)	0.01 (0.37)
EOU	*0.49 (0.31)	–	–
Constant	13.48 (6.23)	10.11 (6.76)	2.26 (4.66)

Note Instrumented: lrev; Instruments: lsize lage mnetwork acquisation reconfig lnetwork EOU q49 skildev; *, **, *** indicate significance at 10%, 5% and 1% levels respectively; *Data source* BIDS Survey (2009)

that *resource reconfiguration* capability contributes to the higher productivity of EOUs. On the other hand, for NEOUs, dynamic capability indicators are not significant to productivity; rather, output and company age is significant to productivity.

In another attempt, we categorize firms into two categories: highly productive firms (if firm's productivity exceeds 75th percentile level, particularly if the logarithm of productivity >12.0) and average productive firms (if firm's productivity exceeds 50th percentile level, which is 11.5) to examine which factors matter for highly productive firms. We run 2SLS probit regressions based on the categorization. to tackle endogeneity bias. The results are shown in Table 7.

The results show that while reconfiguration capability is positive and significant for highly productive firms, resource acquisition capability is negative but significant. Other capability indicators, such as learning and marketing networks, are not significant even for these highly productive firms. On the other hand, none of the capability indicators are significant for average productive IT firms. Comparing the results of the two specifications, it may be concluded that resource acquisition capability is significant to productive firms but not highly productive. This supports the hypothesis that these categories of firms are at the early stage of development.

7 Concluding Remarks

This chapter examines the capabilities of ICT firms in Bangladesh by analyzing survey data of ICT firms collected in 2009 and 2020. Firm capabilities are associated with higher labor productivity, which depends on management experience and education, and the maturity of firms is also indirectly associated with a firm's incentive structure. Most firms are domestic-oriented and heavily dependent on e-commerce, website development, and e-governance projects for higher revenues and profits. Firms gain productivity over time; however, there are no differences between export-oriented and non-export-oriented firms. The government's "Digital Bangladesh" initiative is expected to generate more demand for IT applications and software in both the public and private sectors, which will thus help firms to achieve maturity and competitive capabilities.

Technical efficiency analysis suggests that firms established on or after 2000 were competitive and export-oriented. The estimates suggest that skilled labor, capital, and electricity are the key factors of production.

Table 7 Probit model estimates with endogenous covariates

	High Productive Firms	*Average Productive Firms*
	Coef. (Std. Err.)	Coef. (Std. Err.)
Log (size)	0.41 (1.34)	1.34*** (0.56)
Log (company age)	0.34 (0.53)	0.60*** (0.27)
Marketing network (mnetwork)	0.00 (0.47)	−0.05 (0.42)
Resource acquisition (acquisition)	−0.40** (0.20)	−0.16 (0.16)
Reconfiguration network (reconfig)	0.31* (0.18)	0.14 (0.15)
Learning network (lnetwork)	0.20 (0.54)	−0.27 (0.30)
Export oriented (EOU)	0.08 (0.58)	0.60*** (0.25)
Const	0.24 (15.18)	12.30* (7.34)
/athrho	0.44 (0.88)	1.61 (1.19)
/lnsigma	−0.40 (0.08)	−0.40 (0.08)
Rho	0.41 (0.73)	0.92 (0.18)
Sigma	0.67 (0.05)	0.67 (0.05)
Wald test of exogeneity	chi2(1) = 0.25 Prob > chi2 = 0.61	chi2(1) = 1.84 Prob > chi2 = 0.17

Note Instrumented: lrev; Instruments: lsize lage mnetwork acquisation reconfig lnetwork EOU promotional_activities skildev; *, **, ***indicate significance at 10%, 5% and 1% levels respectively; *Data source* BIDS Survey (2009)

Therefore, policies are needed to build capabilities to produce more high-quality IT graduates and provide easy access to finance with collateral-free credit and uninterrupted electricity supply for further development of the ICT industry.

Although the dynamic capabilities of ICT SMEs are necessary for enhancing innovations and productivity of the sector, it is almost non-existent. Two types of capabilities, namely "resource reconfiguration capability" and "resource acquisition capability" have contributed to the enhanced productivity of export-oriented firms. However, "learning network" and "marketing network" capabilities are important for innovations and greater market access. Owners with foreign engineering degrees and experience are important for increasing the export capabilities of firms as they can build an effective market network. Firms in the IT parks do not significantly differ from non-IT park firms. However, the clustering of firms has some positive impacts on profitability and export performance, though productivity does not matter. The analysis indicates that the ICT industry in Bangladesh is still at its initial stages of development in terms of maturity, product specialization, and market access. Innovation, product and process up-gradation through knowledge, and network building capabilities are some of the key strategies that may improve the productivity of firms.

References

BIDS Survey. (2009). *Assessment of the impact of clustering on IT industries*. Bangladesh Institute of Development Studies (BIDS).

BIDS-SEIP Survey. (2020). *Labor market and skill gap in the ICT sector in Bangladesh*. Bangladesh Institute of Development Studies (BIDS) and Skills for Employment Investment Program (SEIP), Finance Division. Ministry of Finance.

Black, J. A., & Boal, K. B. (1994). Strategic resources: Traits, configuration, and paths to sustainable competitive advantage. *Strategic Management Journal, 15*, 131–148.

Borch, O. J., & Madsen, E. L. (2007). Dynamic capabilities facilitating innovative strategies in SMEs. *International J. of Technoentrepreneurship, 1*(1), 109–125.

Brush, C. G., Greene, P. G., & Hart, M. M. (2001). From initial idea to unique advantage: The entrepreneurial challenge of constructing a resource base. *Academy of Management Executive, 15*(1), 64–78.

Chatterjee, S., & Harrison, J. S. (2001). Corporate governance. In M. A. Hitt, R. E. Freeman, & Harrison, J. S. Harrison (Eds.), *Blackwell handbook of strategic management* (543–563). Blackwell.

Clark, K. B., & Fujimoto, T. (1991). *Product development performance: Strategy, organization and management in the world auto industry*. Harvard Business School Press.

Cohen, W. M., & Levinthal, D. A. (1990). Absorptive capacity: A new perspective on learning and innovation. *ADministrative Science Quarterly, 35*, 128–152.

Dougherty, D. (1995). Managing your core incompetencies for corporate venturing. *Entrepreneurship Theory and Practice, 19*(3), 113–135.

Eisenhardt, K. M., & Brown, S. L. (1999). Patching: Resticing business portfolios in dynamic markets. *Harvard Business Review, 77*, 72–82.

Eisenhardt, K. M., & Martin, J. K. (2000). Dynamic capabilities: What are they? *Strategic Management Journal, 21*, 1105–1121.

Gebreeyesus, M., & Mohnen, P. (2013). Innovation performance and embeddedness in networks: Evidence from the Ethiopian footwear cluster. *World Development, 41*, 302–316.

Gnyawali, D. R., & Madhavan, R. (2001). Cooperative networks and competitive dynamics: A structural embeddedness perspective. *Academy of Management Review, 26*(3), 431–445.

Grant, R. M. (1996). Toward a knowledge-based theory of the firm. *Strategic Management Journal, 17*, 109–122.

Greene, P. G., Brush, C. G., & Hart, M. M. (1999). The corporate venture champion: A resource-based approach to role and process. *Entrepreneurship Theory and Practice, 23*(3), 103–122.

Hall, R. (1993). A framework linking intangible resources and capabilities to sustainable competitive advantage. *Strategic Management Journal, 14*, 607–618.

Hansen, L. P. (1982). Large sample properties of generalized method of moments estimators. *Econometrica, 50*(4), 1029–1054.

Hausman, J. A. (1978). Specification tests in econometrics. *Econometrica, 46*(6), 1251–1271.

Helfat, C. E., & Peteraf, M. A. (2003). The dynamic resource-based view: Capability lifecycles. *Strategic Management Journal, 24*, 997–1010.

Hitt, M. A., Ireland, R. D., Camp, S. M., & Sexton, D. L. (2001). Strategic entrepreneurship: Innovative strategies for wealth creation. *Strategic Management Journal, 22*, 479–491.

Hulten, C., Bennathan, E., & Srinivasan, S. (2006). Infrastructure, externalities, and economic development: A study of Indian manufacturing industry. *World Bank Economic Review, 20*(2), 291–308.

Koka, B. R., & Prescott, J. E. (2002). Strategic alliances as social capital: A multidimensional view. *Strategic Management Journal, 23*(9), 795.

Liberman, M. B., Lau, L. J., & Williams, M. D. (1989). Firm-level productivity and management influence: A comparison of U.S. and Japanese automobile producers. *Management Science*, *36*, 10.

Levinthal, D. A., & March, J. G. (1993). The Myopia of learning. *Strategic Management Journal*, *14*, 95–112.

Mauri, A., & Michaels, M. (1998). Industry effects within strategic management: An empirical examination. *Strategic Management Journal, 19*(3), 211–219.

Nahapiet, J., & Ghoshal, S. (1998). Social capital, intellectual capital, and the organizational advantage. *The Academy of Management Review, 23*(2), 242–266.

Pisano, G. P. (1994). Knowledge, integration, and the locus of learning: an empirical analysis of process development. *Strategic Management Journal*, *15,* 85–100.

Shinkai, N., & Hossain, M. (2011). Productivity and performance of the IT sector in Bangladesh: Evidence from firm-level data. *Bangladesh Development Studies, 34*(2), 1–22.

Teece, D. J., Pisano, G., & Shuen, A. (1997). Dynamic capabilities and strategic management. *Strategic Management Journal, 18*(7), 509–533.

Venkataraman, S., MacMillan, I. C., & McGrath, R. G. (1992). Progress in research on corporate venturing. In D. L. Sexton & J. D. Kasandra (Eds.), *The state of the art of entrepreneurship*. PWS-Kent.

Zaheer, A., & Bell, G. G. (2005). Benefiting from network position: Firm capabilities, structural holes, and performance. *Strategic Management Journal, 26*(9), 809–825.

Zollo, M., & Winter, S. G. (2002). Deliberate learning and the evolution of dynamic capabilities. *Organization Science, 13*(3), 339–351.

CHAPTER 8

Cluster-Based ICT Industry Development in Bangladesh: National and International Perspectives

1 Introduction

Software Technology Park (STP)[1] development is now considered an important policy instrument for the development of the IT industry after the success of Silicon Valley in the USA and Software Technology Park (STP) in Bangalore, India. Silicon Valley of the USA and IT Park in Bangalore, India, are some of the most notable examples of success in clustering and networking-based IT sector development. In what follows, many countries started building IT parks with different names to develop their IT industry. Even India has so far established some 60 STPs all over the country. Countries tried to imitate the success of Silicon Valley or Bangalore IT park by offering tax breaks, policy and regulatory support. Considering the benefits of agglomeration economies, IT parks can bring benefits through collective efficiency, establishing networks with larger producers, and excel into national and global markets. However, there are also some negative aspects of agglomeration. In addition to agglomeration benefits, it is easier for the government of developing countries to provide various policy and infrastructure supports to firms located in a cluster or park, such as uninterrupted electricity

[1] STPs are established in many countries with different names, such as IT/ICT parks, high-tech parks, etc.

M. Hossain, *Digital Transformation and Economic Development in Bangladesh*, https://doi.org/10.1007/978-981-19-2753-9_8

and internet, tax benefits, office space, satellite uplinks, import certifications, and market analysis. Undoubtedly, IT parks provide a spatial manifestation of the digital revolution, being a source of attraction for customers and facilitating networking among firms through cost and resource sharing (Fujita & Thisse, 1996).

Following other countries' experiences, Bangladesh also considers building STPs as one of the important policy agendas for developing the ICT industry. Though the development of STPs started in early 2000, it has accelerated in the early 2010s as part of the Digital Bangladesh vision. The initial thought was to provide uninterrupted electricity, internet, and other infrastructure benefits to IT firms located in a cluster. However, with improved electricity and internet coverage across the country, current motivation is perhaps associated with agglomeration economies' benefits. This chapter attempts to analyze the policy of establishing STPs and related aspects from national and international perspectives in order to facilitate informed policy making.

It is to be noted that cluster-based IT industry development has not been successful in many countries. IT Park has both merits and demerits. IT Park offers some agglomeration benefits as suggested by Marshall, commonly known as Marshallian triad (Marshall, 1890): Market-size effect, thick labor market effect, and external market effect. The market-size effect refers to demand and cost benefits through creating backward and forward linkages. A local concentration of firms allows creating a large local market that also makes effective demand for locally produced goods and services. At the same time, cost-benefit arises out of locally produced intermediate goods that essentially lower the production costs of other producers. The thick labor market effect refers to a local concentration of a thick labor market, where employees and employers are readily matched. Third, the pure external economies effect denotes spillover benefits from the local concentration that benefits all firms in the agglomeration.

Despite the Marshallian benefits of agglomeration, there are potential negative sides of agglomeration, as identified by Krugman (1998). For example, immobile factors, such as land, natural resources, and, to some extent, labor, might slow down the process of agglomeration. The concentration of economic activity drives up the cost of land and discourages further concentration. Moreover, pure external diseconomies refer to the concentration of economic activities and population are likely to lead to increased traffic, congestion, pollution, and crime. These factors might affect private-sector-led initiatives of IT parks. However, in most cases, the governments facilitate and establish parks with serviced land and other benefits, such as tax incentives etc. to promote the ICT industries. In many cases, the negative aspects of agglomeration, as Krugman (1998) mentioned, are surpassed by the positive outcomes. However, as Shinkai and Hossain (2011) found, many of the IT firms in Bangladesh were not willing to relocate them in an IT park from the concerns of driving out of their contract to other firms given a scarcity of supply of orders.

Against the backdrop, Bangladesh has established its first IT Park, namely ICT Incubation Center, in 2002 at the BSRS (Bangladesh Shilpa Rin Sangstha) building in Dhaka to provide infrastructure supports to about 50 firms. This incubation center later turned into an IT cluster as many older firms are located there. Another IT cluster was established in a building named Janata Tower in Dhaka in 2010 as the government could not find a good place for a high-tech park in Dhaka city due to land disputes. Later, to expedite IT park projects, the government of Bangladesh enacted the "Bangladesh Hi-Tech Park Act-2010," through which the government established the Bangladesh Hi-Tech Park Authority (BHTPA). This authority is entrusted with overseeing hi-tech park, software technology Park, and IT training and incubation center projects. These hi-tech parks are designed to be the hub of ICT in the country, acting as mediums to further augment IT/ITES industries (Bangladesh Hi-Tech Park Authority, 2019). The BHTPA has already begun implementing six projects while also building and designing the infrastructure for 28 hi-tech parks or software technology parks in 2017.

With this background, Sect. 2 discusses theoretical and international perspectives of IT parks. Section 3 highlights the current status of IT parks in Bangladesh, and Sect. 4 analyzes the performances of IT firms in the IT parks. Section 5 highlights the opinions of entrepreneurs on the IT park facilities and benefits, and Sect. 6 concludes the chapter.

2 Theoretical and International Perspectives of IT Parks

Many countries attempted to establish IT parks following the successes of Silicon Valley and Bangalore IT parks by offering tax breaks, improving infrastructure, and regulatory relief to firms; however, they could not succeed in the way they anticipated (Rodriguez-Pose & Hardy, 2014). The history of successful IT park development might guide us in this context. The author got a mixed understanding while talking to various experts and stakeholders about the success of Bangalore during paying a visit to Bangalore IT parks in 2011. The common perception is that Bangalore has not become successful just because of government policy intervention in developing IT infrastructure; instead, it has a historical perspective (Parthasarathy, 2015). For example, many thought that the success of Bangalore IT Park was not based on a systematic policy intervention and, therefore, it cannot be replicated or imitated. Bangalore IT park has been benefitted from Bangalore's heavy-industrial base, which was the hub of some notable heavy industries, such as the Hindustan Aeronautics Limited (HAL), Hindustan Machine Tools (HMT), and Indian Telephone Industries (ITI). In what follows, to meet the demand for technical workforce and engineers for these industries, a large number of outstanding education and research institutions were established in Bangalore that plays a significant role in supporting and promoting the ecosystem. Institutes like the Indian Institute of Science (IISc), Indian Institute of Management-Bangalore (IIMB), Institute of Bioinformatics and Applied Biotechnology (IBAB), and National Centre for Biological Sciences (NCBS) is based in Bangalore and have their own Technology Business Incubators (TBIs) to nurture entrepreneurship. These institutions worked as a boon for IT sector development in Bangalore. Furthermore, the Park facilitates alliances, clustering, and networking to help small firms to compete, grow, and cooperate with large firms in IT parks (Kolko, 2001). By working together, firms gained the benefits of collective efficiency, which enabled them to link with larger producers and connect to global markets. Therefore, the key to success in a cluster depends on three aspects: customer-oriented focus (supply chain), a mutually supportive approach, and a cumulative effort to ensure continuous improvements. More importantly, the lack of a mutually supportive culture among the firms in developing countries is a cause of concern, which often leads to lower benefits for industrial or IT clusters.

Another interesting aspect is that the entry of Texas Instruments into Bangalore in 1984 has been instrumental in attracting numerous IT Multi-National Companies there. With the right policies in place, the Karnataka state government started effectively using the experience to build an ecosystem supporting technology start-ups' emergence, sustenance, and growth. As Kolko (2001) noted, the success of Silicon Valley or Bangalore IT Park is not because of just ICT's unique features, rather it facilitates sharing the high-skilled workforce and IT industry benefits among the firms. High skills and rapid turnover directly explain concentration and persistence, and from this perspective, ICT clusters are not very different from other industrial clusters. Kolko (2001) pointed out that clusters are relatively less likely to remain for ICT industries, though it is yet to be validated. This argument perhaps reflects to the fact that why other IT parks in India have not been successful to that level of Bangalore.

Theoretically, if one geographical region becomes specialized in software making, then increasing returns to scale will lead software-making firms profitable to cluster there. The underlying idea is that with increasing returns, producers and consumers may not switch from there if the technological superiority of the park can establish a beach-head presence (Arthur, 1994; David, 1985). Venables (1996) pointed out that natural spatial clustering and agglomeration can happen in the new economic geography with inter-connections in the production chains. As Internet and telecommunications infrastructures improve, workers no longer have to be together in one physical place for certain collaborative communications. These arguments, *ceteris paribus*, predict decreasing spatial agglomeration defying the private or public initiatives of developing the IT industry through IT parks.

The discussion in this chapter clarifies that although spatial clustering of ICT firms is evident worldwide, some other forms of inter-relationships (or networking) might prevail in this sector, which ultimately reduces the necessity of ICT spatial clustering. Taking evidence from the firms located in Bangladesh's lone IT incubator, BSRS building, Hossain et al. (2012) showed that spatial integration is evident among the firms only if they hire international IT experts or collaborate on a project in the same cluster, making IT cluster a restrictive choice.

3 Software Technology Parks in Bangladesh

Despite proper assessment of the benefits of IT Parks, establishing IT/Hi-Tech or Software Technology Parks has taken an important place in Bangladesh's ICT sector development policy. The Bangladesh government has taken initiatives to develop many IT parks. The creation of the Bangladesh Hi-Tech Park Authority (BHTPA) in 2010 is a big step forward. In Dhaka, at present, two IT parks do exist. The oldest IT Park, initiated as an ICT incubator, operates at Dhaka's BSRS building, where only about 50 firms have been accommodated. In 2010, the government allotted the Janata Tower, a 12-storied building located at Karwan Bazaar in the Capital with 72,000 square feet of floor space for establishing the second IT Park in Dhaka, which is now in operation with 15 firms. This also includes ten start-up companies conducting their modes of operation rent-free. The Park employs around 800 individuals, according to BHTPA. However, the existing IT parks at Dhaka are no longer full-fledged IT parks. In addition, the government has the vision to establish HTPs (Hi-Tech Parks)/STPs in each of the 64 districts in phases. Currently, the BHTPA has been working on a project to build a hi-tech park in 12 districts: Rangpur, Natore, Khulna, Barishal, Dhaka, Gopalgonj, Mymensingh, Jamalpur, Cumilla, Chattagram, Cox's Bazar, and Sylhet.

The proposed *Bangabandhu Hi-Tech City*, previously known as Kaliakoir High-Tech Park, is considered its biggest and full-fledged IT Park. The government initiated this first state-level Hi-Tech Park in 2011. The proposed Hi-Tech Park is located at Kaliakoir Upazila in Gazipur district, about 40 km. north from Dhaka city, and the total land area is 355 acres. The Park will be considered a specialized economic zone (SEZ) to attract foreign and local investors. To establish a world-class business environment and enrich the facilities, a project named "Support to Development of Kalikoir Hi-Tech Park at Kaliakoir, Gazipur" has been taken up at BDT 2.23 billion. However, the project's progress is unsatisfactory as it takes longer than expected to develop due to tailback in the bureaucratic and procurement process.

Sheikh Hasina Software and Technology Park were inaugurated in Jessore in 2017. The park stands on a land of 12.13 acres accommodating a building of 15 storied, facilitating a dormitory and other utility services for local and foreign investors. The Park has already assigned corporate spaces to 36 companies while creating around 5000 employment opportunities.

Establishing STPs in all the districts may not be a feasible policy option considering the complex sector-specific dynamics of spatial integration involved in new economic geography that is evident in other countries. There are multiple challenges. For example, as the government undertook initiatives to build ICT infrastructure all over the country including broadband connectivity, it will lower the internet prices making it affordable and easily accessible. This will enable IT firms to operate from any location other than IT parks. Affordable connectivity all over the country may attract IT firms in the parks if other agglomeration benefits prevail. Furthermore, considering the slow growth of the IT sector in the last decade, without complementary and supportive policies, it will be difficult to attract IT firms in STPs built in different locations of the country, and in that case, STPs would be proved to be counterproductive. Therefore, the government may take a slow-go approach by establishing a few IT parks in big cities in the first phase, and then after an assessment of their performances, further initiatives may be taken to develop more new IT parks gradually. It is relevant here to cite the example of the BSCIC industrial estates where many plots remained unallotted due to a lack of interest from genuine entrepreneurs even though BSCIC estates are open to all types of entrepreneurs.

3.1 IT Training Centers

Every industry needs a steady inflow of skilled workforce to flourish, and for the IT industry, the labor force needs to be specifically skilled depending upon the service. Bangladesh has a demographic dividend with 60% youths, a vast resource waiting to be trained and employed. With the aim to create a more skilled IT workforce, the Sheikh Kamal IT Training and Incubation Center project was proposed. The ICT ministry plans to establish 8 IT training and incubation centers with adjacent hi-tech parks so that graduated trainees have easy access to employment and IT parks have access to workers. The proposed institutes will be spread across eight districts, including Sylhet, Cumilla, Chattogram, Barishal, Natore, Magura, Netrokona, and Rangpur. So far, the only training center to be completed under this project is Natore. The project was expected to reach completion in 2021. The current status of ongoing and existing IT Parks is given in Table 4 in Appendix.

While the thrust of the initiative of the Government to establish high-tech parks at various districts is well endorsed, the lack of a proper action plan is a cause of concern. Since only one of the proposed high-tech parks has been implemented, it is unclear whether ICT firms will be interested in investing or operating in various other district level IT parks. However, establishing IT, training institutes appear to be a good initiative. Therefore, training institutes should be established in each district to develop and ensure a smooth supply of human capital for the ever-expanding IT industry. A few centers of excellence in IT and computer science should be in the offing.

4 An Analysis of Firm Performances in IT Parks

There was only one ICT cluster in 2009, located in the Bangladesh Shilpa Rin Sangstha (BSRS) building in Dhaka, accommodating about 50 IT firms. Although it was initially established as an ICT incubator, it has become an ICT cluster as both new and old firms are located there. Later several ICT parks were established in different parts of the country in anticipation that firms in the cluster would enjoy the benefits of agglomeration economies, such as government subsidies in space-rent, uninterrupted electricity, and its tariff, specialized labor pool, networking, etc. Therefore, these firms are expected to perform better than those located outside the cluster.

Survey-based results of some 18 firms from the BSRS ICT cluster (conducted in 2009) are reported below to indicate firms' performances in IT clusters. The average age of the sample firms in the cluster is estimated to be around ten years. This suggests that new entry in the cluster has not happened that much. Most of the surveyed firms in the cluster except the micro firms are involved in outsourcing with varying degrees (Table 1).

Next, we compare selected firms' performances from the ICT clusters in both surveys, 2009 and 2020. In 2020, we collected information from several IT parks, such as the BSRS building, Janata Tower, and Jashore IT Park. Gross profit as a percentage of revenue is relatively higher for the firms located in a cluster than the non-cluster firms in both periods (Fig. 1). A large portion of their revenue comes from domestic sales, indicating that cluster firms are mostly domestic-market oriented.

In terms of labor productivity, the difference between clustered and non-clustered firms is significant in 2020, with higher productivity among the non-clustered (IT park) firms but insignificant in 2009 (Table 2). However, in terms of export orientation, the differences in productivity among the clustered and non-clustered firms are insignificant in both periods. This finding could be important for rethinking the government's strategy to establish IT parks in various districts or places. Despite the smaller sample size from IT parks, results are still justified because the drawbacks of agglomeration might be crucial for the early-stage IT firms in Bangladesh that are located in the IT parks (the average age of firms in IT parks is ten years compared to fourteen years for the firms outside IT parks in 2020). Matured firms might take advantage of agglomeration benefits; however, new firms in the IT parks are affected by increased

Table 1 Characteristics of firms in an incubator (cluster), 2009

Size	*Age of firms (in years)*	*Activities*	*Export as % of revenue (average)*	*Domestic sales as % of revenue*
Cluster (n = 18)				
Micro ($n = 2$)	8.5	E-commerce	0	100
Small ($n = 13$)	9.5	E-commerce, E-governance, GIS (Geographic Information System), BPO (Business Process Outsourcing), ERP (Enterprise Resource Planning)	12.08	87.92
Medium ($n = 3$)	17	E-commerce, GIS, BPO	19.7	80.3

Note n indicates sample size; *Source* BIDS Survey, 2009

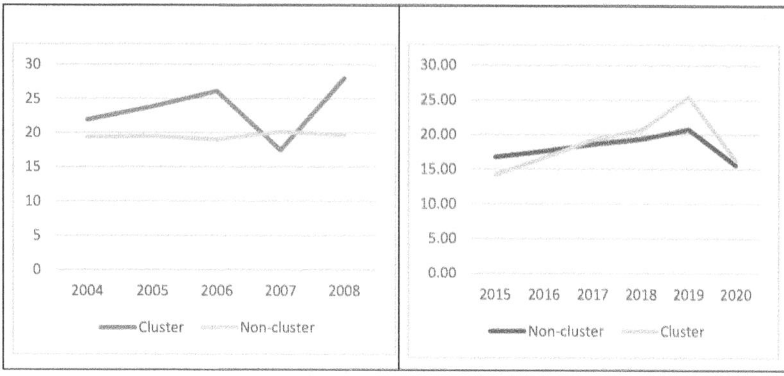

Fig. 1 Comparison of gross profit as % of revenue (*Source* BIDS survey, 2009 and BIDS-SEIP survey, 2020)

Table 2 Labor productivity comparisons, 2009–2020

Log (labor productivity)	*All*		*Export-oriented firms*		*Non-export-oriented firms*	
	2020	*2009*	*2020*	*2009*	*2020*	*2009*
Non-cluster	13.6 (127)	12.54 (167)	13.73 (60)	12.73 (74)	13.63 (67)	12.40 (93)
Cluster	13.31 (17)	12.63 (17)	13.32 (7)	13.17 (7)	13.30 (10)	12.26 (10)
Difference	0.366*	−0.09	0.41	−0.43	0.33	0.14

Note Number of firms in parentheses; *indicates significance at 1% level; *Sources* BIDS Survey, 2009 and BIDS-SEIP Survey, 2020

competition in the IT parks for specialized labor pools, a network of customers, etc.

5 Firms' Perception Regarding IT Parks: Survey Opinions

One aspiration for establishing more IT parks is that it could solve the infrastructure bottlenecks for the ICT industry. About 87% of respondents opined that an IT Park is necessary for developing the IT industry in Bangladesh (Table 3). They suggest that the Park should have the facili-

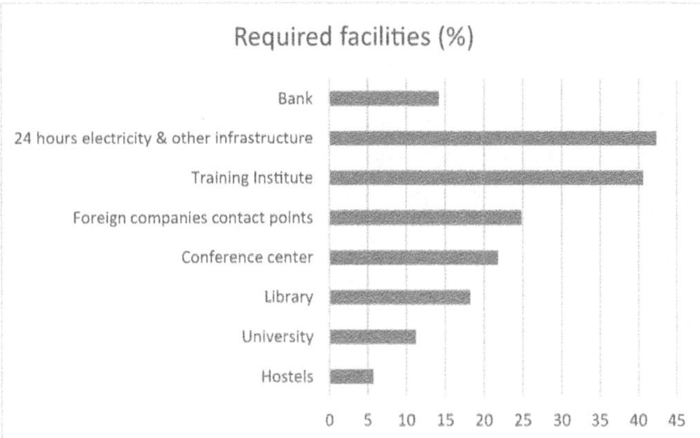

Fig. 2 Opinion on required facilities in IT parks (%) (*Source* BIDS survey 2009)

Table 3 Perceived benefits of IT parks

	Percent
Availability of skilled workforce	50.32
Availability of facility (infrastructure)	83.66
Availability of supply chain	17
A big attraction for customers/buyers	34.65
Sharing human resources	39.87
Govt. support	63.4

Source BIDS survey (2009)

ties like a training institute (41%), uninterrupted electricity (42%), foreign company contact points (20%), etc.

More specifically, in any IT park, most of the respondents (over 40%) felt that uninterrupted electricity must be ensured and there must be a training institute in an IT park. About 25% of respondents wanted to see a foreign companies contact point, and about 20% argued for a conference center in the IT park (Fig. 2). Other facilities include a bank (14%), library (18%), university (11%), and hostel (5%). It is good to know that the planned IT parks include most of these facilities.

However, the main concern is whether firms are willing to relocate in the IT parks if established. A recent employer survey of Asian Development Bank (ADB, 2018) shows that 59% of software firms, 60% of ISPs

(Internet Service Providers), and 61% of call centers are willing to relocate to the nearest IT parks. However, the firms that are not willing to relocate to IT parks cited probable reasons, such as the requirement to stay near clients in Dhaka (57%), limited local business opportunities (42%), lack of connectivity (60%), and lack of human resources (52%). Therefore, the government should take these concerns seriously while identifying the locations for IT parks.

6 Conclusion

Though the IT Park establishment has become an important supportive policy agenda of the government for developing the IT industry in Bangladesh, some supportive and complementary discretionary policies are needed to make the IT parks capable of attracting IT firms and become successful in providing agglomeration benefits. It is to be noted that only building infrastructure will not serve the purpose of IT sector development, rather, the IT park establishment policies should follow international best-practices and take local potentials into cognizance. Though there is a debate whether the success of the Silicon Valley or Bangalore IT Park can be imitated, the following issues appear to be important for establishing STPs in Bangladesh.

Firstly, the wholesale policy of IT park establishment in each district does not appear to be a feasible option. It is more likely that it will not fulfill the intended objectives. Instead, four or five full-fledged IT parks should be established on a priority basis in big cities where Engineering or Science and Technology Universities are available so that a stable supply of human resources can be ensured. Each IT Park must have an IT training institute and start-up incubation centers.

Secondly, necessary efforts and collaboration are needed with international IT tech giants for investment in IT parks. Without attracting FDI (Foreign Direct Investment) in the IT sector, it would not be easy to attract local IT firms in the IT parks and move the country's IT sector forward.

Finally, instead of establishing more IT parks in each district, the government should promote IT education and training by establishing IT training institutes in each district. Later, IT parks can be selectively established based on the availability of human capital/freelancers considering the success of the training centers and industrial base.

Appendix

Table 4 IT parks at a glance

Name of IT park	*District*	*Year of initiation*	*Area (in acre)*	*Expected year of completion*	*No. of firms located*
Bangabandhu HI-Tech City, Kaliakoir	Gazipur	2011	355	Under construction	25
Bangabandhu HI-Tech City, Rajshahi	Rajshahi	2016	43	2021	
Bangabandhu HI-Tech City, Sylhet	Sylhet	2016	162	2021	
Sheikh Hasina Software Technology Park	Jessore	2010	12.13	Completed in 2017	48
Bangladesh Shilpa Rin Shangstha (BSRS)	Dhaka	2002		One IT cluster formed in 2009	50
Software Technology Park, Janata Tower	Dhaka	2010		Completed in 2016	31
Sheikh Kamal IT Training & Incubation Center	Natore	2017	1.239	Completed in 2018	

(continued)

Table 4 (continued)

Name of IT park	*District*	*Year of initiation*	*Area (in acre)*	*Expected year of completion*	*No. of firms located*
Hi-Tech Park, (Sylhet Electronics City)	Sylhet	N/A	162.83	Under construction	
Sheikh Kamal IT Training and Incubation Centre	Several districts*	2017		2021	
IT/–Hi-Tech Park at District Level (12 districts)	Several districts**	2017	N/A	2021	
IT Business and Incubation Centre, CUET (Chattogram University of Engineering and Technology)	Chattogram	N/A	4.7	Under construction	
IT Business and Incubation Centre,	Rajshahi	N/A	4	Under construction	
ICT Incubator Cum Training Cente, KUET (Khulna University of Engineering and Technology)	Khulna	N/A	8	Under construction	

Notes *Sylhet, Natore, Netrokona, Barishal, Magura, Cumilla and Chattagram; **Rangpur, Natore, Khulna, Barishal, Dhaka, Gopalganj, Mymensingh, Jamalpur, Cumilla, Chattogram, Cox's Bazar and Sylhet

References

Asian Development Bank. (2018). *Employer survey of IT/ITES industry in Bangladesh.* Manila.

Arthur, W. B. (1994). *Increasing returns and path dependence in the economy.* The University of Michigan Press.

Bangladesh Hi-Tech Park Authority. (2019). *Hi-tech park—Prospective gateway of investment & employment.*

BIDS Survey. (2009). *Assessment of the impact of clustering on IT industries.* Bangladesh Institute of Development Studies (BIDS).

BIDS-SEIP Survey. (2020). Labor market and skill gap in the ICT sector in Bangladesh. Bangladesh Institute of Development Studies (BIDS) and Skills for Employment Investment Program (SEIP), Finance Division. Ministry of Finance.

David, P. A. (1985). Clio and the economics of QWERTY. *American Economic Association Papers and Proceedings, 75*(2), 332–337.

Fujita, M., & Thisse, J. (1996). Economics of agglomeration. *Journal of the Japanese and International Economies, 10*(4), 339–378.

Hossain, M., Shinkai, N., Yunus, M., & Bakht, Z. (2012). Integration of ICT industries and its impact on trade and market access: The case of Bangladesh and India. In Rahman, Brunner & Khatri (Eds.), *Regional integration and economic development in South Asia*. Edward Elgar Publishing.

Kolko, J. (2001). *Silicon mountains, silicon molehills: Geographic concentrations and convergence of internet industries in the US* (WIDER Working Paper Series DP 2001–2002). World Institute for Development Economics Research (UNU-WIDER).

Krugman, P. E. (1998). Whats new about the new economic geography. *Oxford Review of Economic Policy, 14*(2), 7–17.

Marshall, A. (1890). *Principles of economics*. London: Macmillan.

Parthasarathy, B. (2015). The ICT service industry in Bangalore, India: Its changing structure and characteristics. In Hirakawa et al. (Eds.), *Servitization, IT-ization and innovation models: Two-stage industrial cluster theory*. Routledge.

Rodriguez-Pose, A., & Hardy, D. (2014). Technology and Industrial Parks in Emerging Countries. Panacea or Pipedream? Basel: Springer.

Shinkai, N., & Hossain, M. (2011). Productivity and performance of the IT sector in Bangladesh: Evidence from firm-level data. *Bangladesh Development Studies, 34*(2), 1–22.

Venables, A. J. (1996). Equilibrium locations of vertically linked industries. *International Economic Review, 37*, 341–359.

CHAPTER 9

Human Capital, Labor Market Outcomes, and Skills Gap in the ICT Sector

1 Introduction

The relatively small IT sector in Bangladesh employs over 0.30 million IT professionals. The IT industry revenue grows at about 17% and labor demand is projected at 10% per year. With the rate of 10% growth of IT professionals, the projected human resources will be doubled by 2025 (Hossain, 2016, 2018). Over 95 universities and 200 polytechnic/technical institutes provide support to the ICT sector by supplying about ten thousand IT graduates every year (Asian Development Bank, 2019), though about twenty thousand graduates are needed to meet the projected labor demand of the sector. Moreover, there is a demand-supply gap as fresh graduates are not adequately acquainted with the required skills of the industry. A substantial mismatch in academic knowledge and industry-level competencies poses a threat to the expected growth of the IT industry. The skills gap in the current pool of IT professionals and consequential skills mismatch is manifested in the inadequate linkage between industry and academia.

Against this backdrop, in the context of the 4th Industrial Revolution and the country's demographic dividend position, an understanding of the industry's employment, productivity, and skills level are necessary to articulate a proper strategy for developing human capital for the ICT sector. This chapter thus systematically analyzes the following aspects of

M. Hossain, *Digital Transformation and Economic Development in Bangladesh*, https://doi.org/10.1007/978-981-19-2753-9_9

ICT employment and skills using data from several surveys: (i) employment and labor market outcomes; (ii) the current level of skills and the gap in skills in terms of availability (shortage), job-specific skills, and skills mismatch; (iii) the supply-side capacity constraint of the academic and training institutions; (iv) the emerging thrusts of the ICT sector, and (v) the training needs and ways of implementing the training programs.

The chapter is structured as follows. After the Introduction, Sect. 2 describes the basic characteristics of IT firms. Section 3 highlights the current state of the ICT labor market in Bangladesh, and Sect. 4 provides a firm-level analysis of occupations and gender dimensions. Section 5 provides an analysis of skills and skills shortages in the sector. Section 6 discusses the ways and strategies of mitigating the skills gap, and Sect. 7 analyzes the supply side constraints of skills of IT professionals. Section 8 highlights the IT education and training in Bangladesh and Sect. 9 concludes the paper.

2 Basic Characteristics of ICT Firms in Bangladesh

In this section, the firms' performances will be highlighted by comparing their basic characteristics between 2009 and 2020. This study considers only software firms providing IT and IT-enabled services (ITES). Several important features of Bangladeshi software firms are discernible here. The domestic firms still dominate the IT sector and there are only a few FDI (Foreign Direct Investment) firms. The scenario has not changed in the last ten years.

2.1 Ownership Pattern

According to a 2009 survey (BIDS Survey, 2009), about 85% of firms are owned by domestic entrepreneurs, and the remaining 15% are entrenched through a joint venture with overseas companies. However, in 2020, while 90% of firms belong to domestic ownership and 8.22% are joint ownership, only 1.33% of firms are owned by foreign entrepreneurs

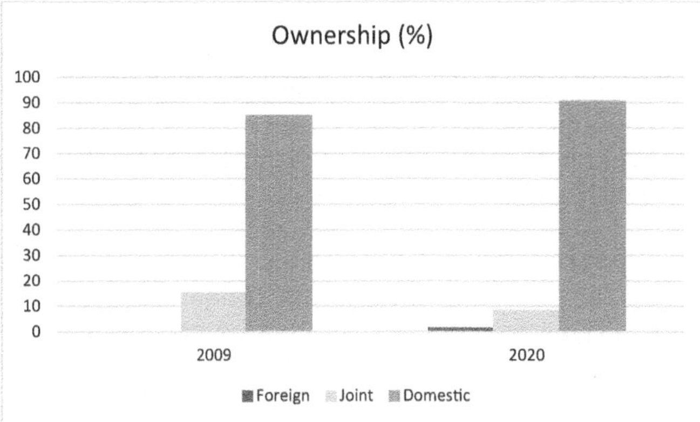

Fig. 1 Ownership pattern of the firms (*Source* BIDS Survey, 2009 & BIDS-SEIP Survey, 2020)

(BIDS-SEIP Survey, 2020).[1] The majority of the ICT firms were established in 2000 onward (about 80%) as per both the surveys. With over 95% of firms, male CEOs (Chief Executive Officers) dominate the industry. About 30% of owners have engineering bachelor's degrees, more than 25% have above M. A./M.Sc. (Masters of Arts/Masters of Science) degrees and a similar percentage of owners have an MBA (Masters of Business Admiration) degree. The educational qualification of owners/CEOs reveals that IT graduates turn into entrepreneurs, returning after higher education in overseas educational institutions.

2.2 *Firm Age and Owner's Age*

The age of owners is mainly concentrated in the 40s, and the average age of the firms is 13.5 years indicating that the owners started their enterprises in their 30s. Most of the firms (over 80%) were established on or after 2000 when the government undertook various liberalization policies for this sector, including the digital Bangladesh agenda, which created many opportunities for this sector (Fig. 1). About 35% of the

[1] Of the surveyed firms in 2020, 58% were the same one we surveyed in 2009. Therefore, including the newly surveyed firms, the ownership pattern of the ICT industry, remained almost unchanged.

surveyed firms were established after 2009. The favorable policies were coupled with the market's positive prospect, an increasing the number of graduates from polytechnic institutes and engineering departments. In the early 2000s, the industry gained an advancement due to its positive image of modern industry and advanced technology. Therefore popularity among students was created for studying computer science and IT-related subjects.

However, the initial adoration appears to be diminishing as the industry gains maturity with greater competition and saturated market opportunities. This is revealed by the new entries and exits in this industry. Considering our survey of 202 firms in 2009, about 15% of the firms have closed their businesses or switched to other businesses, while a similar proportion of firms could not be traced. Apart from that, 400 new firms entered the industry following the new BASIS (Bangladesh Association of Software and Information Services) membership after 2009. One positive aspect is that the owners of IT firms are relatively younger and have good educational qualifications that could be instrumental for the industry's dynamism. This has been reflected in the age distribution of exporting firms, as the average age of owners of exporting firms is lower than domestic-market-oriented firms (Figs. 2 and 3).

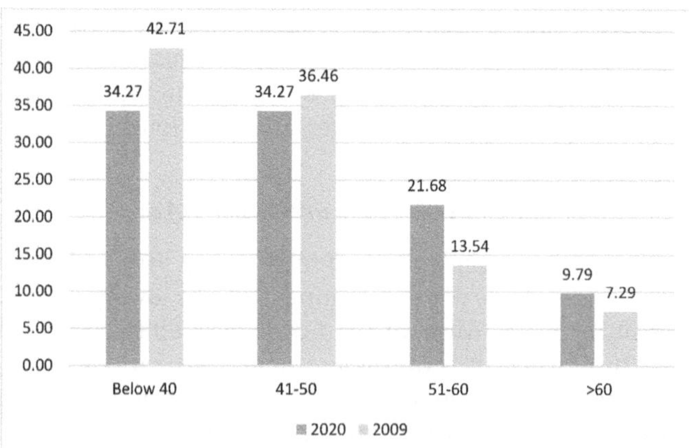

Fig. 2 Changes in the age distribution of owners, 2009–2020

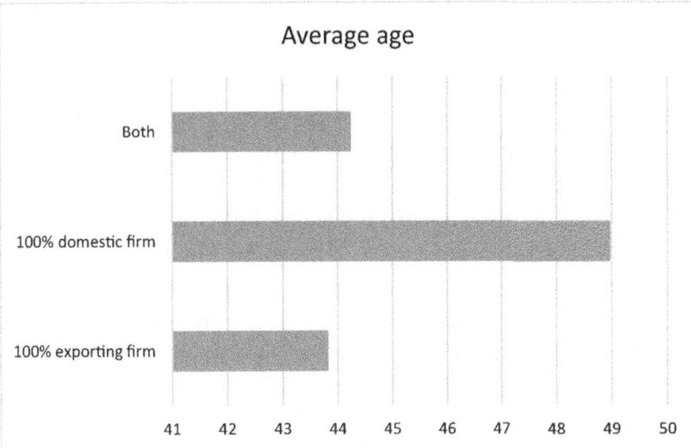

Fig. 3 Age distribution in terms of export orientation of firms, 2020

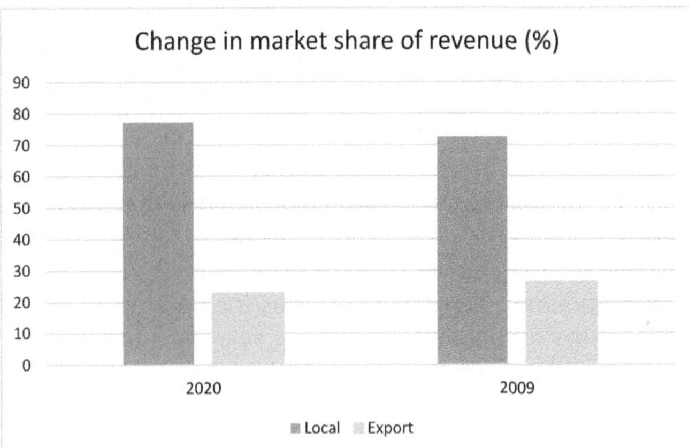

Fig. 4 Change in market share of revenue, 2009–2020

2.3 *Sales Revenue and Profitability*

In terms of the market share of revenue of the ICT firms, no significant change was observed over 2009-2020; instead, the export share declined somewhat. As Fig. 4 suggests, the major revenue share comes from the domestic market (about 75%), and the rest are from exports. The findings in this section are based on a sample survey. Therefore, it may not fully represent the industry's performances, particularly export performances. However, the lower share of exports of the ICT firms indicates less exposure to dynamic capabilities in terms of networking, linkages, and productivity.

About 55% of firms are domestic-market focused, 55% focus on domestic and export markets, and 10% focus on only export markets. However, domestic sales have been instrumental to the rise in industry revenues. On the other hand, North America remains the biggest export market for Bangladeshi firms, followed by the European Union. Domestic and foreign demand for software was driven mainly by the financial sector.

Gross profit as a percentage of revenue of Bangladeshi software firms is reportedly about 20%. Gross profit is relatively higher for the firms that sell their products in domestic and export markets. A slight fall in profitability was observed in 2020 among the domestic market-oriented firms, mainly due to the Covid-19 pandemic. However, overall, ICT firms performed well during the pandemic as demand for digital services grew significantly. One of the reasons behind this high profitability of non-exporting firms could be the government's "Digital Bangladesh" initiative that has led to more e-governance projects and automation of public sector entities. On the other hand, export-oriented firms are in a consolidation process after the global financial crisis that has slowed their profitability.

Table 1 reports the average share of sales revenue according to activities and corresponding percentage of firms for three years, 2017–2019. It can be seen that for about 15% of firms, one-third of sales come from e-commerce services, while for about 10% of firms, websites constitute one-third of their sales. Software development generates 50% of sales revenue for about 25% of firms. About 60% of sales revenue comes from internet services for about 15% of the firms. The results also highlight that a small proportion of firms specialize in a specific area that makes it their primary source of sales revenue (for example, Geographic Information System, game development, mobile app development, web hosting, Enterprise Resource Planning, etc.).

The industry registered a slow but steady increase in profit (Gross profit as % of revenue) ranging between 16 and 21% over 2017–2019 (Table 2). The profit of call centers is relatively higher than other segments. About the IT firms' market share, it is observed that about 50%

Table 1 Percentage share of sales according to activities, 2017–2019

	2017		*2018*		*2019*	
	Average sales revenue share (%)	*% of firms*	*Average sales revenue share (%)*	*% of firms*	*Average sales revenue share (%)*	*% of firms*
E-commerce	33.10	14.79	33.05	14.58	35.68	13.10
E-gov. (e-Governance)	37.22	6.34	40.00	5.56	39.40	6.90
GIS	69.67	4.23	69.67	4.17	70.00	4.14
BPO (Business Process Outsourcing)	58.33	2.11	52.00	2.78	57.33	2.07
Data entry	35.00	1.41	30.00	2.08	32.50	1.38
Website	32.19	11.27	34.64	9.72	36.00	10.34
Graphic	62.50	4.23	68.00	3.47	59.71	4.83
Internet Service	62.09	14.79	61.81	14.58	61.95	15.17
Mobile app development	36.67	4.23	33.33	4.17	32.83	4.14
Game development	70.00	1.41	72.50	1.39	67.50	1.38
Web hosting	60.00	0.70	65.00	0.69	65.00	0.69
ERP	65.00	2.82	60.00	2.78	62.25	2.76
Database	52.50	1.41	46.67	2.08	54.00	1.38
Programming Language	32.00	0.70	30.00	0.69	33.50	1.38
Software Tester	25.00	0.70	30.00	0.69	35.00	0.69
Software Development	53.06	23.94	53.74	24.31	54.00	24.14
DBA (Database Administrator)	40.00	0.70	40.00	0.69	45.00	0.69
Call center	40.00	1.41	41.00	1.39	42.50	1.38

Note Definitions of activities are given in Appendix. *Source* BIDS-SEIP Survey (2020)

Table 2 Gross profit as % of revenue, 2015–2019

	2015	*2016*	*2017*	*2018*	*2019*
Software firms	16.56	17.57	18.80	19.67	21.74
ISPs	16.58	17.35	18.59	19.06	20.42
Call centers	18.03	17.48	20.37	22.14	23.75
All	16.44	17.45	18.65	19.48	21.31

Source BIDS-SEIP survey (2020)

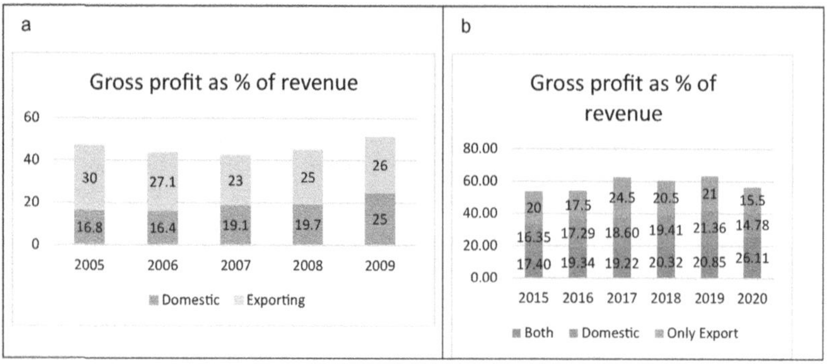

Fig. 5 Gross profit as % of revenue, 2005–2009 (BIDS Survey, 2009) vs. 2015–2020 (BIDS-SEIP Survey, 2020)

of the firms do export, and of them, 25% are 100% export-oriented firms (BIDS-SEIP survey, 2020). Overall, the market share for export is 23% and the rest, 77%, comes from the domestic market, indicating that the sector is mainly dependent on the domestic market (Fig. 5). The majority of the IT firms are SMEs (Small and Medium-sized Enterprises), with a typical software company with about 10–30 individuals. Major export markets are the USA, Canada, Japan, UK, Denmark, Sweden, Norway, Netherlands, Germany, Australia, Saudi Arabia, and UAE. Export volume per annum was around US$ 1 billion in 2018–2019, according to BASIS, though the validity of this claim could not be verified.[2]

2.4 *Major Value-Added Activities of Firms*

The primary activities of the IT firms in 2019 include e-commerce (62.9%) and website development (15.32%) with e-commerce in the domineering position. In contrast, in 2009, e-commerce (26.51%), web development (14.46%), ERP (20.48%), and BPO (Business Process Outsourcing) (12.05%) were the key services of the IT firms. As the results suggest, firm size matters in choosing the activities. Some new activities like mobile app development, robotics, IoT (Internet of Things), etc. have emerged, but the proportion is negligible (Table 3).

[2] The export volume for 2019–2020 is not included as there has been an unusual fall in exports due to the unforeseen circumstances of COVID-19.

Table 3 Major activities by the size of firms, 2009–2020

	2020 (% of firm)					*2009 (% of firm)*				
Activities	*Micro*	*Small*	*Medium*	*Large*	*Total*	*Micro*	*Small*	*Medium*	*Large*	*Total*
E-commerce	50	66.67	45.45	70	62.9	40	28.33	12.5	50	26.51
E-governance	0	6.41	4.55	10	6.45	0	8.33	0	0	6.02
Geographic Information System (GIS)	0	3.85	9.09	0	4.03	0	5	12.5	0	6.02
Web development	0	14.1	22.73	15	15.32	20	16.67	6.25	0	14.46
Graphics	0	2.56	0	0	1.61	0	5	12.5	0	6.02
Enterprise resource planning (ERP)	0	1.28	0	0	0.81	20	18.33	25	50	20.48
Mobile application	25	0	0	0	0.81	–	–	–	–	–
BPO	–	–	–	–	–	20	10	18.75	0	12.05
Others	25	5.13	18.09	5	7.92	0	7.22	12.5	0	8.43
No. of observations	4	78	22	20	124	5	60	16	2	83

Sources BIDS Survey (2009) and BIDS-SEIP survey (2020)

3 ICT Labor Market in Bangladesh

The ICT labor market is not only restricted to the IT/ITeS service sector, it also includes IT professionals engaged in other sectors, such as banks and financial institutions, the manufacturing sector, and other service sectors that handle or use various software and hardware. With the progress of digitalization, the demand for IT professionals is expected to grow over time. Hossain (2016) made a linear projection of the labor demand for the IT/ITeS sector for the period from 2016 to 2025, which is shown in Table 4. Assuming a 10% growth in labor demand in the ICT sector, the number of IT professionals will increase from 0.31 million in 2020 to 0.44 million in 2025.[3] Most of the labor will be absorbed by the

[3] The estimates of the projected IT professionals are based on information provided by the industry associations. No database of professionals is available based on an in-depth survey as of yet.

Table 4 Estimated demand for IT professionals for the ICT sector, 2016–2025 (in million)

	2016	*2020*	*2025*
Annual growth rates of labor demand (%)	11.0	10.0	5.0
Software & ITeS	0.14	0.19	0.27
ISPs	0.05	0.07	0.10
Call centers	0.03	0.04	0.06
Hardware	0.003	0.004	0.007
Total labor	0.22	0.31	0.44

Notes See Hossain (2016; 2018). The estimate of labor demand in the base-year (2016) has been made based on FGDs (Focus Group Discussions) with stakeholders, and then it has been adjusted with the estimated projected sectoral growth rates. A linear projection is made here.

software and ITeS sector, followed by ISPs and call centers. According to the projection, more than twenty thousand IT professionals are needed annually and a substantial skills gap does exist. The gap between supply and demand seriously limits the proper growth of the sector, let alone the quality of graduates.

The key professional occupations in the software and ITeS sector are product or project manager, system analyst or administrator, database administrator, web developer, graphic designer, quality tester/assurance officer, and operators. For ISPs, hardware/networking professionals occupy the major employment, followed by the system administrator, while for call centers, operators or technicians hold the main occupation. In addition to hardware or networking professionals, project or product managers also occupy a major place in the hardware sector.

For the software sector, there is a high demand for the programmer and system analysts, followed by the manager, web developer, and data administrator (Table 5). Therefore, more efforts are needed to train or develop these professional groups to maintain the industry's growth potential. For ISPs, the demand for a manager, system administrator, and hardware or network professionals has been increasing over time, while for call centers, operators/technicians who require soft skills in communications have been growing. Apart from software engineers, there has been a significant demand for hardware and networking engineers.

Table 5 Occupation-wise projected demand for IT professionals (million)

	2016	*2020*	*2025*
Software			
Product/project manager	0.014	0.021	0.035
Programmers/system analysts/software engineer	0.081	0.126	0.211
Database administrator	0.008	0.013	0.021
Web developer	0.009	0.015	0.025
Graphic designer	0.005	0.008	0.014
Quality assurance officer	0.007	0.011	0.018
Operator/Technician	0.011	0.017	0.028
ISP			
Product/ project manager	0.012	0.018	0.030
Programmers/system analyst/software engineer	0.013	0.019	0.033
Database administrator	0.010	0.016	0.026
Hardware/networking	0.025	0.039	0.065
Call center			
Product/project manager	0.005	0.007	0.012
Programmers/system analyst/software engineer	0.002	0.002	0.004
Operator/technician	0.024	0.037	0.063
Hardware			
Product/project manager	0.0019	0.0029	0.0049
Hardware/networking	0.0006	0.0010	0.0016

Source Hossain (2016)

4 Firm-Level Analysis: Distribution of Occupations and Gender Dimensions

The proportion of different IT professionals in an IT firm is as follows. On average, 18.23% are Software developers, 12.42% are Administrative and Managerial employees, 10.12% are App developers, and about 11% are Technicians (Table 6). The proportions closely match with overall projections made in Table 5. In the case of ISP firms, the average percentage of technicians is very high (39%). On average, about 11.72% of employees in Call center & BPO (Business Process Outsourcing) firms are call center agents, and 31% are Web developers and Graphic and multimedia designers. Women's participation in IT labor force is still very negligible as only 15% are female across occupations. Only in the case of call centers, about 30% of employees are female. IT and ISP firms are generally small, having an average employee size of 70 and 85, respectively. On the other

Table 6 Distribution of employees across occupations, 2019

Occupation name	*Average % of employees*		
	IT firm	*ISP firm*	*Call center and BPO*
Administrative and managerial	12.42	9.69	10.31
Working owner/director/shareholder	7.45	4.16	7.01
Accountants, financial and investment advisers	4.48	7.07	3.98
Software developers	18.23	4.53	2.33
Data scientist, IOT professionals, Robotic Process Automation (RPA) developer	2.76	0.75	0.46
Applications developers/programmers	10.12	2.21	0.27
Web developers and graphic and multimedia designers	9.83	2.44	31.07
Database designers and administrators	4.31	1.47	0.36
Systems administrators and computer network professionals	5.86	8.43	7.00
Technicians	10.94	38.59	3.63
Clerical and sales	6.92	10.9	8.78
Call center professional	0.13	0	11.72
Quality assurance manager	0.06	0	3.74
Others	6.45	9.77	9.33
Average number of employees per firm	70.16	84.67	127.89

Source BIDS-SEIP Survey (2020)

hand, Call centers appear to be medium in size, having employees over 100.

4.1 *Average Wage of Professionals*

The average monthly salary of employees of different occupations across job types is shown in Table 7 based on a survey conducted in 2020 (BIDS-SEIP, 2020). Among the job categories, Administrative and Managerial employees, Software developers (including mobile app. game developers and Software Tester), and Quality Assurance managers are relatively highly paid; their average monthly salary is about US$650. Data Scientist, IOT Professionals, Robotic Process Automation (RPA) Developer, Applications developers/programmers, Database designers,

Table 7 Average monthly salary across occupations, 2020

Occupation name	*Average monthly salary (in taka)*	*Average monthly convenience (cash benefit) (in taka)*	*Total in Tk. (in US$)*
Administrative and managerial	52000	5000	57000 (670)
Working owner/director/Shareholder	133000	10000	143000 (1682)
Accountants, financial and investment advisers	36000	3000	39000 (458)
Software developers (including mobile app. game developers, and Software testers)	59000	4000	63000 (741)
Data Scientist, IOT Professionals, Robotic Process Automation (RPA) Developer.	46000	5000	51000 (600)
Applications developers/programmers	50000	5000	55000 (647)
Web developers and graphic and multimedia designers	37000	3000	40000 (470)
Database designers and administrators	39000	3000	42000 (494)
Systems administrators and Computer network professionals	44000	4000	48000 (565)
Quality Assurance Manager	46000	5000	51000 (600)
Technicians	22000	2000	24000 (282)
Clerical and sales	24000	2000	26000 (306)
Call center agent	9000	1000	10000 (117)

Source BIDS-SEIP survey, 2020; Exchange rate: 1US$ = Tk. 85 (as of July 28, 2021)

data administrators, and systems administrators, and Computer network professionals receive a bit lower wage, which ranges from US$450 to US$500. Hossain et al. (2012) found that in 2009, the salary of a senior manager or professional was about 600 US dollar while it was about 500 US dollar for a mid-level professional. This means that the salary of IT professionals has not changed much over the last ten years. The working owner, director, or shareholder receives the highest salary, about US$1700 per month. Call center agents are among the lowest paid (about US$120), The salary level in Bangladesh is still lower than India and

Table 8 Labor mobility and reasons

Activities	*High mobility (in 1 month)*	*High mobility (in 3 months)*	*Reasons for mobility*			
			Many competitors	*Job is not interesting*	*Low salary*	*Others*
E-commerce	6.9	8.4	40.0	6.7	46.7	6.7
E-governance	1.5	4.5	50.0		37.5	12.5
GIS	0.5	2.5	20.0	20.0	40.0	20.0
BPO	3	5	40.0	10.0	40.0	10.0
Data entry	3	0	20.0	20.0	50.0	10.0
Web site	11.9	11.4	30.0	15.0	45.0	10.0
Graphic	5.4	3.5	18.2	9.1	72.7	
Multimedia	3	2	40.0		60.0	
ERP	7.4	6.9	25.0	18.8	43.8	12.5
Center	0	0.5	100			
ISP	5	10.9	26.9	15.4	50.0	7.7

Source BIDS survey (2009)

China. Various web sources indicate that the salary of a software engineer in China or India is way above US$1000, even in 2009 (Hossain et al., 2012) .

4.2 *Job Switching Pattern*

Labor mobility or frequent job switching is an important concern for software firms. They often face this because of a shortage of skilled labors as well as competitive market structure. Job switching is evident more among the professionals working on ERP, e-commerce, and website development. Fierce competition among the firms in these activities paves the way for employees to switch jobs and bargain for better salaries (Table 8). This, in other words, reflects the scarcity of an appropriately skilled workforce in this sector.

4.3 *Job Placement*

A graduate tracer study of Asian Development Bank (ADB, 2019) shows that about 77% of CSE/IT graduates from 2012 to 2018 got jobs, and among them, 35% got jobs within one year of graduation, and the rest needed more than one year to get the preferred job. Most of them (about

92%) were employed full-time. This suggests that CSE/IT graduates have a high scope for job placements, indicating a vibrancy of the IT sector.

5 Skills Shortage and Skills Gap in the ICT Sector

It is often argued that the IT sector in Bangladesh has been suffering from both shortage and low-skilled workforce, for which the industry could not grow at its full potential. Various studies attempt to assess the skills gap in the sector. However, assessing the skills gap is not straightforward, particularly for the ICT sector. There are various dimensions in identifying skills gaps in the industry. Capelli (2015) argued that skills gap may be determined in terms of three aspects: (i) shortage of job-specific skills; (ii) skill shortfalls arising from faults in education; and (iii) skills mismatch—oversupply or undersupply caused by skill shortfalls and skill shortage. Hossain et al. (2022) have followed this approach while assessing the skills gap in the IT sector in Bangladesh. A brief snapshot is taken from their study as well as the primary data of the survey has been analyzed to substantiate the analysis.

5.1 Shortage of IT employees

The shortage of employees may be reflected by the number of a filled post. Overall, 90% to 100% posts are filled across firms indicating a shortage of below 10%. However, in the case of Call centers and BPO firms, on average, only 67% of Software developers (including mobile app. game developers and Software Tester) posts are filled, which is the lowest among the three types of firms. However, as Fig. 6 shows, the IT firms' shortage of skills (in terms of unfilled positions) is relatively lower, in particular, less than or around 5% in key occupations, such as web developer and graphic designer, software developer, and applications developer. A more or less similar extent of shortage is observed in the case of ISP firms. However, a higher percentage of shortage is reported by the call centers & BPO firms for the positions of data scientist/analytics (17%), accounting and financial (6%), administrative and managerial (6%), and so on, though these are not their key technical positions. Overall, the shortage of manpower is below 10% in the Bangladeshi IT sector.

Fig. 6 Job-specific employee shortage (*Source* BIDS-SEIP Survey, 2020)

5.1.1 *Activity-Specific Skills Shortages*

Though there are about 5% to 10% of shortage of employees in the IT industry, in terms of job-specific skills, the industry faces a serious shortage of skills. Around 50% of the professionals in the areas of GIS, BPO, Multimedia, AI, IoT, and Robotics are unskilled and semi-skilled, and a similar proportion is unskilled/semi-skilled in assembling, repairing, and manufacturing for the hardware sector (Table 9). About 50% in call centers and 67% in ISPs are semi- or unskilled, which may be due to the low wage structure in these firms, otherwise this is not consistent with the overall IT sector. The results also indicate that the IT industry lacks an adequate skilled workforce for some emerging areas of activities, such as Robotics, AI, IoT, etc.

Over 60% of skilled/high-skilled professionals belong to e-commerce, e-governance, BPO, data entry, website, graphic, multimedia, ERP, and IoT. About 50% of employees are skilled/high-skilled for hardware assembling and repairing, and so for internet service providers. The data indicates that though there is almost no shortage of employees, the lack adequate skills.

5.2 *Skills Gap*

The employers were asked to assess the skill gap of the employees on a scale of 1–5 (1–5: very low to very high). The lowest skill gap is at

Table 9 Skills level across activities

Activity of the employees	*Percentage of firm rating the overall skill level of employees*			
	Unskilled	*Semi-skilled*	*Skilled*	*Highly skilled*
E-commerce	5.32	8.51	46.81	39.36
E-governance	17.86	16.07	35.71	30.36
GIS	29.27	19.51	34.15	17.07
BPO	24.39	19.51	21.95	34.15
Data entry	13.04	11.59	39.13	36.23
Website	1.75	2.63	31.58	64.04
Graphic	11.96	8.7	38.04	41.3
Multimedia	27.42	3.23	30.65	38.71
ERP	8.93	10.71	39.29	41.07
Robotics	57.58	6.06	27.27	9.09
AI	57.14	7.14	17.86	17.86
IoT	30.23	6.98	27.91	34.88
Hardware				
Assembling	43.59	7.69	28.21	20.51
Repairing	44.74	10.53	28.95	15.79
Manufacturing	68	4	20	8
Internet services	20	2.22	15.56	62.22
Call center	45	5	27.5	22.5
ISP	61.9	4.76	23.81	9.52

Source BIDS-SEIP survey (2020); multiple responses are reported (row-wise)

the Entry-level employees across all occupations except Game developers (Fig. 7). At the intermediate-level professionals, 30% of firms identified a moderate level skills gap. For the senior-level professionals, 30% identified a moderate skills gap and 20% identified a high skills gap. More specifically, the BIDS-SEIP survey data revealed that a very high skills gap exists at all levels of game developer professionals, while a moderate level skills gap was identified at the senior-level applications developer (38%), system administrator (37%), and Data Scientist (39%). For mid-level professionals, a moderate level of skills gap has been identified by over 30% of firms for applications developers (34%), web developers (32%), database designers (33%), system administrators (26%), and Data Scientist (37%) is RPA developer (44%). The high skills gap has been identified at the mid and senior levels by over 20% of firms, particularly for mobile app developers, game developers, database designers, data scientists, IoT professionals, software testers, and RPA developers (for details, see Hossain et al., 2022).

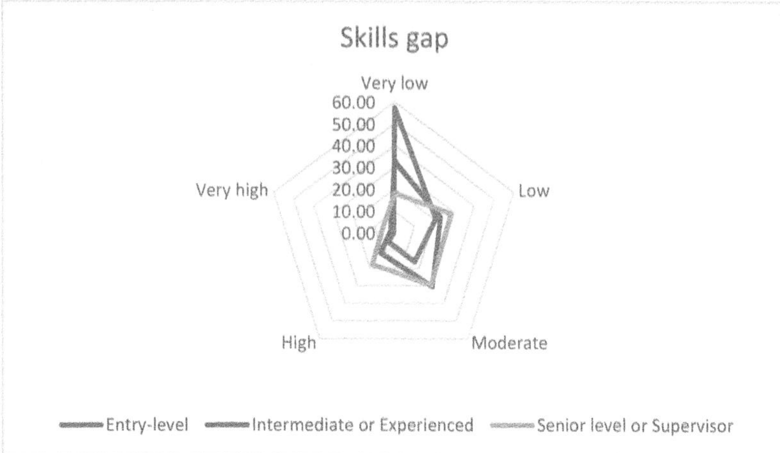

Fig. 7 Skills gap identified by the firms (%) from very low to very high (*Source* BIDS-SEIP survey, 2020)

6 Mitigating Skills Gap: Training and Skills Development Programs

One possible way to mitigate the skills gap is to provide training through some skills development programs. Various training programs are offered at the private level, though the quality of these private training centers is questionable. A significant government skills development program named the Skills and Employment Investment Program (SEIP) has been undertaken with donors' support since 2014. So far, SEIP has trained over fifty thousand IT professionals at various levels through various training institutes; of them, the job placement rate was over 66%.

Another possible way to improve the skills of IT professionals is through upgrading and modernizing the IT education curriculum, which may be done through an effective industry-academia linkage. This is also important for IT firms to provide on-the-job training for fresh recruits and off-the-job training for mid to senior-level professionals. As Hossain et al. (2022) have observed, firms, in almost all cases, provide on-the-job training, but only a few spend money on providing training to their employees at the mid to senior level. The pertinent question is whether private sector training or SEIP-sponsored training are adequate to meet the industry requirements. A three-month short training course may not be sufficient to cater to the needs of the IT industry. What is important is to establish some centers of excellence in IT education, which could be supported by the SEIP. SEIP may also provide support to different Universities to upgrade and modernize their CSE or IT curriculum.

The study by Hossain et al. (2022) also identified very poor linkages between TVETS and the IT industry, which is also a source of the skills gap. One problem for the TVETs is that they do not have adequately trained trainers. Therefore, a comprehensive Training for Trainers (ToT) should be devised to make an impact of the TVETS on the industry. The shortage of skilled workforce and the required professionals for the emerging thrusts of the IT sector are two key challenges for the IT sector. Since the country currently faces a shortage of a certain amount of skilled workforce for specific tasks, industry growth and investments are likely to be severely affected in the future. Given the existing skills gap and future demand for skills in emerging areas, appropriate policies, effective industry-academia linkages, and adequate training programs are the desirable options for human capital development in the IT sector.

The IT education institutions are required to adjust their curriculum to accommodate the emerging thrust sectors/issues keeping in mind the existing skills mismatch and shortage of skilled IT professionals in emerging areas, such as IoT, AI, Robotics, Gaming, big data analytics, etc. Theory and empirical evidence suggest that the skill level is positively associated with the performance of the firms. It is to be noted that the demand for IT skills is ever-changing with the emergence of new areas of technologies and content. The industry has a high demand for professionals for the activities, such as E-commerce, website/web analytics, Enterprise Resource Planning (ERP), and graphic analysis. The professionals are expected to be acquainted with the following software/programming languages: JAVA, HTML5, ASP, JSP, Net, Ruby, C/C++/VC, CSS3, Python, Mongo DB, Node JS, Postgre, SQL, Big Data, and database software/applications such as MS SQL, Oracle, UNIX/Linux/Solaris, XM. Also, there is a high demand for professionals having expertise in mobile applications, such as Android, iOS, and J2ME. On the other hand, ISP and call center professionals need to be acquainted with basic computer literacy, and some programming languages, such as C/C++, JAVA, HTML5, and database applications.

An important caveat is that about 90 percent of IT firms are highly satisfied with their employees' current level of skills, though a certain skills gap does exist. This level of satisfaction with the human capital is a reflection of the promise of the youths and the future potential of IT and related industries in Bangladesh.

7 Supply-Side Aspects of IT Professionals

The employment demand in the ICT sector has been manifested with the potential growth and development of the IT/ITeS sectors. For example, the IT industry has set a target to achieve US$5 billion in exports by 2025, and the BPO industry also sets a target to reach US$1 billion by the same time. Therefore, these sectors roughly have to increase their exports by US$1.50 billion per annum in the next three years, and the consequent increase in employment would be approximately 20–25% per annum. These targets, however, look ambitious and, therefore, would likely remain unfulfilled given the current slow growth of the sector. To be consistent with the expected growth of the sector, the supply of IT professionals, particularly skilled, has to be increased.

A sharp rise in the demand for IT skills in some emerging areas may be anticipated in the context of the 4th Industrial Revolution (4IR). In particular, skills for the Internet of Things (IoT), Cyber Security, Artificial intelligence (AI), Gaming, Cloud Computing, etc., would likely escalate substantially in the near future. However, some potential constraints such as the lack of up-to-date curriculum, industry-academia linkages, shortage of R&D labs and quality trainers, and inadequate training facilities impede human capital development in this sector. Moreover, deficiencies in soft skills, such as English proficiency and business communications are also acute among the IT professionals. Therefore, complementary training courses on soft skills could be made mandatory along with regular IT training courses (Table 10).

8 Human Capital Development Programs in Bangladesh

A basic understanding of IT human capital can be obtained from the recent survey results (Hossain, 2018). "On the job" training is required for almost all newly recruited staff, while two-thirds received training from external training institutes. On the other hand, about two-thirds of firms offer short-term (3 to 6 months duration) apprenticeship/internship facilities for fresh graduates. After successfully completing the program, outstanding participants are also offered jobs in the firm.

Table 10 Supply-side constraints of IT skills

	Less important constraint (%)	*Neutral (%)*	*More important constraint (%)*
Lack of up-to-date IT-related curriculum	–	42.86	57.15
Lack of industry-academia linkage	11.11	–	88.89
Shortage of quality teachers/trainers	44.44	11.11	44.44
Inadequate quality and facilities in IT training institutes	20	30	50
Shortage of R&D labs	12.50	12.50	75
Limited range of courses offered by IT training institutes	33.33	33.33	33.33

Source Hossain, 2016

As already mentioned, over 95 universities, 200 colleges and institutions, and 300 IT centers currently offer various IT courses and produce about ten thousand IT graduates with various competencies (Ministry of Finance, 2017). The quality of IT education varies substantially across public and private universities. Only a handful of public universities and a few private universities produce quality graduates in computer science and engineering disciplines. Polytechnic and Vocational Training Institutes also produce some IT graduates though they are not well-trained. Various computer and IT training institutes mushroomed in the country to provide training on basic computer skills, but their quality of training is questionable due to the lack of proper monitoring and a unified curriculum.

The BASIS also started a training institute in 2012, namely the BASIS Institute of Technology & Management (BITM), with donor support. The BITM mainly provides training with financial and technical support from the government's Skills for Employment Investment Program (SEIP). It has trained so far 23,000 IT professionals over the last few years, and they plan to train several thousands in the next few years. BITM's training programs are short-term in nature, and therefore, it does not have a significant impact on the development of IT human capital needed for the IT industry. Like the BITM, similar types of institutes need to be established under the aegis of BACCO and ISPAB. An undergraduate-level BPO course may be introduced in business studies, which might enhance the graduate's opportunities to get jobs in the BPO sector.

Apart from these training programs, the public and private sectors also initiated various other training programs. However, the main concern is that the short-term courses may not be sufficient to mitigate the skills gap of the IT professionals. It is important to establish some centers of excellence in IT education to cater to the emerging needs of the IT human capital and support the potential growth of the IT industry and digitalized economy.

9 Conclusions and Recommendations

The discussion and analysis in this chapter suggest that the current supply of IT professionals is adequate though they lack skills and competencies to varying degrees. The supply and demand for IT professionals almost converge indicating a slow growth of the IT industry. The proportion of unskilled or semi-skilled employees in some IT segments is alarming. Around 50% of the professionals in GIS, BPO, Multimedia, AI, IoT, and Robotics are unskilled and semi-skilled, and a similar proportion is unskilled/semi-skilled in assembling, repairing, and manufacturing for the hardware sector. About 50% in call centers and 67% in ISPs are semi- or unskilled. The IT industry thus lacks an adequate skilled workforce for some emerging areas of activities, such as Robotics, AI, IoT, etc.

Though fresh graduates are available, there is a shortage of skilled mid-level professionals and managers. Job placement in the IT sector is reasonably good, and there is a good demand for IT graduates in the country. The wage structure is apparently has not changed much in the last ten years, and it is much lower compared to India and China. Therefore, wage structure needs to be competitive. Otherwise, it would be difficult to retain or attract skilled professionals in emerging IT areas. The relatively lower wage compared to India and China might give Bangladesh certain leverage to attract foreign direct investments in this sector. Low-wage structure is not enough to attract FDIs if the sector could not supply enough competent IT professionals. The shortage of skilled workforce is an important impediment to FDI attraction in this sector. Furthermore, the shortage of the managerial and technical leadership levels is reportedly acute, which might drag the firms into a vulnerable situation in their pursuit of industrial growth. Based on the existing skills gap and skill mismatches, it is recommended to build some top-quality IT training institutions, update the respective curriculum, and devise proper strategies for linkages between academia and industries. The government may invest in this direction for a long-term sustainable supply of quality IT graduates.

In the context of the 4IR, there is a fear that a substantial amount of manual labor will be redundant, leaving a big sunk of unemployment. Robotics, AI, and similar other technologies will take the place of human labor. Though the fear is more valid for non-IT sectors, the IT sector professionals need to be acquainted with capturing the growing markets of robotics, AI, and so on. Therefore, better preparation is needed by providing training on upskilling and reskilling of the existing IT professionals.

References

ADB. (2019). *Bangladesh: Computer and software engineering tertiary education in 2018*. Asian Development Bank.

BIDS Survey. (2009). *Assessment of the impact of clustering on IT industries*. Bangladesh Institute of Development Studies (BIDS).

BIDS-SEIP Survey. (2020). *Labor market study for skills for employment investment project (SEIP)—IT sector*. Bangladesh Institute of Development Studies.

Capelli. P. (2015). Skill gaps, skill shortages, and skill mismatches. *Industrial and Labor Relations Review.*

Hossain, M. (2016). Labor market and skills gap in the ICT sector in Bangladesh. In *BIDS study report: Labour market and skill gap in Bangladesh* (Macro and Micro Level Study). Dhaka. Skills Employment Investment Program, Ministry of Finance, Government of Bangladesh.

Hossain, M. (2018). *Labor market and skills gap in the ICT sector in Bangladesh: An exploratory study*. Presented in the Asian Think Tank Development Forum, Canberra, Australia, August 22–23, 2018. The paper can be downloaded at: https://events.development.asia/materials/20180822/labor-market-and-skills-gap-ict-sector-bangladesh-exploratory-study

Hossain, M., Shinkai, N., Yunus, M., & Bakht, Z. (2012). Integration of ICT industries and its impact on trade and market access: The case of Bangladesh and India. In Rahman, Brunner and Khatri (Eds.), *Regional integration and economic development in South Asia*. Edward Elgar.

Hossain, M., Chowdhury, T. T., & Shashi, N. A. (2022). *Analysis of skills gap in the ICT sector in Bangladesh*. Bangladesh Institute of Development Studies, Unpublished.

Ministry of Finance. (2017). *Progress on Digital Bangladesh, 2017*. Finance Division, Bangladesh Government. https://mof.portal.gov.bd/sites/default/files/files/mof.portal.gov.bd/page/044ef203_53ca_489d_bc3b_60989c8b163a/Digital%20Bangladesh%2022-05-2017%20Final.pdf

PART III

Digital Transformation, Economic Growth and Development

CHAPTER 10

Transformative Impact of Digitalization on Selected Sectors

1 Introduction

The underlying benefits of digitalization may be realized through its transformative impact on various economic sectors in terms of its use, productivity gains, and GDP growth. The digital transformation meaningfully takes place if sectors could integrate digital technology into all areas of a business and production, in particular changing the production process through innovations and delivering value to customers. As the supportive policies are in place with the Digital Bangladesh vision of the government, it is expected that industries move aggressively to integrate new digital applications and build new markets for digital products and services. Though service sectors appear to be adopting digital technologies more quickly, making services more efficient, their contribution to GDP has remained almost the same for a long time. The adoption of digital technologies by the high productive manufacturing sector is of paramount importance to achieve higher growth in the sector and its diversifications. Digital finance is a complementary sector that might have various spillover effects on other sectors, including manufacturing.

Given the background, this chapter highlights the current status of digital transformation in various sectors, its impact on productivity growth, and future supportive actions that might complement the digitalization process. The chapter is organized as follows. Section 2 discusses the transformative effect of digitalization on the service sector, and

M. Hossain, *Digital Transformation and Economic Development in Bangladesh*, https://doi.org/10.1007/978-981-19-2753-9_10

Sect. 3 identifies six promising sectors for digital transformation. Section 4 discusses the state of digitalization in the manufacturing sector in detail. Section 5 discusses the state of digital finance, and Sect. 6 discusses various digitalization efforts in the agriculture, livestock, and fisheries sectors. Section 7 discusses the impact of digitalization on job losses, and Sect. 8 concludes the chapter.

2 Transformative Impact of Digitalization on the Service Sector

Internet and software used in the service sector enhance productivity through R&D, product design, marketing, sourcing and supply chain management, sales, and after-sales services. A vast digital transformation has taken place in the service sectors in Bangladesh, which is now contributing to GDP by over 50%. The automation leaped various service sectors, including public administration and services, including revenue collection (VAT and Customs), military administration, financial sectors, and so on. Apart from that, health, education, tourism, multimedia, etc., have been increasingly adopting digital content to gain efficiency and productivity (Fig. 1). The demand for banking software and applications has remained unchanged for the last ten years or so, indicating that the financial sector has already attained a certain level of digitalization, which enables them to enjoy productivity and efficiency gains from digitalization.

More importantly, the value creation in the manufacturing sectors is expected from intangible assets and services, leading to the servitization of manufacturing. A good example is Taiwan, where the growing importance of digital services to mobile devices and cloud computing prompted the servitization of manufacturing, leading them to take the upper place in global production networks and innovation networks (Chen et al., 2013; Vandermerwe & Rada, 1988).

The internet has now unleashed a remarkable innovation in consumer electronics that have created an opportunity for cutting-edge digital content development and new business processes. Currently, 34 TV channels and 25 FM radio channels in Bangladesh are using various software and multimedia digital content that has opened up a big digital market for media services. During the Covid-19 pandemic, the over-the-top (OTT) platform became popular, and the OTT marketplace saw enormous growth. The OTT platform, with support from video

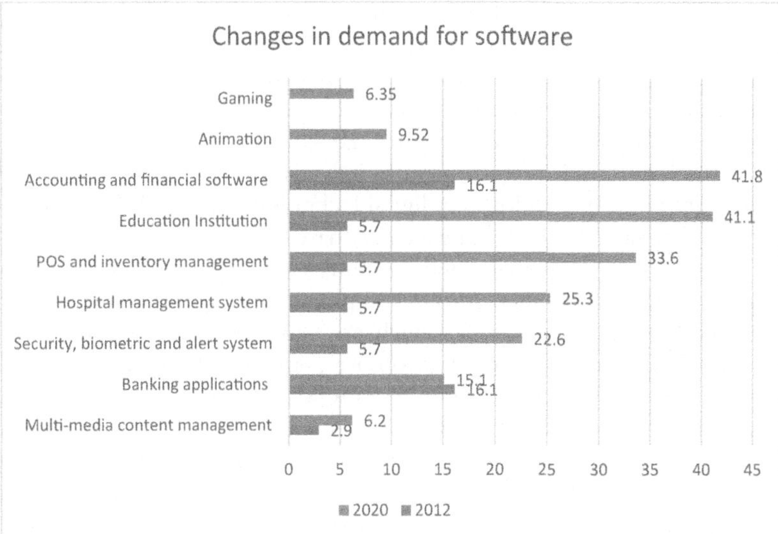

Fig. 1 Changing demand for software services, 2012–2020 (*Sources* BASIS, 2012 and BIDS-SEIP Survey, 2020)

streaming tools, helps the film sector continue its business. The newly emerged digital platforms for web series, IPTV (Internet Protocol Television), OTT, etc., have created enormous scopes for new businesses. The digital advertisement market earns around Tk. 2,000 crore per year in Bangladesh, and this market is growing substantially with a big customer base in the digital space, which is approximately 3.5 crore (Islam, 2019).

The health care sector has been booming in Bangladesh, which might take advantage of digital technologies to improve its service quality. A recently conducted "Survey of Private Healthcare Institutions" (BBS, 2021) shows that there has been a phenomenal growth of private hospitals and clinics since 2000. Currently, there are 4452 private hospitals, 2236 private clinics, and 10,291 diagnostic centers in Bangladesh. With the increasing demand for healthcare facilities and rising foreign investments in this sector, demand for digitalized hospital management systems has escalated. During the COVID-19 pandemic, various mobile-based applications have been developed to support the covid patients. Notably, the Surokha (surokha.gov.bd) application has made the vaccination drive of the government to a new height with efficiency. Digitalization of health services reduces transaction costs by a substantial amount. Other countries' experience suggests that 2–10% of health costs are saved through digitalization. However, it may also reduce around 2% of employment in the sector (McKinsey Global Institute, 2014).

In the education sector, private universities and English-medium schools are pioneers in adopting digital technologies in education content and management. Private universities have been using various software and education management systems to provide better and more efficient education services. About 103 private universities are now operating in the country, most of which are squinted with the digitalized education management system. Moreover, online delivery of education through various platforms, such as ZOOM, Microsoft teams, Google Meet, etc., during the COVID-19 pandemic enhances the usability of digital platforms by the students and educational institutions. To capture a share of the revenue from the digital video conferencing platform, the ICT division has attempted to develop some local video conferencing tools. However, public universities and colleges are still lagging in adopting digital education management systems. Apart from an education management system, demand for digitalized education content is an ever-expanding area, contributing to this sector's enhanced quality of education and productivity.

In Bangladesh, the financial sector is the leader in adopting digital technologies. Almost all the banks are now automated, providing electronic banking services. The banking and financial sector has created much value by analyzing data on credit and non-performing loans, customers' identities, quick disbursement of funds, etc. These have reduced transaction costs and increased productivity. Various other manufacturing sectors have also been adopting accounting and financial software that have contributed to the better financial management of those sectors. With the growth of the corporate sector, the demand for security, biometric and alert systems has been growing, which has been reflected in software firms' activities.

The animation sector is an emerging sector in Bangladesh with huge potential to gain from the untapped market. The sector has been growing very fast with the growth of streaming digital content. This sector is witnessing double-digit growth worldwide (see Global Animation, VFX & Video Games: Strategies, Trends & Opportunities, 2021–2025). The market size of animation, VFX, and video gaming was estimated at US$261 billion in 2020. An estimate shows that the animation industry has been growing at the rate of 2–3% per year. The market size of the

Global Video Gaming industry was US$ 105 billion in 2020, which is attributed to the growing number of online video viewers worldwide and due to the availability of cable and satellite TV, availability of low-cost internet access, penetration of mobile devices, and the growing popularity of streaming video. This is an emerging area from which the Bangladeshi software industry can take advantage. A trend is evident that the software industry of Bangladesh, though very small in size, has been specializing in gaming and animation activities. Local demand-driven content development might help the industry capture a significant portion of the local market apart from outsourcing opportunities.

3 Six Promising Sectors for Digital Transformation

In this section, six promising sectors have been identified that have a high potential for growth through automation and digitalization. The current demand for IT/ITeS (Information Technology/Information Technology Enabled Services) is driven, apart from health and education service sectors, mainly by the six sectors, such as the manufacturing (clients of 30% of IT firms), wholesale and retail trade (26%), accommodation, and food service (11.64%), real estate (10.96%), construction (8.22%), and transport and storage (8.9%). These sectors are contributing to higher productivity and GDP (Gross Domestic Product) growth of the economy, and therefore, they have shown promises to grow further (Table 1). Some of these sectors' share of GDP has remained stagnant over time, which could be overcome by adopting appropriate digital technologies. This is evident in Table 1 as the acquisition of IT software and applications by these sectors has been growing. The manufacturing sector is at the top level of the value chain of the IT/ITeS industry now, which is similar to the case of India in 2010, indicating that the servitization of the manufacturing sector is on the rise (Hossain et at., 2012). The other five sectors, have the potential for growth though the level of adoption of ICTs by these sectors is low. The manufacturing sector is a high-growth sector with increasing shares of GDP, and therefore, a separate section is devoted to analyzing the state of digitalization in the manufacturing sector.

The wholesale trading sector has been using IT/ITeS services at a high rate contributing to higher sectoral GDP growth (8.14%) though its share of GDP has remained almost the same in the last ten years.

Table 1 Major activities of the clients of IT firms, 2020

	Percent of IT firms	*Sectoral GDP growth (%)*		*Sectoral share to GDP (%)*	
		2010–2011	*2018–2019*	*2010–2011*	*2018–2019*
Manufacturing	30.14	10.01	14.2	17.75	24.08
Agriculture, forestry, and fishing	6.85	3.89	3.15	14.27	10.15
Electricity, gas, steam, and air conditioning supply	9.59	15.82	10.33	1.36	1.34
Water supply, sewerage, waste management, and remediation activities	2.05	8.23	11.57	0.08	0.09
Construction	8.22	6.95	10.25	6.67	7.63
Wholesale and retail trade	26.03	6.69	8.14	14.02	13.92
Transportation and storage	8.9	8.44	7.19	11.23	11.01
Accommodation and food service activities (Hotel and restaurants)	11.64	6.20	7.57	0.75	0.74
Financial and insurance activities	20.55	10.44	7.38	2.99	3.42
Real estate activities	10.96	3.88	5.38	7.41	6.13
Professional, scientific and technical activities	7.53				
Administrative and support service activities	17.12				
Public administration and defense, compulsory social security	9.59	8.84	6.40	3.33	3.65
Education, teaching	28.77	5.63	7.66	2.21	2.44

(continued)

Table 1 (continued)

	Percent of IT firms	*Sectoral GDP growth (%)*		*Sectoral share to GDP (%)*	
		2010–2011	*2018–2019*	*2010–2011*	*2018–2019*
Human health and social work activities	6.85	6.34	11.79	1.95	1.89
Arts, entertainment, and recreation	2.74				
Other Service Activities	7.53				
Back office support	2.05				
Business Process Outsourcing (BPO)	4.79				
No. of valid cases	146				

Source BIDS-SEIP Survey (2020); Bangladesh Economic Review, various issues, Finance Division, Ministry of Finance.

The increase in e-commerce during the pandemic is noteworthy. The annual revenue generated from around 2,500 e-commerce companies is about \$2 billion in Bangladesh (Daily Star, 2020[1]). Facebook commerce or F-commerce has also become a popular platform with more than 0.3 million online business stores based on Facebook (IDLC Monthly business review, 2019[2]). Since Bangladesh's economy is turning into more of a consumer economy with local enterprises in the driving seats, there is a high prospect of the wholesale trading sector becoming a more significant contributor to GDP with greater adoption of ICTs.

The other promising sectors are construction and real estate which could take advantage of digital services. Both sectoral GDP and share of GDP of the construction and real estate sectors have been increasing with relatively higher adoption of digital services (about 8.22% of IT firms

[1] https://www.thedailystar.net/editorial/news/the-dark-side-e-commerce-1967709.

[2] https://idlc.com/mbr/article.php?id=192.

are their clients). Construction and real estate are interrelated, and therefore both can gain productivity and growth using digital technologies. As the real estate sector has been booming over time, and so does the construction, a digital marketplace with digital advertisements, inventory management, and e-commerce are some of the areas through which both sectors can benefit from digital technologies.

The transport and storage sector is another growing sector that might be benefitted from the adoption of various digital technologies. For example, adoption of vehicle tracking systems, inventory management, online ticketing for public transportation, and online platform for booking cargo, trucks, and other vehicles for goods transportation, etc., might contribute to reduced transaction costs, profitability, and productivity of this sector. Hotels and restaurants are other promising sectors that have high growth potential with the country's journey towards a middle-income economy. Tourism will get prominence in the coming days, so the demand for various software and applications for hotel management, tour operators, and other stakeholders will likely rise.

4 Manufacturing Sector

A disaggregated analysis of the manufacturing sector clientele reveals that food products (47%), RMG (40%), textile (23.4%), computer, electronics, and optical products (21%), and beverages (15%) are the key clients for software and other IT services (Fig. 2). RMG and textiles together accounted for 64% of the IT firms' services, while Food and beverage together accounted for 61% of the IT services. Other notable clients in the manufacturing sector are pharmaceuticals, metal products, and chemicals and chemical products. Thus, IT/ITeS technology adoption has contributed to the country's key value-added industries.

The RMG Industry, being the leading export earning industry in the country, has been slowly adopting IT/ITeS applications for attaining higher productivity (Fig. 3). The basic information technology or software that is used in the garment industry are CAD/CAM systems for pattern making or plotting, computerized cutting machines, online FIT approval, ERP (Enterprise Resource Planning) for inventory tracking in the production management, mailing solution, preparation of MIS (Management Information System) reports, voice chatting, semi-automatic and fully automatic sewing machines and real-time communication with buyer through online video platforms, Skype or ZOOM.

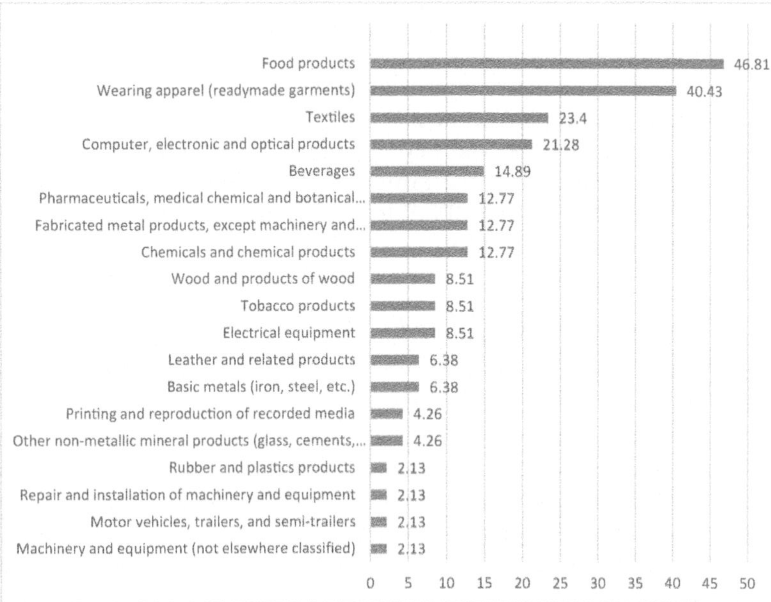

Fig. 2 Major manufacturing clients (*Source* BIDS-SEIP Survey, 2020)

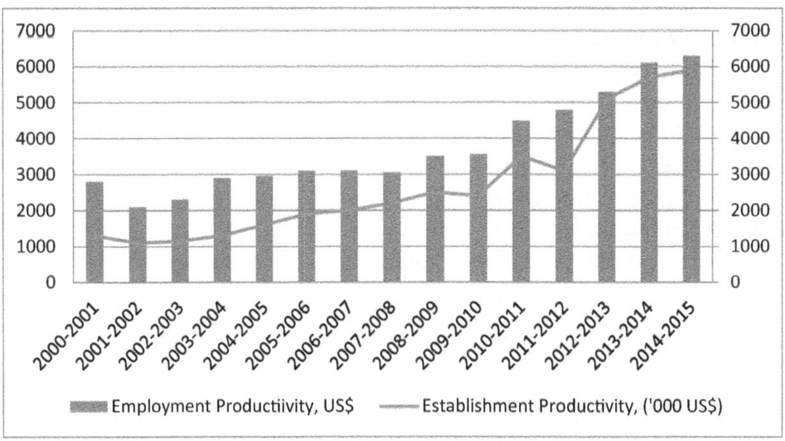

Fig. 3 Productivity growth in the RMG sector (*Source* Uramoto and Naschum [2018])

In addition, IT applications are used for office management, such as employee attendance (clocking in), shipment dispatching, and ERP. The use of IT/ITeS has been improving the sector's productivity significantly though such capital deepening might reduce employment to some extent. Similarly, the food and beverage industry has been using various software and e-commerce platforms for improving product processes, marketing, and ERP. IT and ITeS technologies help the manufacturing sectors move up the value chain.

4.1 Consumer Electronics and Automotive Sectors Are the Future Drivers of Growth

The adoption of digital technologies has a two-way impact on consumer electronics for a country like Bangladesh which is mainly dependent on imported electronics items. Digitalization enhances the use of various electronic devices, such as smartphones, smart TV, home appliances, and gadgets, and has a consequential impact on their production and R&D activities. Rapid digitalization leads to innovations in the manufacturing of this sector. For Bangladesh, the market for consumer electronics has been ever-expanding, estimated at US$1.8 billion in 2017.[3] At the same time, some local manufacturing units, such as Walton, Fair Electronics, etc. have emerged. With proper incentives, currently operating numerous electronics assembling units could venture into manufacturing units. On the other hand, the human capital with skills and education in CSE/IT and Engineering could supplement a specific need of the consumer electronics industry. This argument follows the product space theory of diversification floated by Hidalgo et al. (2007) which underlies the concept that a new product is dependent on the ability to produce similar products with similar capabilities.

Industrial development is a process of continuously improving the production of the same goods, but a continuous accumulation of the capabilities needed to upgrade production by transferring resources with higher productivity levels through structural transformation. In Bangladesh, thousands of assemblers of electronics items currently assemble Chinese electronics products locally and sell them to the market. The challenge here is to transform the assembler into a manufacturer

[3] https://databd.co/profiles/industries/profile-consumer-electronics.

with technology acquisition and policy support. What is needed is to create a conducive environment to facilitate establishment of joint manufacturing units in Bangladesh. The same argument may apply to the automotive industry, which is dependent on both electronics/electrical inputs with digital technologies, including software and hardware. Recently, fair electronics has started manufacturing electric cars locally and Samsung smart mobile phone sets in the country.[4] Therefore, following the East Asian path of development, Bangladesh can excel in the electronics and automotive industry that could take the place of the lead exporter, which is now the low-productive RMG (Ready-made Garments) sector. The current digitalization policy should focus on such transition from low value-added manufacturing to high-value-added diversification in the medium to long term.

4.2 *Manufacturing SMEs*

SMEs (Small and Medium Enterprises) are making the backbone of the industrial structure in Bangladesh. While SMEs comprise over 95% of all economic units, and its contribution to GDP is about 25% (ADB, 2015) with 86% of industrial employment. The shares of micro, small and medium enterprises in manufacturing employment are 7.8, 16.2, and 6.5%, respectively; however, their contribution to manufacturing gross value added (GVA) was estimated at 5.9, 23.7, and 23.3%, respectively (BBS, 2013; Hossain & Chowdhury, 2022; SMI, 2012). This sector has enormous potential to use digital technologies and the marketplace to gain productivity through innovations. A 2012 survey of manufacturing SMEs throughout Bangladesh showed that about 50% of SME manufacturing units use computers, the internet, email, and 100% have mobile access (INSPIRED, 2013). On the other hand, as only 12% have websites, 3% sell output online, 2.5% use internet banking, and 1.6% do video conferencing (Fig. 4), it indicates firms' very low involvement in gaining value-added services through digital footprint. However, the situation has slightly improved in 2020, as 15% have websites, 14% sell online, and 31% use mobile money transfer platform (Table 5).[5]

[4] https://www.tbsnews.net/economy/industry/auto-industry-get-boost-fair-technology-enters-deal-hyundai-111550.

[5] Though sample size is different and smaller than 2013 survey, the situation portrays that the adoption of digital platform in productivity enhancing activities perhaps has not yet improved to a great extent.

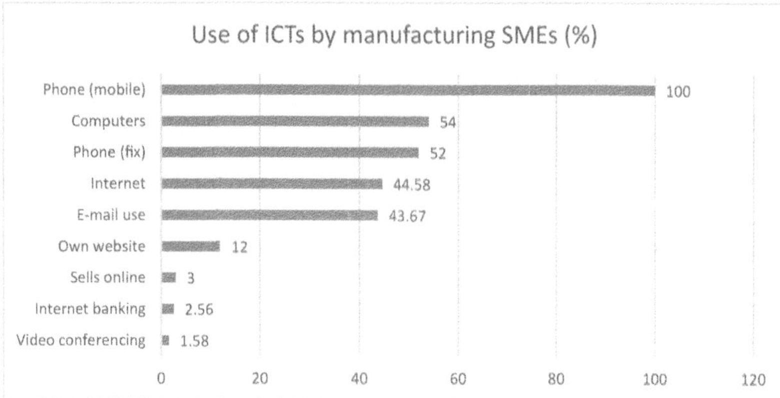

Fig. 4 Use of ICTs by manufacturing SMEs (%) (*Source* INSPIRED [2013])

The manufacturing sectors adopting ICTs in their production and business process, particularly those that extensively use computers, the internet, and emailing and websites, have high gross value-added (GVA) and labor productivity growth (Table 2). Though some sectors have high gross value-added and productivity growth with less adoption of ICTs, the ICT-using sectors might have gained more with improvements in efficiencies in production over time through better adoption of digital technologies. In particular, RMG, paper and paper products, chemicals and chemical products, computer and electronics, basic pharmaceuticals, rubber and plastic products, and furniture are high-value-added and productivity-enhancing sectors, and their rate of digital technology adoption is also high.

5 Digital Financial Services

Digital financial service (DFS) is another area that has successfully taken advantage of digitalization in transforming the financial sector. This helps achieve greater financial inclusion in Bangladesh by providing individuals and firms easy access to finance with lesser transaction costs.[6] Currently, digital financial services have been taking a bigger shape in transforming the financial ecosystem of the country.

[6] Digital Financial Services may be applied to various financial services such as payments, credit, savings, remittances as well as insurance using the digital platform. The services are provided using digital channels such as the internet, smartphones and feature phones,

Table 2 Use of ICTs by manufacturing SMEs across sectors (%)

Sector	*Phone (fix)*	*Computer*	*Internet*	*Mobile phone*	*Have website*	*E-mailing*	*GVA growth*	*Productivity growth*
Food	46.71	36.53	28.74	100	12.31	8.9	21.97	4.85
Beverage	60	20	20	100	0.77	0.21	35.16	5.94
Textile	44.36	66.92	51.88	100	9.23	15.32	−9.41	4.63
Ready-made garments	70.97	87.1	79.03	100	18.46	19.05	16.08	15.39
Leather	48.65	51.35	45.95	100	3.08	2.28	−59.13	2.50
Wood and wood products	20.55	16.44	13.7	100	0.77	1.66	−25.15	6.28
Paper and paper products	75	82.14	76.19	100	10	12.84	34.12	6.27
Printing and recorded media	59.68	66.13	46.77	100	2.31	5.18	11.10	6.59
Coke and refined petroleum products	100	0	0	100	0	–	34.32	6.91
Chemicals and chemical products	61.4	63.16	56.14	100	8.46	6.42	3.51	9.65
Basic pharmaceuticals	90	90	76.67	100	7.69	4.35	16.12	4.08
Rubber and plastic products	61.8	51.69	39.33	100	4.62	6.21	31.32	11.90
Other non-metallic products	55.17	55.17	48.28	100	6.15	2.9	5.86	4.31

(continued)

Table 2 (continued)

Sector	*Phone (fix)*	*Computer*	*Internet*	*Mobile phone*	*Have website*	*E-mailing*	*GVA growth*	*Productivity growth*
Basic metals	56.6	52.83	43.4	100	3.08	4.14	−19.29	2.44
Fabricated metal products	44	46	36	100	2.31	3.31	−23.50	7.83
Computer, electronics, and electrical products	68.18	54.55	54.55	100	4.62	2.28	−22.20	-8.97
Machinery and equipment	43.48	26.09	21.74	100	2.31	1.04	−20.11	8.60
Motor vehicles, trailers, and semi-trailers	100	100	0	100	0	0.21	141.01	12.50
Other transport equipment	20	60	20	100	0	1.04	53.75	16.52
Furniture	41.18	52.94	35.29	100	1.54	0.62	−17.50	15.90
Repair and installation	23.16	20	10.53	100	0.77	2.07	105.52	7.53
N	1200							

Source INSPIRED Survey (2013); GVA and productivity growth are estimated by the author.

In particular, mobile financial services (MFS) makes a difference in the financial landscape in Bangladesh. Starting in 2011, MFS became highly popular among individuals and firms for money transfers. According to World Bank's Global Findex data, although only 5.3% of individuals (aged 15 or above) in the developing world had a mobile money account in 2017, the figure is 21.2% for Bangladesh. Access to mobile phones and mobile financial services have expanded rapidly in Bangladesh, thereby allowing people and firms to save, borrow, make payments and manage risk (Jack & Suri, 2014). While the percentage of MSMEs (Micro Small and medium-sized Enterprises) using online platforms for sales in 2019 in Asia was 8.7%, and 7.1% use digital payment system (Sonobe et al., 2021), the percentages are higher for Bangladesh (Hossain and Chowdhury, 2022). Nevertheless, the rapid growth of mobile phone ownership and MFS-use has opened up the potential for expanding MFS and its various value-added services for smaller businesses.

The COVID-19 pandemic has seen phenomenal growth in usage of the digital financial platform. The banking sector in Bangladesh has also encouraged electronic funds transfer (EFT) during the COVID-19 pandemic. The volume of EFT transactions substantially increased during the pandemic, and banks have witnessed significant growth in online transactions (BEFTN, Bangladesh Bank, 2020).[7] The COVID-19 pandemic has triggered Bangladesh's digital finance surge like other countries. The government's policy to disburse the salaries of readymade garments workers under the Covid stimulus packages and transfer safety net funds to remote areas using MFS created momentum for the MFS sector (Table 3). Given the financial vulnerability of MSMEs, it is of interest to understand how and to what extent MSMEs could utilize Fintech in their recovery process during the pandemic.

Status of Digital Financial Services in the SME Manufacturing Sector

A recent study by Hossain and Chowdhury (2022) showed that only one-third of the manufacturing SMEs use MFS for business transactions. MFS

Automated Teller Machines (ATMs), Point-of-sale (POS) Terminals, Kiosks, Near field communication (NFC)—enabled devices, chips based cards, biometric devices, tablets as well as any digital instrument (afi, 2016).

[7] The overall development of Fintech in Bangladesh is not encouraging yet, as Bangladesh's rank is 78th among 83 in Global Fintech Index, 2021). Only MFS gained popularity in Bangladesh (Hossain & Chowdhury, 2022).

Table 3 MFS trends in Bangladesh

	June 2015	*July 2019*	*December 2020*
No. of banks in the services	20	16	15
No. of agents	538,170	942,648	1,058,897
No. of registered clients (in millions)	28.6	73.09	99.33
No. of active accounts (in millions)	12.2	33.57	32.32
No. of the total transaction (in millions)	96.2	227.4	299,506,884
Total transaction in taka (BDT in millions)	129,700	374,780	565,568.8
No. of average daily transaction, million	3.2	7.34	9,661,512
Average daily transaction (BDT in millions)	432	12.9	18,244.2
Product-wise information (count in '000 s)			
Inward remittance	4.09	28.77	1347.8
Cash-In transaction (BDT in millions)	54,620	134,600	173,466.5
Cash-Out transaction (BDT in millions)	47,770	129,990	154,442.3
P2P transaction	2287	8122	169,821.5
Salary disbursement (B2P)	101	943	20,937.2
Utility bill payment (P2B)	120	519	8341
Merchant payment	0	371	21,472.4
Government payment	0	416	413.9
Others	219	616	15,326.5

Source Bangladesh Bank website

has played the role of an important facilitator of their business during the COVID-19 pandemic increasing their sales by over 60%. However, only 15% of firms have e-commerce websites, and only 13.6% sell products online. Both online businesses and MFS users agreed that Fintech and digital platforms have contributed to an increase in their sales during the COVID-19 pandemic though only a small proportion of SMEs is accustomed to the fintech ecosystem in Bangladesh (Hossain & Chowdhury, 2022).

Digital Commerce

Digital commerce and digital payment have been progressing forward, however, at a rapid pace during the pandemic (Tables 4–6). During the initial three quarters of 2020, digital transactions amounted to more than US$65 million, among which 72% included MFS. With over 90 million registered MFS users and US$202 million in daily MFS transactions, digital finance can tap into new potentials of the digital commerce industry in Bangladesh (Islam et al., 2020). Digital transactions will facilitate the expansion of the digital commerce industry as the e-commerce market, including f-commerce, grows in a steady manner reaching US$2.1 billion in 2020. Online-based platforms have experienced exponential growth during the pandemic. The sector has connected 1,200 e-commerce companies, 60,000 SMEs, 35,000 individuals, 25,000 enterprises, among which 2,000 are web-based and 50,000 active f-commerce merchants. In the next five years, the country's e-commerce sector may generate around five hundred thousand jobs and holds the potential to be a key driving force of the economy.

The COVID-19 pandemic has altered consumer purchase patterns and spending habits with a paradigm shift toward a more digitized world. Some sectors, such as Pharmaceuticals, Agriculture, ICT/ITeS, Logistics and Digital Financial Services showed their promises with growth and digital transformation, and expected to continue with better performances in the coming days.

The lockdown, imposed at the beginning of the pandemic in early 2020, affected many sectors, however, some sectors such as e-businesses, groceries, fintech sectors, and logistics have experienced exponential growth. In 2020, the e-Commerce sector grew by 300% compared to the pre-pandemic period, while 8% of the companies began retailing

Table 4 Digital platforms, 2020

Description	*Amount*
Local e-commerce market (USD in billions)	2.1
ICT exports (2018–2019) (USD in millions)	802
Mobile Penetration	
Mobile subscribers (in millions)	168
Internet users (in millions)	111
MFS Penetration	
Daily MFS Transaction (USD in millions)	9.1
Average daily volume of MFS transactions (in millions)	3.2
MFS registered users (in millions)	95
Govt. e-Service Penetration	
Monthly Govt. e-service users (in millions)	2
Digital cards issued (in millions)	100

Source World Bank Data; BTRC; Bangladesh Bank; a2i; Light Castle Partners, 2020

Table 5 Growth of e-commerce market size (2016–2020)

Year	*Market Size (USD in billions)*	*Growth (%)*
2016	0.066	–
2017	1.1	1567
2018	1.2	9
2019	1.6	33
2020	2.1	31

Source ECAB; Statista; Light Castle Partner, 2020

Table 6 Growth of digital payment

Year	*Payment (USD in millions)*	*Growth (%)*
2016	20	–
2017	152	660
2018	185	22
2019	233	26
2020	471*	102

Source ECAB; Statista; Light Castle Partner, 2020; * = *projected*

groceries, 300 companies started online services, and daily e-commerce orders increased to more than 100,000 with a 25% increase in the average orders for essential products (Hossain & Chowdhury, 2022). Using the digital financial services, transactions related to remittance and insurance continued to grow while online payments and lending grew exponentially (Islam et al., 2020). However, during the pandemic, digital commerce has faced a setback with fraudulent practices of some e-commerce companies, attributed mainly to weaknesses in the regulatory framework.

With its growing importance, it has become imperative to establish secure, quick, and efficient tools for digital transactions. Digital transactions should be guided by the existing laws and regulations. Digital transaction plays a catalytic role for the e-commerce, and therefore, to protect consumer rights, much importance should be given to the secure transactions. Fundamentally, the digital commerce policy of the government should aim to convert and facilitate the transformation of all trade into digital trades to create a cashless society.

6 Digitalization in Agriculture, Livestock, and Fisheries

Crop Agriculture

Bangladesh's economy is still heavily dependent on agriculture, with around 80% of the rural households entirely or partly reliant on agriculture. About 50% of the labor force is engaged in agriculture. However, the sector's contribution to GDP has declined over time with decreased mechanization and productivity. There are some distortions, such as illegal tolls (rents) collection, extortion during transportation, hoarding, smuggling, the commission charged by the intermediaries, wholesalers' syndicates, and the creation of artificial supply shortage that affect the welfare of the farmers. The Food and Agriculture Organization (FAO) Experts' meeting underscored the need to adopt ICTs in agriculture to facilitate the fair distribution of products across markets (Alexander, 2005). ICT adoption in product distribution will enable farmers to make planting decisions, and permit traders to make better decisions regarding the viability of seasonal storage (Shepherd, 1997). Access to information enables farmers, fishers, and herders to make informed decisions about supplies, prices, markets, rural services, and entitlements, as well as local weather (USAID, 2005).

Bangladesh has made attempts to develop agricultural market information systems (AMIS). Soil Research Development Institute (SRDI) has developed an "Online Fertilizer Recommendation System (OFRS)" through which farmers get suggestions through SMS. Other initiatives, such as online paddy procurement, e-Krishok, etc., have been developed to support the farmers. Bangladesh ICT in Development (BIID) has developed the e-Krishok initiative to bring the benefits of ICT to the farmers' community of Bangladesh through knowledge sharing, adopting sustainable, climate-resilient farming practices, capacity building, and providing innovative and smart solutions. However, in most cases, information is collected, but such information has not been made available and readily usable to farmers (Islam & Gro¨nlund, 2007). This is a potential problem in leveraging the benefits of ICTs in Bangladesh.

An integrated information system for agriculture stakeholders could solve various problems and address a wide variety of information needs. A good review of international best practices was made in the Bangladesh

National Conservation Strategy (Hossain, 2016). A Kenyan integrated system, "DrumNet," is a good example that provides information supports through the delivery of financial, marketing, and other information (Van Zyl et al., 2012). Ghana developed a mobile application-based index, namely the Esoko Ghana Commodity Index (EGCI) in 2005 (Van Zyl et al., 2012) to publish a cash market price index composed of data on physical commodities. The weekly index tracks wholesale and retail prices and is now operational in more than ten African countries. These are good examples that may be followed in Bangladesh to ensure fair prices of agricultural commodities. Geoinformatics or Geographic Information System (GIS) can be used for soil analysis and topography mapping (Farounbi, 2013). Therefore, there are various ICT tools and applications that can be used for better marketing, distribution, fair pricing, soil testing, etc.

In 2003, under the "Support to ICT" taskforce program, the agriculture ministry set up an agricultural information system. Initially, this system used the data of ten different districts of Bangladesh to collect and disseminate information on the products produced by the various agricultural sectors. (Liton et al., 2017). Geoinformatics or Geographic Information System (GIS) is now being used by DAM and Agricultural Ministry to assess crop production. There are about 30 GIS installations in the country so far. For example, the soil and land resource information system (SOLARIS) by SRDI, a GIS-based multipurpose database on soil structure, is operational; it can be used for natural resource management, hazard mapping, land zoning, etc. It can analyze data on various levels.

Agriculture Information and Communication Centre (AICC) was established during 2009–2010 to share agricultural information with the people of farming communities. There are currently 245 AICCs countrywide, covering all AEZs (Agro-Ecological Zones), which provide services such as weather information, crop cultivation techniques, insect disease information, and latest price information to 40–50 farmers per day per AICCs. A few mobile phone-based web services are launched; primary examples include Krishoker Bondhu Phone Sheba, Krishi Call Center, e-Purjee, "Banglalink Krishi bazaar," "Krishi Jigyasha," etc. Moreover, various android apps are available to aid farmers in their agricultural endeavors.

Fisheries Resources

Fishery plays a vital role in the lives of millions in Bangladesh. The government adopted the National Fisheries Policy in 1998, which provides the framework for conserving and managing fisheries resources to ensure supply and enhance production (Bangladesh Planning Commission, 2015). In fisheries, various ICT tools are used worldwide for various purposes, including mapping fishery resources, processing capture, and/or culture and marketing (FAO, 2008–2016). A wide range of technologies such as GPS, Sonar, etc. can be used for various useful purposes of fisheries (Hossain, 2016). To ensure the viability of the blue economy in Bangladesh with a vast scope of utilizing fisheries resources in the Bay-of-Bengal, it is essential to apply appropriate ICT tools and technologies.

Livestock

Livestock production accounts for about 1.5% of GDP and about 14% of agricultural GDP (2018–2019). It is a crucial income component for poorer households and employs approximately 20% of the rural labor force. To ease the service delivery mechanism, the Department of Livestock Services undertook a project titled "Service Delivery of Department of Livestock Services Through SMS" with funding support under the Service Innovation Fund of A2I. However, there are still loopholes in the system that impede better services from the Department. Like other agricultural sectors, various ICT tools for market information, locating food availability, and quickly identifying diseases may be applied. Various African countries have been applying software and ICT tools to improve livestock production and marketing (Hossain, 2016). Bangladesh still lags in adopting ICTs in an important and growing livestock sector. There is a vast scope for utilizing ICTs in the agricultural sector to facilitate the growth and development of ICTs in Bangladesh.

7 Digitalization and Job Losses

Digitalization might have a neutral or slightly positive impact on jobs as suggested by a study on China's labor market. While automation leads to some job losses, these losses may be partially or fully offset by the new market creation and increased consumption due to ICTs. A cross-country study of MGI (McKinsey Global Institute, 2014) found that 2.6 jobs were created for every lost job due to the internet economy.

Service sectors and ICT-using manufacturing sectors might retrench some jobs due to the adoption of digital technologies. However, with proper policies, if digital technologies enhance productivity and market access (see Chapter 11), it will create additional jobs for enhanced business activities, even if not for the previous labor-intensive production process. It can introduce entirely new products and services while allocating capital more efficiently and boosting demand across the economy. The Internet's positive impact on start-ups and SMEs could further add some jobs. Another potential area is e-tailing, which could generate incremental consumption, and so does employment (McKinsey Global Institute, 2014).

It is true that with the widespread adoption of digital technologies and servitization of manufacturing, the composition of the labor market and the nature of work are likely to change. On the one hand, jobs associated with activities that are automated could be lost (or redefined); on the other hand, the economy will need more workers with digital skills. Thus, policymakers and business leaders need to find avenues for the displaced workers, and reforms are needed for retraining and upskilling so that enough high-tech and specialized talent can meet the economy's future needs. Growth in the SME sector will be especially critical in Bangladesh in managing this transition for making the Fourth industrial revolution (4IR) meaningful. The complementary sectoral development should be in place to accommodate additional jobs in line with newly emerged sectors.

8 Concluding Remarks

The service sector has largely gone through a digital transformation over the years, for which its impact on the economy has been growing. The banking and financial sector, public services, including revenue departments, media, education, health, and transport, are some of the notable service sectors that have adopted digital technologies to a great extent. The digitalized financial sector is now serving the retail and business segments more efficiently than before, and hence is saving transaction costs and reducing the asymmetry of information to some extent. Such sectors are now providing efficient services and gaining productivity.

However, a slow digital transformation in the manufacturing sector deters the expected productivity gains. In particular, digital footprints are largely absent in the SME sector due to their opaqueness and lack of incentives. Going digital can solve some of the disadvantages that the SME sector faces. Investment in innovations could help them gain productivity and greater market access. In contrast, digitalization can help build networks with suppliers and become price competitive by gathering information from other similar markets. E-commerce might help them increase sales, and adoption of Fintech might facilitate business transactions and pave the way for modern cashless society.

Though there have been enormous potentials to adopt digital technologies in crop agriculture, fisheries, and livestock sector, in reality, these sectors suffer from appropriate policies and efficient placement of technologies. Policymakers in this sector need to work effectively to adopt some digital technologies used in other countries successfully. Adoption of digital technologies is expected to reduce information asymmetry, transaction costs, time and increase data sharing in these sectors and sub-sectors.

Despite the significant development of ICT infrastructures in Bangladesh, the use of the internet and digital content is still limited, not only among individuals but also among businesses and investors. Digital transformation is yet to take a leap that could leapfrog the country into the next level of development. Incentives for innovation and automation, big data analytics, crowdfunding, online sourcing, marketing, and a proper regulatory framework, are necessary to expedite the digital transformation in productive sectors. Collaboration with cross-cutting sectors is needed to make digitalization more productive and growth-enhancing.

References

ADB. (2015). Second small and medium-sized enterprise development project. *Asian Development Bank.*

Alexander, G. F. (2005). *Participation and partnership in rural information networks: Lessons learned from five Asian countries*. FAO Experts' Meeting on Rural Information Networks in Asia-Pacific: Innovative Practices and Future Directions. Bangkok, Thailand.

Bangladesh Bank. (2020). *Bangladesh electronic fund transfer network.*

Bangladesh Bank. (2021). *Mobile financial services (MFS) comparative summary statement.*

Bangladesh Bureau of Statistics (BBS). (2013). *Survey of manufacturing industries (SMI) 2012.* Statistics and Informatics Division (SID). Ministry of Planning.

Bangladesh Bureau of Statistics (BBS). (2021). *Report on the survey of private.*

Bangladesh Planning Commission. (2015). *Environment, forestry and biodiversity conservation: Background paper for seventh five year plan*. Bangladesh Planning Commission.

BIDS-SEIP Survey. (2020). *Labor Market and Skill Gap in the ICT Sector in Bangladesh*. Bangladesh Institute of Development Studies (BIDS) and Skills for Employment Investment Program (SEIP), Finance Division. Ministry of Finance.

Business Wire Report. (2021, January 21). *Global animation, VFX & video games market report 2021: Strategies, trends & opportunities 2020–2025*. Business Wire.

Chen, S., Wen, P., Yu, P., & Yang, C. (2013). *The servitization of Taiwan's ICT manufacturing and its industrial upgrading*. In K. Lal, H. Hirakawa, N. Tokumaru, & S. Paul (Eds.), *Servitization, IT-ization and innovation models*. Routledge.

Databd. Co. (2018, October 9). *Consumer electronics*. Databd. Co.

ET LMIS. (2005). *Ethiopian livestock market information system*.

FAO. (2008–2016). *FAO fisheries and aquaculture department*. Food and Agriculture Organization.

Farounbi, A. I. (2013). Application of information and communication technology (ICT) in ecosystem conservation in Nigeria. *Journal of Research in Education and Society., 4*(3), 13–18.

GSMA. (2014). *Country overview: Bangladesh*.

Healthcare Institutions 2019. (2019). *Statistics and informatics division (SID)*. Ministry of Planning.

Hidalgo, C. A., Klinger, B., Barabási, A. L., & Hausmann, R. (2007). The product space conditions the development of nations. *Science, 317*(5837), 482–487.

Hossain, M. (2016). *Bangladesh national conservation strategy: Information and communication technology*. Ministry of Environment, Government of Bangladesh. https://paperzz.com/doc/9364982/bangladesh-national-conservation-strategy

Hossain, M. S., Chowdhury, S. R., Navera, U. K., Hossain, M. A., Imam, B., & Sharifuzzaman, S. M. (2014). *Opportunities and strategies for ocean and river resources management: Background paper for preparing the 7th five year plan*. Food and Agriculture Organization of the United Nations. Bangladesh Country Office.

Hossain, M., & Samad, H. (2021). Mobile phones, household welfare, and women's empowerment: evidence from rural off-grid regions of Bangladesh. *Information Technology for Development, 27*(2).

Hossain, M., Shinkai, N., Yunus, M., & Bakht, Z. (2012). Integration of ICT industries and its impact on trade and market access: The case of Bangladesh and India. Rahman, Brunner and Khatri (Eds), *Regional integration and economic development in South Asia*. Edward Elgar.

Hossain, M., & Chowdhury, T. T. (2022). *COVID-19, fintech, and the recovery of micro, small, and medium-sized enterprises: Evidence from Bangladesh* (ADBI Working Paper 1305). Tokyo: Asian Development Bank Institute. Available: https://www.adb.org/publications/covid-19-fintech-and-the-recovery-of-micro-small-andmedium-sized-enterprises-evidence-from-bangladesh

INSPIRED. (2013, June). *The survey of manufacturing SME sector in Bangladesh*. Mott MacDonald, INSPIRED Bangladesh.

IDLC Monthly business review. (2019). *Emergence of F-commerce startups: Serving customers at their doorsteps*.

Islam, M. Z. (2019, August 31). DIGITAL MARKETING: A two thousand crore taka market! *The Daily Star.*.

Islam, B., Haque, M., & Rozarlo, S. (2020, December 31). Digital commerce in Bangladesh: Policies & possibilities. *Light Castle Partners*. Retrieved from https://www.slideshare.net/LightcastlePartners/lightcastle-partners-digital-commerce-in-bangladesh-policies-possibilities

Islam, S., & Gro¨nlund, A. (2007). Agriculture market information e-service in Bangladesh: A stakeholderoriented case analysis. In Wimmer et al. (Eds), *Proceedings of EGOV 2007* (167–178). LNCS Series, Germany: Springer publications.

Jack, W., & Suri, T. (2014). Risk sharing and transaction costs: Evidence from Kenya's mobile money revolution. *American Economic Review., 104*(1), 183–223.

Kabeer, N. (1999). Resources, agency, achievements: Reflections on the measurement of women's empowerment. *Development and Change, 30*, 35–464.

Liton, A. I., Azad, M. M., & Mohammed, N. K. (2017). The ICT in agricultural development in Bangladesh. *International Journal of Engineering and Applied Sciences (IJEAS), 4*(7), 2394–3661.

Mahmud, S., Shah, N. M., & Becker, S. (2012). Measurement of women's empowerment in rural Bangladesh. *World Development., 40*(3), 610–619.

Marine Spatial Planning. (2015). *Marine spatial planning initiative*. UNESCO-IOC.

Meena, H. R., & Singh, Y. P. (2013). Importance of information and communication technology tools among livestock farmers: A review. *Scientific Journal of Pure and Applied Sciences., 2*(2), 1–9.

McKinsey Global Institute. (2014). *China's digital transformation: The Internet's impact on productivity and growth*.

McKinsey Global Institute. (2012, November). *Manufacturing the future: The next era of global growth and innovation*.

Miah, H. (2015). *Agriculture sector development strategy: Background paper for preparation of 7th Five Year Plan*. Bangladesh Planning Commission.

Ngouambe, N. (2013). *How can ICT improve livestock sector in Africa: Case studies from Ethiopia and Kenya.*

Pitt, M. M., & Khandker, S. R. (1998). The impact of group-based credit programs on poor households in Bangladesh: Does the gender of participants matter? *Journal of Political Economy, 106*(5).

Robbins, P., & Ferris, S. (2000). Design of a market information system for small scale producers and traders in three districts of Uganda (Study Report—8019). *The Netherlands: Technical Centre for Agricultural and Rural Cooperation (CTA).*

Shepherd, A. W. (1997). Market information services—Theory and practice. *Food and Agriculture Organization of the United Nations (FAO).* Rome, Italy.

Shepherd, A. W. (2003). Making marketing information services relevant to farmers. *Journal on Agricultural Marketing., 45*(4), 4–6.

Silva, H. D. (2005). *An innovative fruit and vegetable market information system in Sri Lanka: The Govi Gnana (farmer knowledge) service.* Post IAMA Conference on "Building New Partnerships in the Global Food Chain." University of Illinois.

Sonobe, T., A. Takeda, S., Yoshida, & H. T. Truong (2021). *The impacts of the COVID-19 pandemic on micro, small and medium enterprises in Asia and their digitalization response* (ADB Working Paper 1241). Tokyo.

TBS Report. (2020). *Auto industry to get a boost as Fair Technology enters deal with Hyundai.* The Business Standard. July 26, 2020.

The Daily Star. (2020, September 26). The dark side of e-commerce: No law to protect compliance, consumer rights and brand reputation. *The Daily Star.*

Tollens, E. F. (2006). *Market information systems in sub-Sahara Africa challenges and opportunities.* International Association of Agricultural Economists Conference. Gold Coast.

Ugwuishiwu, C. H., Udanor, C., & Ugwuishiwu, B. O. (2012). Application of ICT in crop production. *International Journal of Soft Computing and Engineering (IJSCE)., 2*(4), 227–231.

Uramoto, Y., & Nachum, L. (2018). *Corporate governance & sustainability of the global value chain: Bangladesh ready-made garment industry.* Research and Publications, City University, New York.

USAID. (2005). *Supporting gender and ICTs: Opportunities for women in Bangladesh.* United States Agency for International Development.

USAID. (2012). *USAID uses ICT to strengthen livestock trade in Ethiopia.*

Vandermerwe, S., & Rada, J. (1988). Servitization of business: Adding value by adding services. *European Management of Journal., 6*(4), 314–324.

Van Zyl, O., Alexander, T., De Graaf, L., & Mukherjee, K. (2012). *e-transform Africa: The transformational use of ICTs in Africa.* World Bank, African Development Bank & African Union.

Wichen, R., Hausner, U., & Chiwele, D. K. (1999). *Impediments to an agricultural growth in Zambia* (TMD Discussion Paper No. 47). *Zambia Trade and Macroeconomics Division and International Food Policy Research Institute*. Washington, DC.

CHAPTER 11

Innovations, Market Access and Productivity of Smaller Firms: Examining the Role of Financial Development

1 Introduction

The growth of a firm depends on its dynamic capabilities in exploiting niche markets and investment in innovations linked to firm productivity and profitability. As Teece et al. (1997) argued, growth-enhancing dynamic actions of firms are attributed to reconfiguration and transformation of resources to evaluate markets and competitors. Innovations and market access are important factors that influence firm productivity and growth, *albeit* disproportionately (Ito & Tanaka, 2015). Using firm data from Italy, Benfratello et al. (2008) find a stronger positive impact of regional banking development on smaller firms' innovative activities. However, the type of innovations that firms in developed countries undertake would differ from those undertaken by developing countries' firms.[1] While financial access is considered one of the crucial factors behind a firm's effort for innovation, this study attempts to link this effect of firm growth with local financial development to better understand the finance-growth nexus at the local level via innovation channel. This study also

[1] Ayyagari, Demirgüç-Kunt and Maksimovic (2011) observed from an enterprise surveys of over 19,000 firms across 47 countries that imitation and adaptation type innovations have better results than modern technological innovations. They showed that apart from firm, industry, and country factors, finance, governance, competition, and human capital play crucial role in firm's innovation.

M. Hossain, *Digital Transformation and Economic Development in Bangladesh*, https://doi.org/10.1007/978-981-19-2753-9_11

highlights what innovations are prominent in smaller firms in developing countries like Bangladesh that spur firm growth with market access.

However, what is important is to have access to finance for the firms to invest in innovations. As Hossain et al. (2021) suggest, one possible solution is developing the financial sector locally so that locally concentrated MSMEs can easily access finance. Various studies show that increasing the number of bank branches (or financial institutions or any form of digital finance) at a locality reduces both transaction costs and asymmetry of information about the borrowers, which enhances the opportunity for the firms, especially small and medium firms, to get access to credit (Hossain et al., 2021; Kendall, 2012; Fafchamps & Schündeln, 2013; Dehejia & Lleras-Muney, 2006; Guiso et al., 2004). We argue that local financial development provides firms with an opportunity to accumulate capital, which is used by good firms in skills development and technology accumulation for further growth.[2] Therefore, local financial development broadly facilitates firms' investment in innovations and greater market access in several ways. Firstly, external finance is needed for good firms to invest in innovations to be more productive through skills development and labor-saving capital deepening. This argument is supported by some earlier studies that showed that access to finance disproportionately affects innovation by small firms (Benfratello et al., 2008; Sharma, 2007). More importantly, innovation could be one channel that might lead to the heterogeneous impact of finance on firm growth—lower spending on innovation leads to higher productivity in smaller firms. Thus, access to finance through local financial development could lead to a more optimal inter-firm allocation of the expenditure on innovation.

Secondly, firms' access to market (internationalization) is linked with productivity and innovations because more productive firms have greater access to external markets. A large body of literature showed that the less productive firms might have access to only the domestic market, while more productive firms succeed in entering the international market (Helpman et al., 2004; Melitz, 2003). So, a productive firm with greater market access will likely benefit most from the local financial development. Since SMEs are geographically concentrated, and most of them focus

[2] As Solow (1957) showed, technological advances and skill, rather than capital accumulation, are the prime drivers of labor productivity. Solow argues that approximately 80% of the increase in labor productivity in the United States over the period 1909–1949 was due to more productive use of capital in increasing the skill level of the labor force.

on the sub-national level local market, it is fair to assume that relatively more productive firms tend to have access to the national market (beyond the localized market). Therefore, local financial development may be an associated policy to motivate firms to invest in innovation or digital technologies that will ultimately contribute to enhanced productivity and growth.

This chapter thus attempts to assess the factors that facilitate a firm's innovation strategies and enhance productivity; in particular, it focuses on the role of financial development on firms' innovation, highlighting the interrelations between digital finance and technologies. We use nationwide firm-level survey data of 1100 manufacturing SMEs from Bangladesh for the analysis.[3] Considering Bangladesh as a fast-growing developing nation with SMEs contributing to the country's GDP by 25% or more (ADB, 2015), the case of Bangladesh fairly represents the developing country context. Like other developing countries, bank placement, particularly private bank placement in Bangladesh at the local level, is very selective and therefore may be non-random. The bank chooses to expand its branches in growth centers where the viability of the business is apparent. This situation leads to the case of endogeneity of bank placement, which prompts us to apply the instrumental variable (IV) regression method and the propensity score method (PSM) to encounter observed and unobserved heterogeneity in the analysis.

The results suggest that local financial development significantly improves firms' investment in innovations and facilitates their access to external markets, which in turn improves their productivity and growth. In particular, local financial development determines the types of innovations based on firms' market orientation, whether they target the local market or the external market for their products. While local market-oriented firms undertake various simple training programs, external market-oriented firms undertake sophisticated innovation activities, such as replacing inputs, acquiring patents, trademarks, digitization of enterprise resource management, and skills development training to staff to remain competitive and productive in the external market. Therefore, local financial development has a disproportionate impact on the choice

[3] While the focus of Hossain et al. (2021) was to identify the channels and instruments of financial sector that favors LFD and subsequently firm growth, this paper focuses on the channels through which LFD favors firm growth.

of innovations by the smaller firms based on their market access. Furthermore, our results corroborate that innovations in the context of a certain level of LFD significantly improve firms' output and labor productivity, confirming the existence of the threshold effect of LFD. The findings of this study reassure the conclusions of other earlier studies on the positive role of local financial development on smaller firm growth and explain the transmission channels through which LFD works in favor of strong growth. Not only by increasing bank branches at the local level, but also the introduction of mobile financial services, agent banking, online transaction facilities, etc. facilitate local financial development by providing individuals and firms greater access to finance from remote locations. The findings in this chapter are, therefore, highly relevant to the context of the book as digital finance could promote financial development at the local level, and firms' IT adoption would lead to innovations.

The chapter is organized as follows. After Introduction in Sect. 1, Sect. 2 discusses the conceptual framework and hypotheses on how financial development is linked to firm innovation and market access. Section 3 describes the data and variables. Section 4 discusses estimation strategies and Sect. 5 discusses the results of econometric analysis. Section 6 concludes the chapter.

2 Conceptual Framework

2.1 Innovation, Firm Productivity, and Financial Development

Hypothesis 1 Local financial development facilitates a firm's investment in innovation, leading to higher productivity.

Access to finance has a positive but disproportionate effect on firm growth. Using firm data from Italy, Benfratello et al. (2008) find evidence of a stronger positive impact of regional banking development on innovative activities for small firms. Their results suggest that financial growth could lead to a more optimal inter-firm allocation of spending on innovation. This hypothesis implies that as financial markets develop, opportunity increases for smaller firms' investment in R&D (Ito & Tanaka, 2015). Therefore, local financial development could also positively impact firms' decisions on investment in innovations. Though the likelihood of smaller firms investing in R&D is lower than larger firms (Cohen & Klepper, 1996), the productivity of innovations is higher in smaller firms (Acs & Audretsch, 1991).

We may further argue that a firm's investment in innovation makes the firm more visible to the lender (say, a bank), giving a signal that the firm is a good performer and thus would be a good borrower. With local financial development, asymmetry of information about the firms (and its investments in innovation *a la* performance) would likely be eliminated. Therefore firms will get access to formal finance more easily compared to before.

2.2 *Financial Development and Market Access*

Hypothesis 2 Local financial development facilitates a firm's greater access to market

There are various ways local financial development could facilitate a firm's greater access to the market. Firstly, as various studies suggest, more productive firms succeed in entering the international market (Helpman et al., 2004; Melitz, 2003). At the same time, the less productive firms serve only the domestic market, and relatively more productive firms export. Therefore, productive firms in the first place can get access to formal finance that might lead them to gain access to the national or international market with their better performances in the second place. This is related to the argument that points to the self-selection of the more productive firms to delve into national/international markets because of additional costs incurred to sell goods in foreign markets (Bernard & Jensen, 1999; Bernard & Wagner, 1997). For example, the extra costs include transportation, distribution, or marketing costs, a skilled workforce to manage foreign networks or production costs in modifying current domestic products for foreign consumption. These costs provide an entry barrier that less productive firms cannot overcome, requiring formal finance. Therefore, access to traditional finance helps firms better access the external market.

Secondly, greater market access by productive firms increases their demand for various financial services, which may be better served by local financial development (Hossain et al., 2021; Chauvet & Luc, 2017). Availing of financial services leads to a better relationship with the banks that would pave the way for further access to finance.[4] Furthermore, such engagement reduces the asymmetry of information about the firm, which

[4] Torre et al. (2010) provides a discussion on various aspects of relationship lending.

reduces banks' credit default risk and hence increases the likelihood of firms' access to credit.

2.3 *Joint Effect of Innovation and Market Access*

Hypothesis 3 Combining hypotheses 1 and 2, we argue that LFD enhances innovation, and innovation enhances productivity, further enhancing greater market access leading to firm growth. Therefore, a combined effect of innovation and LFD will lead to greater productivity and output growth.

Several studies attempted to establish the link between productivity-enhancing investments, such as R&D investments and exporting, and suggest a possible complementarity between these two activities (Yeaple, 2005; Aw et al., 1995; Bustos, 2011). Productive firms with external market orientation may succeed in innovating by using buyer–supplier networks, strategic alliances, or research collaborations with other firms. Ito and Tanaka (2015) examined the relationship between the firm's productivity and joint decision on R&D strategies and exporting among Japanese firms. They find a remarkable heterogeneity among the exporters regarding their internal or external R&D strategies. The exporters with R&D investments, be either purely internal or purely external, are more productive than exporters without R&D investments. Their results suggest that the internal R&D strategy is crucial for access to the international market, while open innovation is essential to promote innovations for international firms further. Nonetheless, the results support that innovations will lead to external market access and enhance the firms' productivity.

3 Data and Variables

3.1 *Data*

Three types of data are combined to perform the analysis. About 1100 manufacturing SMEs firm characteristics are obtained from the Bangladesh INSPIRED Survey, 2013. Bank branch data are obtained from Bangladesh Bank (the central bank) and thana[5] characteristics are obtained from the National Census 2011 data and Household Income and Expenditure Survey (BBS, 2010) data with necessary extrapolation. The details of the INSPIRED survey data can be found in Hossain et al. (2021).

3.2 Description of Variables

Several sets of outcome variables are considered in this paper: (i) different types of innovations; (ii) market orientation: external or local; and (iii) sales revenue and labor productivity. To examine the role of LFD on investment in innovations, we consider information on nine types of innovations: (i) replacements of inputs with materials having improved characteristics (I1); (ii) acquisition of machinery, equipment, or capital goods to improve manufacturing technology (I2); (iii) acquisition of patents, trademarks or know-how from other institutions (I3); (iv) activities to introduce new products or products with improved characteristics (industrial design, product testing, etc.) (I4); (v) provide training to staff to improve production process or final product (I5); (vi) adoption of the new managerial process (I6); (vii) adoption of new marketing procedures (packaging, advertisements, market research, etc.) (I7); (viii) adoption of new channels to distribute the product (new dealers, sales online, etc.) (I8); (ix) training staff to improve managerial and marketing procedures (I9). All the innovation indicators are dummy in nature (yes/no).

Market access outcome variables consist of external market access (1/0). If a firm sells more than 50% of its products outside its own division, it gets 1 and 0 otherwise. The third set of outcome variables includes sales revenue and labor productivity (sales revenue/GVA per worker).

We control for several firm characteristics: membership in business associations, age of firm, an average number of hours lost due to power outage in a month, the ratio of managers over total employees, and other characteristics. In addition, nine sector-specific dummy variables, namely textile, food, metal, plastic, wood, paper, repair, chemical, and leather, and division dummies are used to control sector and division fixed effects. The summary statistics of some firm characteristics are reported in Table 1.

[5] A thana is usually a local level administrative unit with a police station. In a district, the number of thanas vary from 10 to 30 with an average area of 147 sq. km.

Table 1 Summary statistics of firm-level variables

Variables	*Mean*	*Std. deviation*	*Max*	*Min*	N
External market access (if sales >50%)	0.23	0.42	1	0	1,124
External market access (if sales >75%)	0.16	0.37	1	0	1,124
Replacement of inputs (I1)	0.74	0.43	1	0	1,124
Acquisition of machinery, equipment, or capital goods (I2)	0.41	0.49	1	0	1,124
Acquisition of patents trademarks (I3)	0.01	0.13	1	0	1,124
Training to staffs	0.19	0.39	1	0	1,124
Profit margin of firms	8.41	9.05	40.00	−34.00	1,084
Growth of revenue in 2012	11.47	35.77	902.74	−88.89	1,036
Growth of revenue in 2011	10.24	23.34	206.33	−80.00	1,000
Access to formal credit of firms	0.61	0.49	1	0	1,084
Overdraft facility used by firms	0.005	0.067	1	0	1,084
Trade credit facility used by firms	0.06	0.22	1	0	1,084
Interest rate paid	16.94	8.99	22.00	0.00	680
If a member of an association (yes)	0.70	0.46	1.00	0.00	1,084
Experience of top manager (years)	17.28	9.47	60.00	1.00	1,084
Proportion of top female managers	0.03	0.18	1.00	0.00	1,084
Average employee per firm	49.24	58.98	250.00	10.00	1,084
Proportion of skilled workers	0.01	0.03	0.10	0.00	1,084
Hours of power outage (daily)	1.09	0.29	3.00	0.30	1,083

Source INSPIRED survey data (2013)

We use the number of bank branches in a *thana* (sub-district) for 2012 as a proxy for local financial development, consistent with survey data collected in 2012. A high density of bank branches is observed in Dhaka (16 bank branches within a square kilometer) followed by Chottogram, Rajshahi, and so on.

4 Estimation Strategy

The regression model can be specified as follows:

$$R_{ijt} = \alpha_0 + \alpha_1 B_{it} + \alpha_2 C_{ijt} + \alpha_3 T_{it} + \varepsilon_{it} \quad (1)$$

where R_{ijt} denotes the outcome variables for a firm j in region i at time t, C_{ijt} denotes firm characteristics, T_{it} denotes *thana* characteristics, and B_{it} denotes local financial development indicators. Specifically, α_1 measures the impact of financial development on firm performance.

Equation (1) may suffer from the endogeneity of B_{it} because of the non-random placement of bank branches and the selection of firms (borrowers). To address endogeneity, the instrumental variables (IV) technique and propensity score matching (PSM) are used.

4.1 IV Estimation Strategy

The IV method involves finding suitable instruments, though it is quite a daunting task that affects the intervention (access to finance or bank placement in this case), but not the outcomes of interest (e.g., firm revenue). With the availability of suitable instruments, the IV method can yield unbiased estimates of impacts. We follow the instruments used by Hossain et al. (2021) and Kendall (2012). For example, Kendall (2012) uses deposits and population density at the district level and their squared terms as instruments, whereas Hossain et al. (2021) used deposits and the proportion of overseas migrant workers in a district as the instruments. As the locally collected deposits may not be directly associated with lending and therefore the revenue/output of a firm, per capita deposit may be a valid instrument. However, in our analysis, population density does not satisfy all the validity tests of the instrument. The reason is that firms' marketing strategy is also associated with a high population density and therefore may not be a valid instrument for our purpose. The instruments used in this study have passed the statistical tests of validity as reported in the lower panel of each Table.

Though IV regression encounters endogeneity problems with unobserved heterogeneity in the sample observations, we also employ the PSM strategy to address observed heterogeneity among the firms (Rosenbaum & Rubin, 1983). We use p-score regressions instead of the conventional PSM technique to avoid losing a good number of observations.

5 Econometric Results

5.1 *Financial Development and Firms' Market Access*

We estimate Eq. (1) with the IV regression method. Bank branches in a *thana* are our primary treatment variable. As for outcome variables, investments in innovative activities and market access are our main outcome variables. We also consider the logarithm of sales revenue and labor productivity in some specifications as outcome variables. A variable indicating whether a *thana* has a certain number of bank branches is used as a proxy for local financial development following other studies (Fafchamps & Schündeln, 2013; Hossain et al., 2021; Kendall, 2012). The control variables considered are both firm-level and *thana*-level characteristics that are not expected to influence the treatment firm. Firm characteristics include the firm's age, the manager's years of experience, ownership pattern, firm size, power outage status, and others. *Thana*-level control variables include population density, access to electricity (%), distance to the capital city (Dhaka), sanitation facility, safe drinking water coverage, and headcount poverty.[6]

Table 2 reports the IV regression results assigning p-score weights to each regression to address the observed and unobserved heterogeneity. The first stage results and diagnostic tests for endogeneity are also reported in the lowest panel of the table. The first three columns report the IV regression results based on the firms' percentage share of the sales in different markets, such as local (within own division), national (rest of the country), and international (export). Since the sales shares in different markets represent a mirror image of firms' market shares, we obtained almost the same coefficients though the signs are different. In particular, local financial development significantly increases a firm's access to the external (national) market via productivity channels, as the literature suggests. To examine the market access aspect succinctly, we next attempt to create a market access dummy considering if a firm's share of sales proceeds to the external market exceeds 50% (or 75%), and zero otherwise. Since the model involves a binary outcome variable with continuous endogenous regressors, we apply the IV probit regression technique here. All three specifications (with or without p-score weights) suggest that

[6] As our data spans 2010–2012, we use poverty incidence for 2010 from HIES 2010 (BBS, 2010).

local financial development facilitates firms' external market orientation, which ultimately contributes to their output and productivity growth.

Note that reaching out to a national market by SMEs involves similar efforts that the larger firms chip in to reach out to the international market, such as forming the strategic network, developing necessary skills, and improving product quality. The results suggest that firms' greater orientation to the external market has been greatly facilitated by their access to bank finance, which is significantly dependent on the extent of local financial development. This result can be related to existing studies, such as Hossain et al. (2021) and Fafchamps and Schündeln (2013), highlighting that local financial development spurs firm growth.

5.2 *Financial Development and Innovations*

This section attempts to examine the types of innovation determined by local financial development (LFD). Since the innovation indicators, as described in Sect. 3.2, are binary (0/1), we run IV probit regressions with and without PSM weights to check the robustness of the results. The results without weights suggest that local financial development has a positive and significant effect on I5 and I8 and a negative and significant effect on I6 and I7. However, with PSM weights, we see that local financial development has a positive and significant impact on only two types of innovations, such as I5 and I7, that is, the "training to staff" and "adoption of new marketing procedures." In both specifications, providing training to staff is a common innovation applied by the smaller firms—such types of investments are facilitated by easy access to bank finance. For all the significant results, the tests of exogeneity confirm the evidence of endogeneity of local financial development (Table 3).

5.3 *Innovation and Market Diversification*

Firms usually undertake various innovations based on their market accessibility to remain competitive in the respective market. The role of external finance via local financial development thus could be different for the firms in terms of their investment in innovations based on their market orientation. Therefore, the choice of innovations depending on their market exposure is expected to be facilitated by local financial development. We, thus, create an interaction outcome variable by multiplying the types of innovations (I) with market share (M). Table 4 reports the IV

Table 2 IV regression estimates specifying the impact of local financial development on SME's access to different markets

	(1)	(2)	(3)	(4)	(5)	(6)
	IV Regression results			*IV Probit estimates*		
Variables	*Local Market*	*National Market*	*Export (intl. market)*	*Access to external market (if ex. Market share >50%) [without weight]*	*Access to external market (if ex. Market share >50%) [with p-weights]*	*Access to external market (if ex. Market share >75%) [with p-weights]*
Number of bank branches	−0.54** (0.191)	0.45*** (0.16)	0.09 (0.12)	0.018*** (0.003)	0.018*** (0.003)	0.017*** (0.005)
Firm characteristics	Yes	Yes	Yes	Yes	Yes	Yes
Sector dummies	Yes	Yes	Yes	Yes	Yes	Yes
District dummies	Yes	Yes	Yes	Yes	Yes	Yes
Thana characteristics	Yes	Yes	Yes	Yes	Yes	Yes
Observations	1,122	1,122	1,122	1,122	1,122	1,122
Wald Test of Exogeneity (χ^2)	–	–	–	15.23***	11.10***	5.76***
R-squared	0.73	0.116	0.309	–	–	–

Diagnostic tests				*First stage regression results: columns 1–3*	
F-test of excl. IVs	28.89***	28.89***	28.89***	Per capita deposits	98.57***
Kleibergen-Paap rk Wald	51.52***	51.52***	51.52***	Per capita deposits^2	−12.40***
Craig-Donald Wald F	17.31***	17.31***	17.31***		
Sargan–Hansen J-stat	2.49	2.56	0.31		
Endogeneity test of regressors (χ^2)	6.85***	9.15***	0.74		

Notes Figures in parentheses are robust standard errors. *, ** and *** represent statistical significance at the 10% level, 5% level (or better), and 1% level (or better), respectively. Nine sector dummies, such as Textiles and clothing; Food and beverages; Paper and printing; Metal-mechanic; Plastic and non-metallic; Repair and installation; Wood and furniture; Chemicals and pharmaceuticals; and Leather, were also included to control sector fixed effects. District dummies were also added to the model. Some firm-level characteristics, such as company office in multiple locations, top manager's years of experience, whether the top manager is female, duration of power outage in a day (hours), and whether the company exploits its full capacity (yes/no), were added, but to save space, the results are not shown in the table

Table 3 IV Probit estimates on the impact of local financial development on innovations in SMEs

Variables	*(1)* *I1*	*(2)* *I2*	*(3)* *I3*	*(4)* *I4*	*(5)* *I5*	*(6)* *I6*	*(7)* *I7*	*(8)* *I8*	*(9)* *I9*
No. of bank	−0.002	0.001	0.018*	0.006	0.014***	−0.008*	−0.016***	0.013**	0.003
Branches (LFD) (without p-weights)	(0.005)	(0.001)	(0.011)	(0.009)	(0.004)	(0.005)	(0.004)	(0.007)	(0.009)
No. of bank	0.001	−0.004	0.018	−0.006	0.011**	0.001	0.019***	0.007	−0.004
Branches (LFD) (with p-weights)	(0.008)	(0.006)	(0.011)	(0.009)	(0.005)	(0.009)	(0.004)	(0.011)	(0.010)
Firm characteristics	Yes	Yes	Yes	Yes	Yes	Yes	Yes	Yes	Yes
Sector dummies	Yes	Yes	Yes	Yes	Yes	Yes	Yes	Yes	Yes
Division dummies	Yes	Yes	Yes	Yes	Yes	Yes	Yes	Yes	Yes
Thana characteristics	Yes	Yes	Yes	Yes	Yes	Yes	Yes	Yes	Yes
Observations	1,122	1,122	1,122	1,122	1,122	1,122	1,122	1,122	1,122
Wald Test of Exogeneity (χ^2)									
Model-1	0.30	0.02	0.84	0.14	9.62***	2.68*	8.89***	2.45*	0.48
Model-2	0.07	0.57	0.68	0.95	7.17***	0.04	11.88***	0.48	0.00

Notes Figures in parentheses are robust standard errors. *, ** and *** represent statistical significance at the 10% level, 5% level (or better), and 1% level (or better), respectively. Sector dummies, district dummies, some firm-level characteristics, and thana characteristics are added as before

regression results on the joint effect of market orientation and innovation. We separately run regressions for different markets to further explain what types of innovations are needed to have access to local/external markets for the smaller firms in the context of local financial development.

In the first specification, we see that for local market-oriented firms, local financial development increases their investment in essential innovations, such as I5 (training on production process)) and I9 (training on managerial and marketing strategy). On the other hand, for external market-oriented firms, local financial development facilitates investment in some broader innovations, such as in replacement of quality inputs (I1), acquisition of patents, trademarks, etc. (I3) in addition to I5 (training). This is an important finding in the sense that firms need to undertake investments in I1 and I3 type innovations in addition to I5 to remain competitive in the external market, for which access to external finance appears to be crucial. The development of the local financial sector is thus beneficial for the firms to be competitive in their respective market. The results in Table 4 extend the results in Table 3 because LFD has a differential role in the choice of innovations depending on firms' market exposure.

The analysis also suggests that smaller firms are more innovative than their larger counterparts to exploit competitive advantages to excel in external markets. Among the sectors, metal, plastic, and chemicals appear to adopt different innovations to achieve a competitive edge. On the other hand, we do not see any significant variations among the firms regarding innovations across firm size and sectors. Local market-oriented firms adopt basic training programs as part of skills development.

5.4 Robustness Check: Joint Effect of Local Financial Development and Innovations on Firm Output and Productivity

The previous two sections show that local financial development enhances firms' choice of investments in innovations depending on their market access. These two channels appear to be essential for improving the output and productivity of firms. However, the combined effect of local financial development and innovation would be appealing because firms' higher investments (with easy access to credit) in innovations would enhance output and productivity given their market orientation. Therefore, we

Table 4 Impact of a bank branch on the joint effect of innovation and market access (IV Probit)

Variables	*(1)* *I1*M*	*(2)* *I2*M*	*(3)* *I3*M*	*(4)* *I4*M*	*(5)* *I5*M*	*(6)* *I6*M*	*(7)* *I7*M*	*(8)* *I8*M*	*(9)* *I9*M*
Reg-1									
No. of bank	−0.229	−0.023	0.003	0.007	0.219**	−0.288**	0.077	0.065	0.146**
Branches (local market)	(0.161)	(0.156)	(0.021)	(0.072)	(0.100)	(0.143)	(0.073)	(0.060)	(0.066)
Reg-2									
No. of bank	0.185*	0.076	0.044*	0.034	0.058*	0.063	0.030	0.015	−0.020
Branches (external market)	(0.100)	(0.073)	(0.023)	(0.040)	(0.038)	(0.075)	(0.044)	(0.034)	(0.027)
Firm characteristics	Yes	Yes	Yes	Yes	Yes	Yes	Yes	Yes	Yes
Sector dummies	Yes	Yes	Yes	Yes	Yes	Yes	Yes	Yes	Yes
Division dummies	Yes	Yes	Yes	Yes	Yes	Yes	Yes	Yes	Yes
Thana characteristics	Yes	Yes	Yes	Yes	Yes	Yes	Yes	Yes	Yes
Constant	−74.137	20.264	4.406	−9.671	0.322	−128.567***	−36.675	13.752	41.352
	(52.905)	(49.449)	(14.202)	(27.272)	(36.133)	(40.450)	(28.378)	(26.954)	(25.144)
Observations	1,122	1,122	1,122	1,122	1,122	1,122	1,122	1,122	1,122
R-squared									
Reg. Model-1	0.087	0.091	0.039	0.029	−0.007	−0.025	0.040	0.043	−0.015
Reg. Model-2	0.150	0.079	0.000	0.042	0.031	0.049	0.097	0.065	0.010

Notes Figures in parentheses are robust standard errors. *, ** and *** represent statistical significance at the 10% level, 5% level (or better), and 1% level (or better), respectively. Sector dummies, district dummies, some firm-level characteristics, and thana characteristics are added as before. The detailed results of Reg-1 and Reg-2 are not reported to save space

assess the role of LFD and its interaction with different types of innovations on output (sales revenue) in Table 5 and then on labor productivity in Table 6.

In the first column of Table 5, we see that LFD alone significantly enhances SMEs' sales revenue, which is consistent with Hossain et al. (2021). In the subsequent columns 2–7, we report the results for the interaction of LFD with different types of innovations, in particular, with innovations I1, I2, I3, I5, I7, and I9. We see that the interaction terms LFD*I are significant but negative in all the specifications, while LFD and I are significant and positive separately. The results can be interpreted in a way that firms' investment in innovations enhances its output with local financial development up to a certain level of LFD, indicating the existence of a threshold of financial development (such as bank branch expansion at *thana* level), which is consistent with some other studies (Abdmoulah & Jelili, 2013; Hossain et al., 2021). For example, the coefficient on interaction term in col. 2 is −0.075; that is, the impact of innovation I1 on output would remain positive if the number of bank branches in a *thana* remains lower than 65 [(4.85–0.075*b)* I (=1)]. These results again support the bank competition hypothesis suggesting that smaller firms benefit from an optimal number of branches at a locality (see Hossain et al., 2021; Leon, 2015); otherwise, banks might be selective and support larger firms for their viability. Similar results hold for labor productivity (Table 6). Therefore, the results in this section corroborate the results of earlier studies and explain how firms capitalize on their access to finance in enhancing output and productivity in the context of local financial development. Apparently, smaller firms invest in skills development through training, and relatively better firms go for product and process innovations.

6 Conclusions

This study suggests that digitalization policy would bring greater benefits through productivity if complementary policies, such as local financial development are accompanied. As evident in this chapter, smaller firms' growth is facilitated by firms' investment in innovations for which access to finance and training, and know-how is needed. In particular, it explains how local financial development works in favor of firm growth. The results show that local financial development enhances smaller firms' investment in productivity-enhancing innovations in a disproportionate way in terms

Table 5 Impact of local financial development and innovations on firm output

Variables	*(1)* *Log (rev)*	*(2)* *Log (rev) (LFD*I1)*	*(3)* *Log (rev) (LFD*I2)*	*(4)* *Log (rev) (LFD*I3)*	*(5)* *Log (rev) (LFD*I5)*	*(6)* *Log (rev) (LFD*I7)*	*(7)* *Log (rev) (LFD*I9)*
Local fin. Dev (LFD)	0.014*** (0.004)	0.06** (0.03)	0.05*** (0.024)	0.007*** (0.003)	0.011*** (0.005)	0.011*** (0.003)	0.005*** (0.003)
Innovation type (I)	–	4.87*** (2.09)	0.94*** (0.30)	16.56** (8.07)	4.71*** (1.92)	4.64*** (1.29)	7.15*** (3.68)
LFD*I	–	−0.075*** (0.03)	−0.06*** (0.029)	−0.2*** (0.095)	−0.08*** (0.03)	−0.07*** (0.002)	−0.14*** (0.06)
Firm characteristics	Yes	Yes	Yes	Yes	Yes	Yes	Yes
Sector dummies	Yes	Yes	Yes	Yes	Yes	Yes	Yes
Division dummies	Yes	Yes	Yes	Yes	Yes	Yes	Yes
Thana characteristics	Yes	Yes	Yes	Yes	Yes	Yes	Yes
Constant	10.949*** (1.326)	14.279*** (2.288)	0.166 (4.15)	9.072*** (2.186)	19.977*** (6.385)	10.487*** (2.801)	6.07*** (1.47)
Observations	1,122	1,122	1,122	1,122	1,122	1,122	1,122
R-squared	0.443	0.266	0.94	0.154	−2.018	0.417	−0.12
Kleibergen-Paap rk Wald	69.77***	8.58***	10.71***	6.05**	10.33***	20.03***	11.17***
Sargan–Hansen *J*-stat	0.04	0.47	3.47**	0.248	0.84	0.006	0.28
Endogeneity test of regressors (χ^2)	14.32***	12.02***	9.45***	13.67***	13.12***	13.76***	15.66***

Notes Figures in parentheses are robust standard errors. *, ** and *** represent statistical significance at the 10% level, 5% level (or better), and 1% level (or better), respectively. Nine sector dummies and district dummies were included to control sector and regional fixed effects

Table 6 Impact of local financial development and innovations on labor productivity

Variables	*(1) Labprod (b)*	*(2) Labprod (b *I1)*	*(3) Labprod (b *I2)*	*(4) Labprod (b *I3)*	*(5) Labprod (b *I5)*	*Labprod (b *I7)*
Local Fin. Dev. (LFD)	0.002** (0.001)	0.008* (0.005)	0.002** (0.001)	0.001*** (0.0006)	0.002*** (0.0008)	0.002*** (0.0009)
Innovation type (I)	–	0.59* (0.38)	0.42* (0.23)	2.20 (1.47)	0.62** (0.34)	0.66** (0.33)
LFD*I	–	−0.009* (0.006)	−0.007** (0.003)	−0.027* (0.017)	−0.011* (0.005)	−0.011* (0.005)
Firm characteristics	Yes	Yes	Yes	Yes	Yes	Yes
Sector dummies	Yes	Yes	Yes	Yes	Yes	Yes
Division dummies	Yes	Yes	Yes	Yes	Yes	Yes
Thana characteristics	Yes	Yes	Yes	Yes	Yes	Yes
Constant	0.246 (0.324)	0.834 (0.550)	−0.92 (0.54)*	−0.228 (0.310)	2.640* (1.574)	−0.236 (0.975)
Observations	1,038	1,038	1038	1,038	1,038	1,038
R-squared	0.010	−0.168	−0.09	−0.052	−3.510	0.049
Kleibergen-Paap rk Wald	40.25***	10.72***	10.10***	6.85**	14.80***	20.08***
Sargan–Hansen J-stat	0.56	1.79	0.12	0.23	0.003	0.45
Endogeneity test of regressors (χ^2)	3.75**	1.88	3.43**	3.68**	3.84**	3.72**

Notes Figures in parentheses are robust standard errors. *, ** and *** represent statistical significance at the 10% level, 5% level (or better), and 1% level (or better), respectively. Nine sector dummies and district dummies were included to control sector and regional fixed effects of firms' market orientation, either local or external. The impact of local financial development is lower on local market-oriented firms compared to external market-oriented firms. External market-oriented firms gain to a larger extent by investing in product and process innovations in the context of local financial development.

Local financial development, either in the form of bank branch network extension or digital finance, provides SMEs with an opportunity to be active in the local/global value chains and carve out a niche in their respective markets. Digital finance could be one of the attributes of local financial development as digital finance reduces transaction costs. Easy access to finance through local financial development thus enhances firms' productivity and, consequently, their growth. The results of this study highlight that local financial development enhances inclusive finance and facilitates inclusive growth through promoting value chains and market potentials.

Since SMEs are the most significant source of employment and drivers of growth in developing countries, their development and growth can be enhanced significantly with local financial development (in the form of either expanding bank branches or any forms of fintech) at the sub-national level. Such financial development not only provides firms with an opportunity to accumulate capital but also gives them leverage to innovate and expand. Therefore, financial development strategy at the sub-district level could be an important policy option to achieve the benefits of digitalization-based innovations of the smaller firms, which could pave the way for balanced regional development. As for policy, the analysis in this paper underscores the importance of specific plans and incentive mechanisms for banks to enhance and expand their services to sub-national disaggregated levels to ensure inclusivity and digitalization of finance that will spur innovations and growth within the country.

References

Abdmoulah, W., & Jelili, R. B. (2013). Access to finance thresholds and the finance-growth nexus. *Economic Papers: A Journal of Applied Economics and Policy, 32*(4), 522–534.

Acs, Z. J., & Audretsch, D. B. (1991). Innovation and the size at the firm level. *Southern Economic Journal, 57*(3), 739–744.

ADB. (2015). *Second small and medium-sized enterprise development project.* Asian Development Bank.

Aw, B. Y., & Hwang, A. R. (1995). Productivity and the export market: A firm-level analysis. *Journal of Development Economics, 47*, 313–332.

Ayyagari, M., Demirgüç-Kunt, A., & Maksimovic, V. (2011). Firm innovation in emerging markets: The role of finance, governance, and competition. *Journal of Financial and Quantitative Analysis, 46*(6), 1545–1580.

Bangladesh Bureau of Statistics (BBS). (2005/2010). *Household income and expenditure survey, 2005 and 2010*. Bangladesh Bureau of Statistics.

Beck, T. (2008). *The econometrics of finance and growth*. Policy Research Working Paper No. 4608. The World Bank.

Benfratello, L., Schiantarelli, F., & Sembenelli, A. (2008). Banks and innovation: Microeconometric evidence on Italian firms. *Journal of Financial Economics, 90*(2), 197–217.

Bernard, A. B., & Jensen, J. B. (1999). Exceptional exporter performance: Cause, effect, or both? *Journal of International Economics, 47*, 1–25.

Bernard, A. B., & Wagner, J. (1997). Exports and success in German manufacturing. *Weltwirtschaftliches Archiv/Review of World Economics, 133*, 134–157.

Breshnahan, T., & Reiss, P. (1990). Entry into a monopoly market. *Review of Economic Studies, 57*(4), 531–553.

Bustos, P. (2011). Trade liberalization, exports and technology upgrading: Evidence on the impact of MERCOSUR on Argentinian firms. *American Economic Review, 101*(1), 304–340.

Calem, P., & Nakamura, L. (1998). Branch banking and the geography of bank pricing. *Review of Economics and Statistics, 80*, 600–610.

Chauvet, L., & Luc, J. (2017). Financial inclusion, bank concentration, and firm performance. *World Development, 97*, 1–13.

Cohen, W. M., & Klepper, S. (1996). Firm size and the nature of innovation within industries: The case of process and product R&D. *The Review of Economics and Statistics, 78*(2).

Dehejia, R., & Lleras-Muney, A. (2006). *Why does financial development matter? The United States from 1900 to 1940. Working Paper 9551.* National Bureau of Economic Research.

Fafchamps, M., & Schündeln, M. (2013). Local financial development and firm performance: Evidence from Morocco. *Journal of Development Economics, 103*, 15–28.

Guiso, L., Sapienza,P., & Zingales, L. (2004). Does local financial development matter? *Quarterly Journal of Economics, 119*(3), 929–969.

Helpman, E., Melitz, M. J., & Yeaple, S. R. (2004). Export versus FDI with heterogeneous firms. *American Economic Review, 94*, 300–316.

Hirano, K., Imbens, G. W., & Ridder, G. (2003). Efficient estimation of average treatment effects using the estimated propensity score. *Econometrica, 71*, 1161–1189.

Hossain, M., Yoshino, N., & Taghizadeh-Hesary, F. (2021). Optimal branching strategy, local financial development, and SMEs performances. *Economic Modelling, 96*, 421–4320.

INSPIRED. (2013, June). *The survey of manufacturing SME sector in Bangladesh*. Mott MacDonald. INSPIRED.

Ito, B., & Tanaka, A. (2015). External R&D, productivity, and export: Evidence from Japanese firms. *Review of World Economics, 152*, 577–596.

Kendall, J. (2012). Local financial development and growth. *Journal of Banking & Finance, 36*, 1548–1562.

Khalily, M. A. B. (2017). *Financial inclusion, regulation, and education: Asian perspectives* (N. Yoshino & P. J. Morgan, Eds.). Asian Development Bank Institute.

Leon, F. (2015). Does bank competition alleviate credit constraints in developing countries? *Journal of Banking & Finance, 57*, 130–142.

Melitz, M. J. (2003). The impact of trade on intra-industry reallocations and aggregate industry productivity. *Econometrica, 71*, 1695–1725.

Robins, J. M., Rotnitzky, A., & Zhao, L. P. (1994). Estimation of regression coefficients when some regressors are not always observed. *Journal of the American Statistical Association, 89*, 846–866.

Rosenbaum, P. R., & Rubin, D. B. (1983). The central role of the propensity score in observational studies for causal effects. *Biometrika, 70*(1), 41–55.

Scharfstein, D. O., Rotnitzky, A., & Robins, J. M. (1999). Rejoinder to adjusting for nonignorable drop-out using semiparametric nonresponse models. *Journal of the American Statistical Association, 94*, 1135–1146.

Sharma, S. (2007). *Financial development and innovation in small firms*. Policy Research Working Paper, 4350. The World Bank.

Solow, R. (1957). Technical change and the aggregate production function. *The Review of Economics and Statistics, 39*(3), 312–320.

Teece, D. J., Pisano, G., & Shuen, A. (1997). Dynamic capabilities and strategic management. *Strategic Management Journal, 18*(7), 509–533.

Torre, A., Pería, M. S. M., & Schmukler, S. L. (2010). Bank Involvement with SMEs: Beyond relationship lending. *Journal of Banking & Finance, 34*(9), 2280–2293.

Yeaple, S. R. (2005). A simple model of firm heterogeneity, international trade, and wages. *Journal of International Economics, 65*, 1–20.

CHAPTER 12

ICTs and Economic Growth in Bangladesh

1 Introduction

The role of ICTs in economic growth and development has received prominence with the rapid expansion of ICTs worldwide. For example, IT-producing industries contributed 7.6% of postwar economic growth and 32.8% of postwar productivity growth in the USA (Jorgenson et al., 2016), while in India, software service exports constituted 45% of total e-service exports and 3.5% of GDP (Erumban & Das, 2016). There are various channels through which ICTs can influence growth, albeit directly and indirectly. More specifically, the production of goods and services within the ICT sector directly contributes to creating value-added goods and services in the economy. Additionally, the use of ICT goods and services as inputs in the production of other goods and services increases the productivity of that sector, which contributes to improving the efficiency and productivity of the economy as a whole. Therefore, the impact of ICTs on economic growth is not straightforward and hence needs different approaches to capture the effect. While some empirical studies concluded that the ICT sector is a major contributor to economic growth, some other studies concluded that the ICT sector is both a cause and a consequence of economic growth (Toader et al., 2018).

The economy of Bangladesh has been growing very fast at a rate of over 6% in the last two decades, in tandem with the faster growth of

M. Hossain, *Digital Transformation and Economic Development in Bangladesh*, https://doi.org/10.1007/978-981-19-2753-9_12

mobile phone adoptions and the digitalization process.[1] With a population of over 160 million, the country saw spectacular growth in mobile phone adoption rate (over 100%) and internet use rate (over 25% of the population—mostly mobile-based internet), giving Bangladesh a higher mobile penetration status compared to its other lower-middle-income counterparts. As various studies from other countries suggest, the rapid adoption of mobile phone technology and Internet use, and other ICTs applications might have contributed positively to the impressive economic growth in Bangladesh by improving the country's total factor productivity. The rapid development of ICTs over the past two decades and their adoption across various sectors of the economy have prompted researchers to examine and measure the impact of ICTs on economic growth. However, such an impact, particularly the impact of digitalization on growth, has not yet been captured succinctly. A handful of studies are available on the impacts of mobile phones and teledensity. For example, a study on south Asian countries has shown that a 1% increase in teledensity enhances economic growth by 0.028% in Bangladesh (Tripathi & Inani, 2020). From household survey data, Hossain and Samad (2021) showed that the use of mobile phones increases household income by 3–10%, depending on their occupations.

This chapter takes a modest attempt to capture the impact of digitalization on economic growth in Bangladesh. A potential problem in this exercise is that a massive digitalization process started in the country followed by the government's Digital Bangladesh Vision only in 2009, and therefore a small sample size restricts us from applying any standard econometric technique. Though mobile phone adoption started in the mid-1990s, its benefits became widespread after 2000, followed by liberalization of the sector. Thus, though it is possible to capture the impact of mobile phones or teledensity on economic growth, the impact of overall digitalization on TFP (Total Factor Productivity) is somewhat tricky.

The chapter is organized as follows. Section 2 highlights the digital transformation and economic growth from the perspectives of Bangladesh, and Sect. 3 discusses the same from an international perspective. Section 4 discusses the methodological issues of estimating the

[1] While subscriber penetration was only 1% in 2003, it grew to more than 40% in 10 years (GSMA, 2017) and is expected to grow to 50% by 2020. At present, about 60 million people are using mobile-based internet and the number of MFS agents grew from 9,000 to over 414,000 in just over 2 years after allowing the MFS in 2011.

impact of ICTs on economic growth. Section 5 assesses the contribution of ICT and non-ICT sectors to the aggregate TFP growth. Section 6 identifies the determinants of TFP growth in Bangladesh, and Sect. 7 concludes the chapter.

2 Digital Transformation and Economic Growth: Bangladesh Case

The critical aspect of Digital Bangladesh vision is that it institutionalizes the digital transformation process in the country's development objective, which is reflected in various development policy documents, such as Five-Year Plans, Perspective Plans, and so on.

Average GDP growth over the decades could be the starting point of our discussion (Fig. 1). The country achieved below 4% annual GDP growth in the 1970s and 1980s, as both decades were afflicted by famine, coups, and political instability. However, a certain degree of economic liberalization started in the late 1970s, which was accelerated in the 1980s before taking off in the 1990s. A massive reform in the areas of trade and

Fig. 1 GDP growth and its drivers, 1991–2012. *Note* Average GDP growth over a decade has been considered. Total Factor Productivity (TFP) growth and labor productivity growth are taken from Asian Productivity Organization (APO) Databook 2020

the financial sector was undertaken in the 1990s, the result of which was reflected in a 1% increment in average growth in the 1990s and a further 1% in the 2000s, reaching nearly 6% annual growth. Despite the global financial crisis in 2007–2008 coupled with domestic political unrest in the context of assuming state power by a military-backed caretaker government, a further 1% or more incremental growth in the 2010s might be attributed to the digital transformation that might have been reflected in TFP (Total Factor Productivity) growth and labor productivity growth. From 2010 onward, the shares of two main drivers of growth, such as remittances and RMG (Ready-made Garments) exports, have declined while TFP growth and labor productivity growth have been increasing. On the other hand, the beneficial outcome of ongoing public mega infrastructure development projects initiated in the 2010s is unlikely to be realized soon. Therefore, I hypothesize that digitalization contributes to economic growth in the decade of 2010 through productivity gains. Why and how the digital Bangladesh policy could facilitate economic growth has been discussed in the chapter in particular and at length in this book.

Digital Bangladesh has now become a buzzword for development in Bangladesh. This is, therefore, an important policy that needs to be evaluated succinctly. Bangladesh is poised to become a digital economy with the virtue of its demographic dividend by exploiting its abundant pool of talented youths, favorable policy diffusions, and appropriate technological skills. Nonetheless, ICTs can make the best use of the country's youth population to foster economic growth through at least three channels: (i) increasing efficiencies in product and process development by reducing transaction costs reinforcing the "death of distance"; (ii) facilitating innovations through the adoption of software and information technologies that assist productivity gains across the board, which contribute to total factor productivity and hence higher economic growth; and (iii) developing IT industry with a skilled labor force that can capture a part of growing outsourcing businesses from the developed world with low-cost labor advantage. Thus, low-income countries like Bangladesh have comparative advantages to gain from adopting ICTs and outsourcing IT activities. For example, as the ICT sector mainly relies on human capital and a low level of technologies and investments, it is easier for these countries to build necessary capabilities faster with affordable costs. These advantages of ICT adoption led many countries to invest in ICTs. However, all the countries could not succeed, though China and India are exceptions.

3 ICT AND ECONOMIC GROWTH: INTERNATIONAL EVIDENCE

A vast literature has documented the positive and significant impact of ICTs on economic growth. The studies have examined the role of several aspects of ICTs, including investments, the internet (broadband), and telecommunications, on economic growth. Overall digitalization could lead to GDP growth and a reduction in unemployment. A survey of the World Economic Forum (World Economic Forum, 2013) indicates that a 10% increase in a country's digitization will increase a 0.75% in GDP (Gross Domestic Product) per capita and decreases the unemployment rate by 1.02%. Yousefi (2011) argued that upper-middle-income countries are the most benefitted from digitalization as ICTs have a bigger impact on their GDP growth. Some studies focus on specific issues, such as the impact of broadband infrastructure on growth. These studies found evidence from 25 OECD countries (for the period 1996–2007) that a 10% increase in the broadband penetration rate would increase a GDP per capita growth by 0.9–1.5% (Crandall & Singer, 2010; Czernich et al., 2009; Qiang et al., 2009). Similarly, Nasab and Aghaei (2009) showed from seven OPEC (Organisation of the Petroleum Exporting Countries) member countries for the period 1990–2007 that ICTs have a significant positive impact on economic growth.

The transformations in ICTs, the rapid development of semiconductor technology, investment in ICTs and software along with globalization have become a prominent sources of economic growth for both industrialized and emerging economies (Jorgenson & Vu, 2016). Jorgenson and others provided empirical evidence that ICT intermediaries are critical to stimulating economic growth, taking examples from China and India. China is the hub of ICT hardware manufacturing with a growing export, while India has become the largest exporter of computer software and ICT services (Jorgenson & Vu, 2016). The adaptation of ICT-using services is the source of service sector productivity in India (Erumban & Das, 2016).

Erumban and Das (2016) argued that a significant source of India's growth originates from the productivity from ICT using market services and their share to aggregate productivity growth. India has gained productivity in the ICT-producing sector that contributed to total factor productivity growth (TFPG) with the widespread adoption of telecommunication services. However, the manufacturing sector falls short in

ICT investment. Jorgenson and Vu (2016) provide evidence that total factor productivity (TFP) is important to differentiate the source of the growth between replication and innovation. In another study, Jorgenson et al. (2016) examined the significance of ICT in the postwar growth from 1947–2019 of the U.S economy. The replication of established technologies through investments in both IT (Information Technology) and non-IT capital are the major drivers of US economic growth as opposed to innovation in information technology.

To optimize the advantages in productivity from investments in ICT, additional investments in the organizational composition, employee development, and intangible assets are also important (Chen et al., 2016). Using the industry-level intangible investment data for ten European countries, Chen et al. (2016) showed that intangible capital investment is important to acquire greater benefits from investment in ICTs. Intangible capital subsidizes labor productivity growth, which is more prominent in ICT-intensive industries than in industries with limited ICT adaptation. However, not all intangible assets contribute to higher output in ICT-intensive industries. This is only true for organizational structures and research and development as per the samples investigated by the authors (Chen et al., 2016). Fukao et al. (2016) further emphasized that lack of investment in intangibles was one of the reasons why Japanese firms lagged behind the ICT revolution (Fukao et al., 2016).

Digital finance is an important attribute of ICTs that has a significant effect on economic growth. Zandi et al. (2016) find that electronic payments increased the consumption of goods and services, which in turn increased GDP. Card usage contributes to a 0.4% increase in consumption, leading to 2.6 million additional job opportunities over five years (2011–2015). Moreover, the authors also showed that an increase in electronic payment increases economic growth for emerging markets by 0.11%, while 0.08% for developed countries. The theoretical explanation of electronic payments influencing consumption and thus economic growth was given by Wong et al. (2020) and Hasan et al. (2012). Hasan et al. (2012) observed that electronic payments, including debit cards, credit cards, credit transfers, direct debit, and cheque payments, had significant positive effects on trade and consumption, facilitating higher economic growth for 27 European countries between 1995 and 2009. In another study, Berger (2003) assessed that cashless payments improve banks' productivity by reducing operating costs. This allows banks to gain economies of scale, leading to business expansion, increasing the propensity for greater investments and economic growth (Wong et al., 2020). Putting all these things into perspective, digitalization has a positive and significant impact on economic growth.

4 Estimating the Impact of ICT on Economic Growth: Methodological Aspects

There are two approaches based on production function to assess the impact of ICTs on economic growth. One is the direct impact of ICTs where one can segregate capital into ICT capital and non-ICT capital in terms of investments. The other approach is to assess the value-added created by the ICTs, which can be reflected in TFP growth. Both the approaches have limitations in their own right, highlighted in this chapter.

4.1 *Impact of ICT Investments on Economic Growth*

To estimate the contribution of ICT investment to growth, Jorgenson et al. (2008) and later Jergenson and Vu (2016) decompose the aggregate growth into capital and labor services and total factor productivity (TFP). The production function is defined as the output (Y) as a function of capital services with ICT capital (k_{ICT}) and non-ICT capital (k_{NICT}), and labor services in terms of hours worked (W) and labor quality (l_{Q}).

$$Y = A.F\,(k_{\text{ICT}},\, k_{\text{NICT}},\, W,\, l_{\text{Q}}) \tag{1}$$

Equation (1) can further be decomposed into the growth accounting Eq. (2) with competitive factor market assumption as follows:

$$\begin{aligned} \Delta\ln Y &= \omega_{\text{k}}\,\Delta\ln k + \omega_{\text{l}}\,\Delta l + \Delta\ln A \\ &= \omega_{\text{k}_{\text{ICT}}}\,\Delta\ln k_{\text{ICT}} + \omega_{\text{k}_{\text{NICT}}}\,\Delta\ln k_{\text{NICT}} \\ &\quad + \omega_{\text{l}}\,\Delta\ln W + \omega_{\text{l}}\,\Delta\ln l_{\text{Q}} + \Delta\ln A \end{aligned} \tag{2}$$

Where ω denotes the two-period average share of total factor income, and the assumption of constant returns to scale implies that $\omega_{\text{k}}+\omega_{\text{l}} = 1$ ($\omega_{\text{k}} = \omega_{\text{k}_{\text{ICT}}} + \omega_{\text{k}_{\text{NICT}}}$). From Eq. (2), three features of the GDP growth can be observed:

(i) role of ICT and non-ICT capital: $\omega_{\mathrm{k}}\,\Delta\ln k = \omega_{\mathrm{k_{ICT}}}\,\Delta\ln k_{\mathrm{ICT}} + \omega_{\mathrm{k_{NICT}}}\,\Delta\ln k_{\mathrm{NICT}}$

(ii) role of labor input in terms of hours worked and labor quality: $\omega_{\mathrm{l}}\,\Delta\ln l = \omega_{\mathrm{l}}\,\Delta\ln W + \omega_{l}\,\Delta l$, and

(iii) TFP growth, $\Delta\ln A$.

In this growth accounting framework, as Jorgenson and Vu (2016) argued, capital input is defined in terms of capital services rather than capital stock. The prices of capital are rental prices rather than asset values. This approach, already incorporated into official statistical systems in 2009, is crucial in estimating the impact of the ICTs. On the other hand, TFP may represent the sources of economic growth in terms of replication and innovation in information technologies.

4.2 *Contribution of ICT and Non-ICT Sectors to Aggregate TFPG*

To quantify the relative importance of ICT-producing and ICT-using sectors vis-à-vis non-ICT sectors in driving aggregate productivity growth, one may use the direct aggregation method suggested by Jorgenson et al. (2007). This approach relaxes many assumptions on input and output measurements in the aggregate production function approach. In this approach, the aggregate production function is a value-added function. The aggregate value-added growth is measured as a translog index of industry value-added, with weights being the industry share in aggregate nominal value-added (as in Eq. [3]). The production function at the industry level, however, is a gross output (Υ) function, and therefore, industry output growth can be decomposed into capital (k), labor (l), and intermediate input (F) as

$$\begin{aligned}\Delta\ln Y &= \gamma_{\mathrm{k,i}}\,\Delta\ln k_{\mathrm{i}} + \gamma_{\mathrm{l,i}}\,\Delta\ln l_{\mathrm{i}} \\ &\quad + \gamma_{\mathrm{F,i}}\,\Delta\ln F_{\mathrm{i}} + \Delta\ln A_{\mathrm{i}}\end{aligned} \tag{3}$$

where γ_{k}, γ_{l}, and γ_{F} are, respectively, the share of capital, labor, and intermediate input in total nominal output in industry i. Since the nominal value of gross output is the sum of the nominal value of industry value-added and nominal value of total intermediate inputs, the industry output growth can be obtained as a weighted sum of industry value-added growth and industry intermediate growth with the weights being, respectively, the nominal share of value-added in output and nominal share of intermediate inputs in output. Assuming that aggregate value-added is a translog sum of industry value-added, one can decompose the aggregate value-added growth as follows (see Jorgenson et al., 2007).

$$\begin{aligned}\Delta \ln V &= \sum_i Y_{\mathrm{i}} \Delta \ln V = \sum_i \gamma_{\mathrm{i}} \frac{\gamma_{\mathrm{k,i}}}{\gamma_{\mathrm{V,i}}} \Delta \ln k_{\mathrm{i}} \\ &+ \sum_i \gamma_{\mathrm{i}} \frac{\gamma_{\mathrm{l,i}}}{\gamma_{\mathrm{V,i}}} \Delta \ln l_{\mathrm{i}} + \sum_i \gamma_{\mathrm{i}} \frac{1}{\gamma_{\mathrm{V,i}}} \Delta \ln A_{\mathrm{i}} \qquad (4)\end{aligned}$$

In Eq. (4), aggregate value-added growth is the weighted sum of industry capital input, industry labor input, and industry TFPG. Industry TFP improvement can have a direct effect on industry output, and an indirect effect on output in other industries with intermediate input sold to other industries (Jorgenson et al., 2007).

5 Sector-Wise ICT's Contribution to GDP in Bangladesh

Even though the ICT sector is still small in size in Bangladesh, it has been one of the fastest-growing sectors of the economy since the mid-2000s. However, there is hardly any attempt to quantify the impact of ICT use on Bangladesh's economic growth from a broader perspective. Going by the standard definition of ICT sectors, we define the total market economy into ICT-using sector, ICT-producing sector, and non-ICT sectors following Erumban and Das (2016) (see Table 1). The share of the ICT-producing industries has increased from 1.84% in 2005–2009 to 2.64% in 2015–2019, with the most significant increase being in post and telecommunications services (from 1.3 to 2.6%). In addition, Bangladeshi firms in other sectors, predominantly service sectors such as financial services, also started using the technology heavily to enhance efficiency and reduce communication and coordination costs, which will impact their overall productivity.[2] For instance, a study by

[2] Jensen (2007) shows that, the use of mobile phones by fishermen in the Indian state of Kerala has helped improve both consumer and producer welfare, by reducing price dispersion. Similarly, comparing firms in India and Brazil, Commander, Harrison, and

Table 1 Share of different sectors to GDP attributing to ICTs in Bangladesh

%	*2005–2009*	*2010–2014*	*2015–2019*
ICT-producing sectors	1.84	2.56	2.64
ICT-using manufacturing	0.70	0.61	0.62
Non-ICT manufacturing	15.80	16.19	16.73
ICT-using services	11.29	11.00	10.87
Non-ICT market services	7.36	7.51	7.95
Non-ICT services	34.87	34.71	34.64
Non-ICT others	28.01	26.89	25.22
Total	99.87	99.48	98.67

Note Author's calculation based on data from BBS. Categorization is done based on Erumban and Das (2016) and the detailed estimates are shown in the appendix

Hossain and Samad (2021) found that mobile phone use increases household income from 3 to 10% depending on the occupations, such as small businesses and remittances; improves women's empowerment; and facilitates consumption smoothing during periods of shocks. ICT-using sectors (both manufacturing and services) according to this definition (which includes printing & publishing, machinery, transport equipment, trade, and financial services), contributed to about 12.0% of total GDP in 2005–2009, which decreased to 11.5% in 2015–2019. ICT-producing industries, including electrical and optical equipment manufacturing and telecommunication services, increased their share in GDP from 1.83 in 2005–2010 to 2.64% in 2015–2019. It may be noted that some sectors such as electrical machinery & apparatus, which are included in the ICT-producing category in our industry classification, may not be necessarily ICT producing, and, therefore, might lead to an overestimation of the size of this sector. However, it was hard to split inputs and output into

Menezes-Filho (2011) find robust positive productivity effects of ICT. In particular their findings suggest the importance of better infrastructure and labor market policy for higher rates of ICT adoption.

these sectors from the BBS's (Bangladesh Bureau of Statistics) database for growth accounting analysis.

Clearly, the ICT sector, though the size of the ICT-producing sector is small, shows a remarkable increase both in employment generation and GDP growth over time, substantiating the importance of this sector for Bangladesh's economy. At the same time, it reveals that the contribution from the ICT-using service sectors, predominantly the financial sector, has remained stagnated as the service sector adopted ICTs at an overwhelming rate in the early 2010s. However, the contribution of the ICT-using manufacturing sector remained the same over the years, indicating that the respective manufacturing sectors miserably failed to capitalize on the adoption of ICTs. This also reflects the fact that there is a vast scope of adoption of ICTs in the manufacturing sector to improve its productivity through innovations.

6 Estimating the Determinants of TFP Growth in Bangladesh

As the growth of TFP has been increasing and the trend of TFP has been approaching positive territory from 2010 onward, this motivates us to examine the impact of the adoption of ICTs on the growth of TFP in Bangladesh. With limited literature on the estimation of the determinants of TFP in Bangladesh, previous studies did not attempt to capture the impact of ICTs on TFP growth, mainly because of the prominence of ICTs has been apparent mainly after the late 2000s. For example, Mujeri (2004) assesses relative contributions of labor, capital, and TFP growth in different policy regimes (1974–2006) and concluded that capital accumulation played a significant role in most of the periods since 1970, with a slight dropping in the early 1990s. Moreover, the study examines the role of inflation, public consumption, the real effective exchange rate (REER), and trade openness as the determinants of TFP in Bangladesh. He, however, found that REER and trade openness had a significant impact on productivity growth.

A recent study by Ahmed and Chowdhury (2019), considering both aggregate production function with CRS (Constant Returns-to-Scale) and non-CRS assumptions and intensive form production function of the Cobb–Douglas form, has estimated TFP growth as a residual of growth and then assessed the determinants of TFP growth as follows.[3]

$$D\ln A = D\ln Y - [\alpha(D\ln k + (1-\alpha)(D\ln l + D\ln W] \quad (5)$$

$$D\ln A = D\ln y - \alpha D\ln k \quad (6)$$

For the period 1981–2014, they found that the growth rates of factor accumulation were 5.47 and 5.55%, respectively, which is higher than the GDP growth rates of 4.89% with an impressive capital growth rate of 6.12% coupled with 3.17% effective labor growth rate. This indicates that TFP growth rates are negative over the period. However, the magnitude of negativity in TFP falls from a two-digit number during 1981–1990 to a single digit over the decade 2001–2010, indicating that the efficiency of capital has been increasing over time. One limitation of the Ahmed and Chowdhury (2019) study is that they have extrapolated capital from an old survey of Rahman and Rahman (2002). An ADB (2019) study, however, showed a positive TFP in some periods during our study period.

The findings of Ahmed and Chowdhury (2019) have some discernible features. The improving productivity, though negative, indicates that the country's production processes are getting more efficient over time, given that the change in TFP growth pattern has been positive. It also suggests that Bangladesh has the scope for further enhancement of the economy's growth rate if its productivity growth excels into the positive territory. For the period 2011–2014, Ahmed and Chowdhury (2019) have identified positive TFP in some of their econometric specifications, giving a signal that the contribution of TFP on the growth of Bangladesh will occupy at least some positive impact on GDP growth in this period. This

[3] The study of Ahmed and Chowdhury (2019) have taken government expenditure on schooling and consumption net of schooling (as % of GDP), broad Money (as % of GDP), credit (as % of GDP), Inflation Deflator, Remittance (as % of GDP) data from the World Development Indicators. The GDP value was excerpted from BBS at 1995–96 base prices in million taka. The Human Capital Index and the number of employed persons were adapted from the Barro-Lee database and Penn Table 8 database, respectively. The Capital stock data was replicated following the estimation procedure described in the MIMAP (Micro Impacts of Macroeconomy and Adjustment Policies) study report by Rahman and Rahman (February 2002) published from BIDS. The BBS data was utilized in recalibrating the capital stock, expressed at 1995–96 base prices in million taka. Moreover, Globalization Index data has been taken from KOF database. In addition, data on Voice and Accountability, Rule of Law, Regulatory control, Control of Corruption is taken from the World Governance Indicator dataset.

warrants further investigation of the determinants of TFP to understand what factors have been driving the growth of TFP, particularly in the decade of 2010s. They have identified some determinants, such as government expenditure on education, broad money, voice and accountability, regulatory control though signs vary across the variables. The study fails to capture the important aspects of digitalization from 2000 onward (with high teledensity penetration) and a widespread digitalization since 2010 with the government's Digital Bangladesh vision. As already discussed, many indirect aspects of digitalization, such as enhancement of efficiency in the production process, reduction of transaction costs, and so on, can be captured through the TFP growth.

To assess the role of ICTs in TFP growth, I have used the TFP growth series of Ahmed and Chowdhury (2019)—one is estimated by the OLS (Ordinary Least Square) and the other one estimated by ARDL (Autoregressive Distributed Lag) at their first differences. A few ICT related variables are added to capture the role of ICTs on TFP growth, for example, teledensity, ICT service exports as percentage of total exports and fixed broadband subscribers in addition to some indicators such as voice and accountability, regulatory control, control of corruption, trade liberalization, broad money as % of GDP and government consumption net of schooling.[4] There are various ICT-related indicators that could be added to capture the impact of digitalization. However, the lack of data and small sample years refrained us from using those indicators as potential determinants of TFP growth. Instead, ICT service exports are used to capture the depth of ICT products and services as well as their international market access, which might reflect the overall development of the ICT sector in Bangladesh. Fixed broadband subscribers are considered to capture the quality of internet, which is also available since 2009, and hence it is included in the third and fourth specifications. I have tried to add some more indicators related to e-government; however, data did not permit it. The first difference at their level transformed the variables into an I(0) series that has allowed us to apply OLS estimations.

The results are reported in Table 2. The first two specifications consider data for 21 years, while the last two specifications consider data for ten years as fixed broadband data have been available since then. These variables are taken from the World Development Indicators of the World

[4] The data are mainly taken from the World Bank development indicators and Governance indicators.

Table 2 Determinants of TFP growth

Variables	*(1)* *TFPG1* *(dlna_ols_alpha68beta29)*	*(2)* *TFPG2* *(dlna_ardl_alpha65beta26)*	*(3)* *TFPG1* *(dlna_ardl_alpha65beta26)*	*(4)* *TFG2* *(dlna_ols_alpha68beta29)*
D.teledensity penetration	−0.039** (−2.67)	−0.037** (−2.63)	0.013* (11.06)	0.013* (8.67)
D.ict service exports as % of service export	−0.001 (−0.86)	−0.001 (−0.83)	0.001** (24.52)	0.001** (19.94)
D.govt consumption net of schooling	−0.002 (−1.06)	−0.002 (−1.09)	0.001** (17.47)	0.001** (14.45)
D.voice and accountability	0.045*** (3.89)	0.042*** (3.70)	−0.025** (−26.67)	−0.024** (−21.01)
D.regulatory control	−0.020 (−0.76)	−0.019 (−0.73)	−0.013* (−7.95)	−0.014* (−7.34)
D.control of corruption	0.007 (1.03)	0.008 (1.06)	−0.006 (−5.23)	−0.007 (−4.88)
D.broadmoney	−0.001 (−1.49)	−0.001 (−1.37)	−0.001** (−15.26)	−0.001* (−11.66)
D.trade liberalization	0.000 (1.41)	0.000 (1.45)		
D.fixed broadband subscriptions	–	–	−0.0001** (−39.72)	−0.0001** (−30.58)
Constant	−0.003 (−1.78)	0.001 (0.53)	0.003** (24.31)	−0.001 (−3.69)
Observations	21	21	10	10
R-squared	0.598	0.585	1.000	0.999

Notes Robust t-statistics in parentheses; $^{***}p < 0.01$, $^{**}p < 0.05$, $^{*}p < 0.1$. D stands for the first difference of the variables. TFPG1 represents the TFP growth estimated through the OLS method from the production function with $\alpha = 0.65$ (capital share) and $\beta = 0.26$ (labor share). In contrast, TFPG2 represents TFP growth estimated through the ARDL method from the production function with $\alpha = 0.68$ and $\beta = 0.29$

Bank. In the first two specifications, the change in teledensity penetration and percentage share of ICT exports to total exports have negative effect on TFP growth. However, with the inclusion of the fixed broadband data in the model for 2010 onward, both teledensity and ICT exports appear to be positive on TFP growth. However, fixed broadband is negative to TFP growth. As most people are using mobile data for internet, and fixed broadband remains inaccessible in rural and semi-urban areas, its negative impact on TFP growth may be expected. Though the number of observations is small for the third and fourth specifications, it portrays the expected impact of digitalization on productivity through enhancing efficiency in various sectors. Since the first differences of the indicators are used and estimated TFP growth remained negative in the series, the statistical significance of the determinants is important rather than signs. It is expected that the impact of digitalization would be more prominent in the coming years, which will allow one to employ econometric/regression methods in more appropriate ways.

7 Concluding Remarks

This chapter makes a modest attempt to capture the impact of digitalization on the economic growth in Bangladesh. As discussed in the literature review, ICT and digitalization have a significant growth-enhancing effect, which is evident in many countries. This is a first attempt to capture the impact of digitalization on the TFP growth in Bangladesh and our results show that teledensity and ICTs have a significant impact on TFP growth, vis-à-vis the overall GDP growth. This finding is important because in the absence of any significant reforms in various other sectors of the economy, particularly in the 2010s, the only visible policy changes with necessary investments are made in the ICT sector. Therefore, there are reasons to believe that digitalization contributes to the incremental GDP growth in the decade of 2010, which is evident in our results though the impact is minimal. This also reflects that more efforts should be given to motivate manufacturing sectors to investment in innovation and ICT adoption to improve their productivity so that it can contribute to the total productivity of the economy. As a shifting development strategy, digitalization might have taken place rapidly with a greater growth-enhancing impact. Though this has not happened yet, a rethinking on the digitalization strategies is needed.

To this end, a few issues are discernible. The investments in the telecom sector and ICTs (internet), e-government, and other institutions should have both direct and indirect impacts on GDP growth. Though the descriptive analysis depicted that except ICT-producing sectors, ICT-using manufacturing and service sectors contribution remains almost the same since 2005. This may be true; however, the indirect effects are difficult to capture, and the categorization is tentative. Therefore, there are scopes to invest more in ICT-producing sectors, such as software and BPO/KPO (Knowledge Process Outsourcing) services, mobile phones, computers and internet accessories, etc. Moreover, incentives and policy supports can be given to ICT-using manufacturing sectors to encourage them to use ICTs in their production process to a greater extent and invest in innovation. At the same time, it is important to focus more on ICT end-user perspectives, both individuals and firms, to reap maximum benefits from the digital transformation of the economy. As international evidence suggests, investments in intangible assets, such as organizational restructuring, R&D, IT education, etc. would facilitate digital transformation in quicker and more effective ways.

Appendix

See Tables 3, 4, and 5

Table 3 ICT-based categorization of industries

Industry type	*ICT based categorization*
Agriculture, Hunting, Forestry	Non-ICT others
Fishing	Non-ICT others
Mining and Quarrying	Non-ICT others
Food Products, Beverages, and Tobacco	Non-ICT manufacturing
Textiles, Textile Products	Non-ICT manufacturing
Leather and Footwear	Non-ICT manufacturing
Wood and Products of Wood	Non-ICT manufacturing
Pulp, Paper, Paper Products, Printing and Publishing	ICT-using manufacturing

(continued)

Table 3 (continued)

Industry type	*ICT based categorization*
Coke, Refined Petroleum products	Non-ICT manufacturing
Chemicals and Chemical Products	Non-ICT manufacturing
Rubber and Plastic Products	Non-ICT manufacturing
Other Non-Metallic Mineral Products	Non-ICT manufacturing
Basic Metals and Fabricated Metal Products	Non-ICT manufacturing
Machinery, nec	ICT-using manufacturing
Electrical and Optical Equipment	ICT-producing sectors
Transport Equipment	ICT-using manufacturing
Electricity, Gas and Water Supply	Non-ICT others
Construction	Non-ICT others
Hotels and Restaurants	Non-ICT services
Transport and Storage	Non-ICT services
Post and Telecommunication	ICT-producing sectors
Financial Services	ICT-using services
Public Administration and Defense	Non- ICT market services
Education	Non-ICT market services
Health and Social Work	Non-ICT market services
Other Services	Non-ICT
Wholesale and retail trade	Non-ICT services
Real estate renting and business	ICT-using services

Source Adapted from Erumban and Das (2016)

Table 4 Contribution of TFP to growth (%)

Growth due to-	*Aggregate Production Function*							
	CRS assumption				*Non-CRS assumption*			
	OLS	*VEC*	*FMOLS*	*ARDL*	*OLS*	*VEC*	*FMOLS*	*ARDL*
	TFP	TFP	TFP	TFP	TFP	TFP	TFP	TFP
1981–2015	−13.5	−6.91	−14.01	−12.46	−11.97	−8.71	2.16	−4.28
1981–1990	−22.28	−26.46	−21.96	−22.94	−19.95	−29.21	2.74	−10.45
1991–2000	−14.54	−6.42	−15.18	−13.26	−13.09	−8.13	0.2	−5.49
2000–2010	−13.38	−3.34	−14.17	−11.8	−12.07	−4.89	−0.24	−4.76
2011–2015	−4.87	−5.59	−5.69	−3.22	−3.72	4.24	6.43	2.90

Source Ahmed and Chowdhury (2019)

Table 5 Sector-wise disaggregated contribution to GDP with exposure to capital

Industry	*Industry group*	*GDP share of ICT and non-ICT sectors (%)*				
		2005–2006	*2006–2007*	*2007–2008*	*2008–2009*	*2009–2010*
Agriculture, Hunting, Forestry	Non-ICT others	15.33	15.17	14.89	14.58	14.65
Fishing	Non-ICT others	3.67	3.75	3.79	3.78	3.73
Mining and Quarrying	Non-ICT others	1.53	1.52	1.54	1.62	1.65
Food Products, Beverages, and Tobacco	Non-ICT manufacturing	1.59	1.56	1.50	1.43	1.40
Textiles, Textile Products	Non-ICT manufacturing	8.79	9.32	9.68	9.85	10.36
Leather and Footwear	Non-ICT manufacturing	0.56	0.51	0.45	0.45	0.49
Wood and Products of Wood	Non-ICT manufacturing	0.01	0.01	0.01	0.01	0.01
Pulp, Paper, Paper Products, Printing and Publishing	ICT-using manufacturing	0.43	0.43	0.44	0.43	0.41
Coke, Refined Petroleum products	Non-ICT manufacturing	0.01	0.01	0.01	0.01	0.01
Chemicals and Chemical Products	Non-ICT manufacturing	1.77	1.71	1.54	1.41	1.34
Rubber and Plastic Products	Non-ICT manufacturing	0.37	0.37	0.42	0.40	0.35
Other Non-Metallic Mineral Products	Non-ICT manufacturing	2.15	2.09	2.08	2.24	2.17

(continued)

Table 5 (continued)

Industry	*Industry group*	*GDP share of ICT and non-ICT sectors (%)*				
		2005–2006	*2006–2007*	*2007–2008*	*2008–2009*	*2009–2010*
Basic Metals and Fabricated Metal Products	Non-ICT manufacturing	0.13	0.12	0.12	0.11	0.11
Machinery, nec	ICT-using manufacturing	0.02	0.03	0.02	0.03	0.03
Electrical and Optical Equipment	ICT-producing sectors	0.04	0.04	0.04	0.04	0.04
Transport Equipment	ICT-using manufacturing	0.22	0.24	0.26	0.27	0.26
Electricity, Gas and Water Supply	Non-ICT others	1.21	1.19	1.21	1.23	1.28
Construction	Non-ICT others	6.52	6.49	6.5	6.58	6.65
Hotels and Restaurants	Non-ICT services	0.76	0.75	0.74	0.75	0.75
Transport and Storage	Non-ICT services	8.86	8.76	8.74	8.83	8.93
Post and Telecommunication	ICT-producing sectors	1.3	1.61	1.87	2.06	2.12
Financial Services	ICT-using services	3.11	3.09	3.03	2.88	2.88
Public Administration and Defense	Non- ICT market services	3.08	3.12	3.14	3.19	3.26
Education	Non-ICT market services	2.18	2.21	2.24	2.25	2.23
Health and Social Work	Non-ICT market services	2.03	1.99	1.99	1.95	1.96

Industry	*Industry group*	*GDP share of ICT and non-ICT sectors (%)*				
		2005–2006	*2006–2007*	*2007–2008*	*2008–2009*	*2009–2010*
Other Services	Non-ICT??	12.37	11.91	11.61	11.38	11.08
Wholesale and retail trade	Non-ICT services	13.63	13.78	13.96	14.04	14.02
Real estate renting and business	ICT-using services	8.29	8.03	7.87	7.77	7.61
		99.95	99.80	99.68	99.55	99.75

Industry	*Industry group*	*GDP share of ICT and non-ICT sectors (%)*				
		2010–2011	*2011–2012*	*2012–2013*	*2013–2014*	*2014–2015*
Agriculture, Hunting, Forestry	Non-ICT others	14.27	13.7	13.09	12.81	12.32
Fishing	Non-ICT others	3.73	3.68	3.68	3.69	3.69
Mining and Quarrying	Non-ICT others	1.6	1.61	1.65	1.63	1.68
Food Products, Beverages, and Tobacco	Non-ICT manufacturing	1.34	1.31	1.34	1.36	1.37
Textiles, Textile Products	Non-ICT manufacturing	11.65	13.01	14.1	14.62	14.72
Leather and Footwear	Non-ICT manufacturing	0.48	0.42	0.42	0.44	0.44
Wood and Products of Wood	Non-ICT manufacturing	0	0	0	0	0
Pulp, Paper, Paper Products, Printing and Publishing	ICT-using manufacturing	0.37	0.35	0.36	0.34	0.35

(continued)

Table 5 (continued)

Industry	*Industry group*	*GDP share of ICT and non-ICT sectors (%)*				
		2010–2011	*2011–2012*	*2012–2013*	*2013–2014*	*2014–2015*
Coke, Refined Petroleum products	Non-ICT manufacturing	0.01	0.01	0.01	0.01	0.01
Chemicals and Chemical Products	Non-ICT manufacturing	1.3	1.26	1.26	1.28	1.29
Rubber and Plastic Products	Non-ICT manufacturing	0.35	0.28	0.29	0.3	0.31
Other Non-Metallic Mineral Products	Non-ICT manufacturing	2.11	2.02	2.09	2.03	2.04
Basic Metals and Fabricated Metal Products	Non-ICT manufacturing	0.1	0.09	0.08	0.08	0.08
Machinery, nec.	ICT-using manufacturing	0.03	0.03	0.03	0.03	0.03
Electrical and Optical Equipment	ICT-producing sectors	0.04	0.04	0.05	0.05	0.05
Transport Equipment	ICT-using manufacturing	0.25	0.23	0.22	0.23	0.23
Electricity, Gas and Water Supply	Non-ICT others	1.36	1.41	1.45	1.42	1.42
Construction	Non-ICT others	6.67	6.78	6.9	7.03	7.16
Hotels and Restaurants	Non-ICT services	0.75	0.74	0.75	0.75	0.75
Transport and Storage	Non-ICT services	8.97	9.01	8.94	8.85	8.8
Post and Telecommunication	ICT-producing sectors	2.26	2.48	2.56	2.64	2.63
Financial Services	ICT-using services	2.99	3.21	3.3	3.34	3.38
Public Administration and Defense	Non- ICT market services	3.33	3.35	3.36	3.39	3.49

Industry	*Industry group*	*GDP share of ICT and non-ICT sectors (%)*				
		2010–2011	*2011–2012*	*2012–2013*	*2013–2014*	*2014–2015*
Education	Non-ICT market services	2.21	2.23	2.24	2.26	2.29
Health and Social Work	Non-ICT market services	1.95	1.9	1.88	1.86	1.83
Other Services	Non-ICT??	10.72	10.38	10.09	9.82	9.52
Wholesale and retail trade	Non-ICT services	14.02	14.02	14.03	14.1	14.08
Real estate renting and business	ICT-using services	7.41	7.22	7.07	6.95	6.81
		100.27	100.76	101.24	101.3	100.75

Industry	*Industry group*	*GDP share of ICT and non-ICT sectors (%)*			
		2015–2016	*2016–2017*	*2017–2018*	*2018–2019*
Agriculture, Hunting, Forestry	Non-ICT others	11.7	11.12	10.67	10.11
Fishing	Non-ICT others	3.65	3.61	3.56	3.5
Mining and Quarrying	Non-ICT others	1.77	1.8	1.78	1.77
Food Products, Beverages, and Tobacco	Non-ICT manufacturing	1.38	1.39	1.41	1.43
Textiles, Textile Products	Non-ICT manufacturing	14.84	14.95	15.12	15.32
Leather and Footwear	Non-ICT manufacturing	0.44	0.45	0.45	0.46
Wood and Products of Wood	Non-ICT manufacturing	0.00	0.00	0.00	0.00
Pulp, Paper, Paper Products, Printing and Publishing	ICT-using manufacturing	0.35	0.35	0.36	0.36
Coke, Refined Petroleum products	Non-ICT manufacturing	0.01	0.01	0.01	0.01
Chemicals and Chemical Products	Non-ICT manufacturing	1.30	1.31	1.32	1.34

(continued)

Table 5 (continued)

Industry	*Industry group*	*GDP share of ICT and non-ICT sectors (%)*			
		2015–2016	*2016–2017*	*2017–2018*	*2018–2019*
Rubber and Plastic Products	Non-ICT manufacturing	0.31	0.31	0.32	0.32
Other Non-Metallic Mineral Products	Non-ICT manufacturing	2.06	2.07	2.10	2.13
Basic Metals and Fabricated Metal Products	Non-ICT manufacturing	0.08	0.08	0.08	0.08
Machinery, nec.	ICT-using manufacturing	0.03	0.03	0.03	0.03
Electrical and Optical Equipment	ICT-producing sectors	0.05	0.05	0.05	0.05
Transport Equipment	ICT-using manufacturing	0.23	0.23	0.24	0.24
Electricity, Gas and Water Supply	Non-ICT others	1.5	1.52	1.54	1.57
Construction	Non-ICT others	7.26	7.36	7.5	7.59
Hotels and Restaurants	Non-ICT services	0.75	0.75	0.75	0.47
Transport and Storage	Non-ICT services	8.69	8.65	8.55	8.42
Post and Telecommunication	ICT-producing sectors	2.62	2.61	2.58	2.56
Financial Services	ICT-using services	3.39	3.45	3.45	3.45
Public Administration and Defense	Non- ICT market services	3.63	3.7	3.71	3.65
Education	Non-ICT market services	2.39	2.48	2.46	2.42
Health and Social Work	Non-ICT market services	1.84	1.85	1.83	1.85
Other Services	Non-ICT??	9.18	8.87	8.52	8.16
Wholesale and retail trade	Non-ICT services	13.99	14.01	13.95	13.88
Real estate renting and business	ICT-using services	6.64	6.49	6.31	6.13
		100.08	99.50	98.63	97.29

References

Ahmed, M., & Chowdhury, T. T. (2019). Total factor productivity in Bangladesh: An analysis using data from 1981 to 2014. *Bangladesh Development Studies, 42*(1), 23–75.

Asian Development Bank. (2019). *Computer and software engineering tertiary education in 2018.*

Berger, A. N. (2003). The economic effects of technological progress: Evidence from the banking industry. *Journal of Money, Credit and Banking, 35*(2), 141–176.

Bilan, Y., Mishchuk, H., Samoliuk, N., & Grishnova, O. (2019). ICT and economic growth: Links and possibilities of engaging. *Intellectual Economics, 13*(1).

Commander, S., Harrison, R., & Menezes-Filho, N. (2011). ICT and productivity in developing countries: New firm-level evidence from Brazil and India. *The Review of Economics and Statistics, 93*(2), 528–541.

Chen, W., Niebel, T., & Saam, M. (2016). Are intangibles more productive in ICT-intensive industries? *Evidence from EU Countries. Telecommunications Policy, 40*(5), 471–484.

Crandall, R.W., & Singer, H. J. (2010). *The economic impact of broadband investment.* Broadband for America. Washington, DC, USA:

Czernich, N., Falck, O., Kretschmer, T., & Woessmann, L. (2009). *Broadband infrastructure and economic growth* (CESifo Working Paper 2861).

Erumban, A. A., & Das, D. K. (2016). Information and communication technology and economic growth in India. *Telecommunications Policy, 40*(5), 412–431.

Fukao, K., Ikeuchi, K., Kim, Y., & Kwon, H. U. (2016). Why was Japan left behind in the ICT revolution? *Telecommunications Policy, 40*(5), 432–449.

GSMA. (2017). *Country Overview Bangladesh: Mobile industry and driving growth and enabling digital inclusion.*

Hasan, I., Renzis, T. D., & Schmiedel, H. (2012). *Retail payments and economic growth* (Research Discussion Paper No. 19/2012). Bank of Finland.

Hidalgo Pérez, M. A., Ókean Alonso, J. M., & Rodríguez López, J. (2016). Labor demand and ICT adoption in Spain. *Telecommunications Policy, 40*(5), 450–470.

Hofman, A., Aravena, C., & Aliaga, V. (2016). Information and communication technologies and their impact on the economic growth of Latin America, 1990–2013. *Telecommunications*

Hong, J. P., Byun, J. E., & Kim, P. R. (2016). Structural changes and growth factors of the ICT industry in Korea: 1995–2009. *Telecommunications Policy, 40*(5), 502–513.

Hossain, M., & Samad, H. (2021). Mobile phones, household welfare, and women's empowerment: Evidence from rural off-grid regions of Bangladesh. *Information Technology for Development*, 1–17.

Jensen, R. (2007). The digital provide: Information (technology), market performance, and welfare in the South Indian fisheries sector. *Quarterly Journal of Economics, 122*(3), 879–924.

Jorgenson, D. W., Ho, M. S., Samuels, J. D., & Stiroh, K. J. (2007). Industry origins of the American productivity resurgence. *Economic Systems Research, 19*(3), 229–252.

Jorgenson, D. W., Ho, M. S., & Samuels, J. D. (2016). The impact of information technology on postwar US economic growth. *Telecommunications Policy, 40*(5), 398–411.

Jorgenson, D. W., Ho, M. S., & Stiroh, K. J. (2008). A retrospective looks at the U.S. productivity growth resurgence. *Journal of Economic Literature, 22* (1), 3–24.

Jorgenson, D. W., & Vu, K. M. (2016). The ICT revolution, world economic growth, and policy issues. *Telecommunications Policy, 40*(5), 383–397.

Mujeri, M. K. (2004). Changes in policy framework and total factor productivity growth in Bangladesh. *Bangladesh Development Studies, 30*(3), 1–29.

Nasab, E. H., & Aghaei, M. (2009). The effect of ICT on economic growth: Further evidence. *International Bulletin of Business Administration, 5*, 45–56.

OECD. (2010). *ICTs for development: Improving policy coherence*. OECD.

Qiang, C. Z. W., Rossotto, C. M., & Kimura, K. (2009). *Economic impacts of broadband. In Information and Communications for Development: Extending reach and increasing impact*. World Bank.

Rahman, S., & Rahman, A. K. M. A. (2002). *The estimation of capital stock for Bangladesh economy. Micro impacts of macroeconomy and adjustment policies in Bangladesh*. Bangladesh Institute of Development Studies.

Thompson, H. G., Jr., & Garbacz, C. (2011). Economic impacts of mobile versus fixed broadband. *Telecommunication Policy, 35*(11), 999–1009.

Tripathi, M., & Inani, S. K. (2020). Does information and communications technology affect economic growth? *Empirical Evidence from SAARC Countries, Information Technology for Development*,. https://doi.org/10.1080/02681102.2020.1785827

Toader, E., Firtescu, B. N., Roman, A., & Anton, S. J. (2018). *Impact of information and communication technology infrastructure on economic growth: An empirical assessment for the EU countries*. Sustainability.

World Economic Forum. (2013). *The global information technology report 2013*. Digitization for Economic Growth and Job Creation.

Wong, T., Lau, W., & Yip, T. (2020). Cashless payments and economic growth: Evidence from selected OECD countries. *Journal of Central Banking Theory and Practice*, 189–213.

Yousefi, A. (2011). The impact of information and communication technology on economic growth: Evidence from developed and developing countries. *Economics of Innovation and New Technology, 20*(6), 581–596.

Zandi, M., Koropeckyj, S., Singh, V., & Matsiras, P. (2016). *The impact of electronic payments on economic growth*. Moody's Analytics.

CHAPTER 13

ICTs for Sustainable Development in Bangladesh

1 Introduction

Digitalization and ICT applications can provide support to the sustainable development of a climate-vulnerable country like Bangladesh in various ways. Bangladesh's geographical landscape and riverine position with almost 75% of its territory lying less than 10 m above sea level make it highly vulnerable to climate change risks, such as floods, drought, salinity, cyclones, and sea level rises. The adverse consequences of climate change would be enormous for a densely populated country of over 160 million inhabitants with 1,265 people per square kilometer. The geographical location, climate vulnerability, dense population, and riverine landscape are the characteristics that make a strong case for sustainable development. The agricultural land has been depleting at 1 percent per year mainly for the creation of new homes, roads, educational institutions, industries, etc. The issues of conversion and land degradation due to climate change, unplanned urbanization, environmental consequences, and so on are serious concerns for Bangladesh (Bangladesh Planning Commission, 2015). ICT applications can lend some effective support to address some of these concerns.

This chapter discusses applications of some digital technologies by reviewing international best practices to address some of the environmental and land-related issues for the sake of better management and

M. Hossain, *Digital Transformation and Economic Development in Bangladesh*, https://doi.org/10.1007/978-981-19-2753-9_13

formulating better conservation strategies.[1] The growing adoption of mobile phones and Internet-based applications could play a vital role in raising awareness and education on sustainable development aspects for local communities, and national and international decision-makers. The use of ICTs in conservation activities would be very effective as many of the high conservation sites are relatively remote and undeveloped. Particularly, a steady rise in ICT use for conservation can be observed in areas such as research and monitoring data, remote sensing and communications, increasing public awareness and education.

The ICTs have cross-cutting applications to various conservation strategies, such as conserving biodiversity, tackling climate change, increasing energy efficiency, conserving natural resources, etc. ICTs can be of great help in efficiently collecting, analyzing, and interpreting voluminous data to optimize work processes (Reddy et al., 2017).

ICTs are widely used for environment and climate monitoring, including weather forecasting, and are crucial in early warning and disaster relief communications. Furthermore, ICTs are vital for warning of natural disasters and dealing with crisis-response supports. Given the background, this chapter highlights various aspects of the application of ICTs in the respective conservation areas; particularly, it assesses the existing base of ICTs, future potential, and a roadmap on how to apply ICTs to make the best effort to conservation strategies. It also makes recommendations by taking international good practices into consideration.

2 ICTs use in Environment

The application of ICTs in environment management is necessary to observe, describe, record, and understand the environment-related data analysis that might be crucial for short to medium to long-term environmental planning. Software such as database management systems (DBMSs), and big data analytics are necessary for better understanding the long-term behavior and trends of environmental changes. There are several specific ICT tools that may contribute to environmental information and process management.

[1] This chapter is a revised version of a background paper that was prepared by the author for developing the National Conservation Strategies of the Government of Bangladesh in 2016: Bangladesh National Conservation Strategy (Hossain, 2016). https://paperzz.com/doc/9364982/bangladesh-national-conservation-strategy.

ICTs may help people adapt to climate change through top-down and bottom-up approaches.[2] The possible uses of ICTs for climate adaptation include scientific research and modeling, emergency warning and relief, monitoring and control, deployment of broadband networks, intelligent infrastructure, e-government, and e-services, etc. However, for proper implementation of policies, the adoption of appropriate ICT tools for early warning systems, weather management, remote sensing, meteorological systems, smart and sensor networks, use of GIS and GPS (Global Positioning Systems), and modeling are important. The government needs to improve and implement proper digitalization approaches for better management of environment.

3 Biodiversity and Ecosystem Conservation

Two types of ICT applications are used worldwide for the preservation of biodiversity. The first is the "Mobile Phone Photo System Cloud Service," and the other is the "Birdcall Recognition System." The Mobile Photo System Cloud Service can be used to collect information from a vast area at a time because it allows the general public to participate in the survey by using their mobile phones or smartphones. The census of bumblebees engaged in pollination is an example of Mobile Phone Photo System Cloud Service. To preserve biodiversity, the "Birdcall Recognition System" is used for research on the habitat of endangered species. This software improves survey efficiency and reduces the analysis time. More R&D based on ICTs is needed to improve digitalized biodiversity conservation.

ICT tools can improve practices in agriculture and forestry, monitor air and water pollution, improve the efficiency of the energy, and transportation of goods and services sector. For example, GPS has been widely used in many countries to monitor the movement of large animals, such as elephants, tigers to control their movement toward farmlands. On the other hand, GIS is used in soil analysis and topography mapping. Digital technologies may provide data for vegetation and land cover mapping to get an estimate of production and broad distribution patterns of plants.

[2] Top-down approaches emphasize global climate change scenarios of the kind developed by the IPCC as a planning tool. On the other hand, Bottom-up approaches tend to emphasize vulnerability assessments of specific ecological, economic and social systems as a planning tool.

GPS and GIS can be used for improving solid waste management. Precise estimation of solid waste generation, optimum allocation of commercially available containers could be realized through GIS-based analysis. Digitalizing environmental management will thus minimize the deterioration of ecosystems. What is important is to apply the tools properly with better knowledge. For this, capacity building of respective departments is needed with IT personnel and required software. Moreover, the respective departments' adoption of GPS/GIS, for forestry, agricultural extension, and others, will be helpful to monitor relevant indicators.

4 ICT Applications in Natural Disaster Management

The role played by ICT in natural disaster management has already been recognized in Bangladesh. Mobile-based SMS to make the people aware of the cyclone or floods or earthquakes, use of electronic media, websites, etc., are already in place to disseminate the related information and evacuation of the people in the face of disasters. In addition, the Internet can also play a key role in helping to locate victims, manage information, and reconstruct damaged areas. Social networks, such as Facebook and Twitter are also used widely as means of communication tools. These social networks help disseminate information on disasters and contact people in vulnerable areas through groups and hashtags referring to the disasters. Internet-based messaging and calling options are also used widely to communicate with people at less cost during disasters.

In this context, internet access in public hotspots in coastal areas through Union digital centers, schools, and libraries may enable the community to access the services provided by social networks and the information contained on the web pages. Mobile telephones also offered assistance. With almost 100% access to the mobile phone in Bangladesh, SMS text messages keep people in touch. The use of digital technologies reduces disaster catastrophes substantially in recent days in Bangladesh. An early warning system and log-term weather forecasting with simulation modeling techniques, could help the Weather Department to reap the benefits of ICTs in natural disaster management.

5 The Application of ICTs in Preserving Natural Resources

5.1 Land Resources

The use of ICT tools has vast scopes of improving land administration and management, particularly in developing countries like Bangladesh. ICT can support land markets, land governance, and reform activities in various ways. It reduces information gaps in land pricing, creates network of buyers and sellers, and helps the government plan land use on a sustainable basis. Application of ICTs has an important role in simplifying and systematizing copyright, licensing, and pricing arrangements. As the World Bank highlighted, public–private partnerships can ensure sustainable financing for the adoption of ICT tools in land administration (World Bank, 2011a, b).

In Bangladesh, land use and land management are still following manual procedures that are time-consuming and less user-friendly leading to inefficiency and corruption (Hossain, 2015). Some initiatives have already been taken to digitalize land records and some land management aspects, however, these efforts are not deemed sufficient to reduce corruption and improve efficiency.

For an integrated land administration, an IT-based solution is necessary linking various agencies and departments such as the Assistant Commissioner of Land, the Settlement Officer, and the Sub-Registrar's office. Such an integrated land management system could solve the uncoordinated and disaggregated land administration process. A digitized integrated land system will allow direct access to the land records collected from government agencies, external administrative units, and local autonomous bodies and facilitate various land-related services. The system will reduce time and cost in receiving services, and expectedly reduce the number of land-related disputes. The land trust method can be applied in Bangladesh with digitalized inventory that will improve land management and finance public infrastructure (Hossain & Yoshino, 2019).

Land Information System (LIS) is a long-standing objective for better land management. Such an information system, once developed, could help people to easily and quickly capture, and retrieve different cartographic information. This will also facilitate an accurate geodetic framework and cadastral system with a high degree of measurement accuracy.

5.2 *Water Resources*

Digitalized real-time monitoring and control systems may facilitate optimized real-time operations, alarms management, energy optimization, quality control, and crisis management (European Commision, 2010). Artificial intelligence in water monitoring may detect leaks online while at the same time Automated Meter Reading (AMR) reduces leakage in revenue generation. Smart meters and ICT web tools will benefit both utilities and end-users.

To monitor agriculture water productivity in Africa, the FAO has developed a comprehensive Water Productivity Open-Access Portal (WaPOR) tool (FAO, 2008–2016). This tool provides open access to the water database over underlying maps and provides water and land use assessments. The database is based on satellite data, and Google Earth Engine powers its computation-intensive calculations.

The "Communication for Development (ComDev)" project in Bangladesh attempted to combine participatory communication methods to process various media and tools ranging from rural radio to advanced ICTs (Department of Environment, 2015). However, the project outcome is not well achieved and needs to be broad-based. The Water Resources Planning Organization (WARPO)[3] of the Ministry of Water Resources can take the lead in implementing ICT-based tools in water resource management.

5.3 *Forest Resources*

A comprehensive forest management information system is necessary to improve forest management in Bangladesh. Illegal logging, destruction of wildlife, deforestation, etc. can be minimized through a well-developed forest management system. Nonetheless, deforestation is a major concern in Bangladesh in the context of climate change vulnerability (Forest Department, 2015). A detailed inventory of all major forests can be prepared digitally to analyze the necessary data for research and planning. ICTs may be useful in emerging forest management issues, particularly for dealing with agroforestry, homestead plantation, strip plantation, encroached forest, mangrove afforestation in the coastal area,

[3] http://www.warpo.gov.bd/.

and reducing deforestation and forest degradation. Such a forest management system will help mitigate climate change and conservation area management to preserve wildlife habitat and biodiversity.

6 Urbanization and Urban Development

The concepts of "Smart City," "Intelligent Cities," "Digital City," and "eCity." are widely associated with the application of ICT tools in city management. ICTs may be manifested in managing and developing urban areas with diversified services in an efficient manner (NIUA, 2015; Harter et al., 2010). As already discussed, water management, energy efficiency, transport management, efficient land use, etc. are the characteristics of smart cities that are critically dependent on digital technologies. Different countries have been developing smart cities with the help of technologies. Songdo in South Korea and Masdar in the United Arab Emirates are two examples (Harter et al., 2010). Thus, planned urbanization may be achieved through proper planning with the active use of digital technologies in providing urban services affordable to the people. Internet access, healthcare facilities, and other utility services may be efficiently provided if ICT-based technologies are properly implemented.

7 Conclusions

This chapter highlights some ICT applications in nature conservation and climate-related issues that can be effectively applied for better results. Appropriate application of ICTs can help mitigate the risks and better adaptation and management of natural resources. What is needed is to identify appropriate areas of intervention and take actions to implement ICT tools. As highlighted in this chapter, for sustainable development, various ICT applications and software can be tailor-made for Bangladesh's cause. Land management is an area where ICT applications can make a significant impact in resolving many of the existing conflicts. Though digitalization in land management is in the implementation process, a land information system has not yet been initiated. Digitalization of land administration and management is long-standing demand to increase the welfare of the people, particularly the rural people.

A smart city could be another option to manage urbanization and expedite urban development. *A land trust* is an option to resolve various land-related problems, particularly in land acquisition for major infrastructure development. As highlighted by Hossain and Yoshino (2019), ICTs would play a key role in maintaining a database of land trusts. Similarly, the application of GPS and GIS for biodiversity and conservation, early warning systems for weather forecasting, and so on are essential areas to explore. Necessary capacity building and incentive mechanisms are some of the priority policies that would enhance ICT-based innovations in actions and policies of achieving SDGs.

Nevertheless, ICT applications and investments in environmental conservation and other areas of sustainable development have not yet taken momentum in Bangladesh. A lack of proper understanding of ICT tools in environmental risks and other related areas, inertia in adopting digital technologies, and a lack of investments in ICTs in the areas of sustainable development might have delayed Bangladesh's progress in sustainable development goals.

References

Bangladesh Planning Commission. (2015, January). *Environment, forestry and biodiversity conservation: Background paper for seventh five year plan*. Retrieved January 19, 2016, from Bangladesh Planning Commission Web site http://www.plancomm.gov.bd/wp-content/uploads/2015/02/11b_Environment-Forestry-and-Bioderversity-Conservation.pdf

Department of Environment. (2015). *Fifth national report to the convention on biological diversity*. Dhaka: Department of Environment, Ministry of Environment and Forests, Government of the People's Republic of Bangladesh.

European Commision. (2010). *ICT for water management: Experts consultations, European commission*. https://digital-strategy.ec.europa.eu/en

FAO. (2008–2016, Updated). *FAO fisheries and aquaculture department*. Retrieved January 12, 2016, from FAO website http://www.fao.org/fishery/topic/16618/en

Forest Department. (2015, March 30). *Present forest management*. Retrieved January 13, 2016, from Bangladesh Forest Department Web site: http://www.bforest.gov.bd/site/page/568a5a9b-1321-434b-bc0c-943ad1212d83/Present-Forest-Management

Harter, G., Sinha, J., Sharma, A., & Dave, S. (2010). *Sustainable urbanization: The role of ICT in city development*. Booz & Company.

Hossain, M. (2015). *Improving land administration and management in Bangladesh*. Bangladesh Planning Commission.

Hossain, M. (2016). *Bangladesh national conservation strategy: Information and communication technology*. Ministry of Environment, Government of Bangladesh. https://paperzz.com/doc/9364982/bangladesh-national-conservation-strategy

Hossain, M., & Yoshino, N. (2019). *Implementing land trust in Bangladesh as a strategy for financing infrastructure and sustainable land management* (ADBI Working Paper 1035). Tokyo: Asian Development Bank Institute. Available https://www.adb.org/publications/implementing-land-trust-bangladesh-strategy-financinginfrastructure

Ministry of Environment. (2016). *Bangladesh national conservation strategy*. https://paperzz.com/doc/9364982/bangladesh-national-conservation-strategy

National Institute of Urban Affairs (NIUA). (2015). *Compendium of global good practices: ICT in urban services*. National Institute of Urban Affairs Publishing.

Reddy, S. M. W., Montambault, J., Masuda, Y. J., Keenan, E., Butler, W., Fisher, J. R. B., Asah, S. T., & Gneezy, A. (2017). Advancing conservation by understanding and influencing human behaviour. *Conservation Letters., 2017*(10), 248–256. https://doi.org/10.1111/conl.12252

World Bank. (2011a). ICT for Land Administration and Management. *ICT in agriculture: Connecting smallholders to knowledge, networks, and institutions* (pp. 343–370). World Bank.

World Bank. (2011b). *Using ICT to improve forest governance. ICT in agriculture: Connecting smallholders to knowledge, networks, and institutions* (pp. 373–401). World Bank.

CHAPTER 14

Concluding Remarks: Rethinking Digitalization Strategies for Leapfrogging

Digital Bangladesh vision is one of the important policy frameworks of the Bangladesh government that aims to digitalize the economy to leapfrog into the next level of development. Though many countries have been pursuing ICT-based development policy, Bangladesh's digitalization policy is unique because it gets state-level patronization with utmost importance. As already discussed, the Digital Bangladesh vision satisfies the criteria of the Big Push policy and therefore it warrants an empirical evaluation. The context and timing of this policy suggest that the policy framework has been devised at a turning point in the economic progression of the country. The digitalization strategy may therefore be considered a shifting development strategy. It has been undertaken mainly: (i) to improve the productivity and efficiency of the economy that will help avoid development/middle-income traps in the context of the declining role of traditional growth drivers, such as RMG, remittances, agriculture, etc. and (ii) to utilize the demographic dividend by giving the youth an opportunity to grab the immense potential of digital and technology-driven sectors. Tech-savvy human capital is expected to contribute to knowledge-intensive industries and push forward the 4th Industrial Revolution. Therefore, the digital Bangladesh vision is a farsighted policy, and the continuation of the policy is needed with timely revisions. So far, the government has made significant investments in developing ICT infrastructures, necessary reforms and changes

M. Hossain, *Digital Transformation and Economic Development in Bangladesh*, https://doi.org/10.1007/978-981-19-2753-9_14

in various policies, acts and rules, and created required institutions. However, the outcomes of digitalization are not entirely satisfactory in some cases. For example, despite having 100% mobile phone penetration (54% at the unique subscribers level) and better fixed-broadband connectivity at the rural level, only about 25% of individuals are using the internet. This points to the problems related to internet pricing, reliable connectivity, and affordability of the users. Though e-nothi and e-GP are in place, the government offices still are not making the best use of these services. IT industry revenue has been growing at about 17%, which may not be consistent with the expected high growth as envisioned. The slow growth of the IT industry is not only due to the lack of skilled human capital, it is also due to the lack of dynamic capabilities of firms and, to some extent, policy bottlenecks. Investing in IT parks will thus require further thought. The supply of skilled IT human capital is contingent upon the growth of the IT industry, and therefore, IT education lacks momentum to some extent. Nonetheless, these issues have been reflected in various IT indicators, which is why Bangladesh gets a lower position in IT indicators compared to neighboring countries.

The most encouraging part is that service sectors have been the pioneering in acquiring digital technologies. For example, banking and financial sector, public services including revenue departments, media, education, health, and transport are some of the notable service sectors that have adopted digital technologies to a greater extent. The digitalized financial sector is now serving the retail and business segments more efficiently than before and hence is saving transaction costs and reducing the asymmetry of information to some extent. Such sectors are now providing efficient services and gaining productivity. However, as already discussed, the benefits of digitalization are not translating to different sectors equally due to the slow adoption of digital technologies in production and process management. Therefore, a rethinking in the digitalization strategies would be needed to gain quickly from the process. A few issues are highlighted below that might be useful in getting better outcomes from digitalization strategies.

(i) Digital tarnsformation in the manufacturing sector has been slowly taking place, deterring the expected productivity gains. In particular, digital footprints are largely absent in the SME (Small and Medium-sized Enterprise) sector due to their opaqueness and lack of incentives. Digitalization can solve some of the disadvantages that the SME sector faces. Investment in innovations through easy access to finance could help them gain productivity and greater market access. Digitalization can help build networks with suppliers and become price competitive by gathering information from other similar markets. Faster adoption of ICT applications will enable the manufacturing industry, including manufacturing SMEs, to move up the value chain through more efficient production. With automated production and predictive maintenance, firms can increase the value of products and services, and create new revenue streams. It would thus be a crucial policy for encouraging and incentivizing the manufacturing sector to take advantage of digital technologies to achieve a competitive edge and move up the value chain.

(ii) A strong focus should be given to e-commerce and digital finance. Both sectors have huge potential to grow in the future. During the Covid-19 pandemic, e-commerce grew exponentially, and people became acquainted with e-commerce better than before, which has provided a ground for future uptake of the e-commerce business. To improve and promote businesses through digital commerce, it is crucial for ordinary citizens, new business organizations, and institutions, including government officials and employees, to be aware of digital commerce and business practice and acquire training to obtain detailed knowledge in this field. To protect consumer rights, importance should be given to developing an appropriate regulatory framework to safeguard customers' rights and relieve the grievances of both consumers and traders. Adopting digital technologies in business to a greater extent is expected to reduce information asymmetry, transaction costs, and time and thereby increase revenues. Digital finance, in particular, online banking and mobile financial services, took a leap during the pandemic. Enhancing digital finance will lead to greater financial inclusion and a cashless society, which is important for balanced growth and development.

(iii) Despite the significant development of ICT infrastructures in Bangladesh, the use of the internet and digital content is still limited, not only among individuals but also among businesses and investors. Accessibility and affordability are two crucial concerns for achieving the digital Bangladesh vision. A low level of digital literacy, poverty, and inequality are some of the factors that impede the mass scale digitalization. Economic and financial distresses obstruct a large section of households living in rural areas from buying a computer or smartphone to access the internet connectivity. Easy access to digital devices by the poor and middle-income households and access to easy finance have paramount importance in reducing the digital divide and making digitalization widespread, and for that matter, incentives and motivations are needed. It is now time to focus more on accessibility to get the benefits of already established connectivity to capitalize on digitalization.

(iv) Though the IT Park establishment has become an important supportive policy for developing the IT industry in Bangladesh, a wholesale approach of establishing IT parks in every district would likely be counterproductive. Some supportive and complementary policies are needed to make the IT parks successful. The upshot of building infrastructures in the IT parks will open up the window for corruption for the vested quarters. Therefore, it is important to be selective in building IT parks. Priorities should be given to attract more FDIs (Foreign Direct Investments) in the parks, and an incentive mechanism should be in place to attract local firms. Each park should be a hub of IT human capital. Therefore, establishing modern IT training institutes in IT parks would be a complementary policy to ensure the stable supply of IT human capital in IT parks.

(v) The digital Bangladesh concept still remains unclear to many people, which is not surprising given the lack of appropriate facilities, accessibility, and relevant information regarding IT for development. Training, use of IT devices, and broader dissemination of ICTs can help exchange useful information and provide many related value-added services in rural areas. Engaging rural people with digital technologies at a larger scale is expected to increase output productivity and reduce poverty. Connecting citizens at a broader scale through offering free internet and updating and delivering various IT-related online services in agriculture, health, education, etc., could make digitalization more meaningful. Building awareness about digital services and their utilities is pertinent for the effective utilization of e-services. Most rural people are not aware of the extensive use of mobile phone applications and services, the internet, and computer applications. Without proper awareness of these services, their benefits, and drawbacks, it won't be easy to attract people to use digital services even at the telecenters. Involving

NGOs (Non-government Organizations) and other relevant organs of the government could be effective means to build awareness of various digital contents and their utility.

(vi) The key benefits of digital transformation can be attributed to the growth and development of the IT service industry, which is dependent on the demand for IT services coming through large-scale automation of manufacturing and other sectors. IT industry is still nascent, though it was expected to perform much better. The industry must look beyond application software and focus more on embedded services and new emerging technologies such as blockchain, AI (Artificial Intelligence), IoT (Internet of Things), and robotics for greater value addition. As a supportive policy, the government may provide manufacturing and other industries with proper incentives for automation. These are areas where both public and private sectors could join hands to expedite digital transformation. The IT industry needs adequate support and guidance to undertake productivity-enhancing innovations to capture a particular segment of global IT outsourcing/offshore industry services. The IT industry also needs to invest in enhancing dynamic firm capability and specialize in emerging areas and building effective networking (learning and marketing) linkages, which will help them acquire greater market access.

(vii) Given the enormous potential of the development of the IT industry in Bangladesh leveraging the benefits of demographic dividends, the sector is yet to flourish at its full potential due to the lack of an adequately skilled workforce. Unfortunately, the quality of IT human capital is not up to the mark, and there exists a significant skills gap. Fresh graduates lack appropriate and industry-oriented education, and the training provided by Universities, TVET (Technical and Vocational Education and Training), and other training institutes are poor in their design and quality. To cater to the digital transformation of the economy and leapfrog into a developed nation, it is necessary to transform a large number of educated and energetic youths into a skilled human capital required for the ICT industry. In this context, the up-gradation of the curriculum in IT education with close collaboration between academia and industry could resolve the problem to some extent. If the youths are adequately groomed, Bangladesh can offer a bunch of IT-savvy human capital ready to undertake the 4th Industrial Revolution (4IR) challenges at a competitive wage, given that the salary of the IT workforce in countries like India and China is proliferating. Properly designed training programs for upskilling and reskilling of the existing workforce could mitigate the challenges of the 4IR. Apart from piecemeal efforts on short-term training programs, more efforts should be given to establishing a few centers of excellence (CoE) in IT education. Programs like SEIP can lend support to the respective departments of the Universities in creating CoEs.

(viii) There are huge scopes in Bangladesh to utilize ICTs in achieving sustainable development goals in faster ways. The application of ICTs may improve natural resource management including land, water, energy, etc. As already discussed in this book, Bangladesh could use ICTs more effectively in environmental information and process management, biodiversity and ecosystem conservation, disaster management, etc. ICT applications may facilitate the formation of smart cities, which could solve various bottlenecks of urban development.

(ix) Affordability and accessibility of digital services, particularly in rural areas, are two indicators of the digital divide. Creating digital centers in each village could facilitate access to digital services for the poor and lower-income people. Establishing free internet hot spots in marketplaces and educational institutions may also increase accessibility. More efforts and incentives are needed to make digital services inclusive.

(x) The lack of comprehensive national-level ICT statistics precludes proper estimates of various indicators relating to ICTs contributions to the economy, such as contribution to GDP, gross value added, exports, etc. The A2I conducts a survey of households' access to digital services, which is sample-based and cannot provide a complete picture of the digitalization status of the country. Though the Export Promotion Bureau (EPB) maintains the country's all export-related data, it does not separately account for ICT's contribution to exports, even it does not include ICT exports realized through different channels. Therefore, a national-level uniform database of ICT indicators is necessary to assess this sector's contribution to the economy and formulate proper target-based policies. The Bangladesh Bureau of Statistics (BBS) may be given the responsibility to conduct a national-level survey of ICT indicators every five years, both at the household and industry levels, to properly understand the status of the digital transformation of the country. The EPB needs to improve its reporting on ICT exports by including export earnings from different channels, including earnings from freelancing.

To conclude, the benefits of digitalization should create value for manufacturing and other related industries, such as electronics, semiconductor industry, and high-tech industries. However, the slow progress in digital transformation coupled with the slow growth of the software industry contingent upon a poorly skilled workforce and the lack of dynamic capabilities deters the expected development outcomes of digitalization. Policymakers thus need to rethink the current digitalization strategies and take proper steps to capitalize on digitalization policies. The analysis in this book draws on the digitalization process over the last ten years or so, and therefore, the findings in this book could serve as a basis for future evaluation of the digitalization strategies of the Bangladesh government.

Index

M. Hossain, *Digital Transformation and Economic Development in Bangladesh*, https://doi.org/10.1007/978-981-19-2753-9

E

F

N

The manufacturer's authorised representative in the EU is Springer Nature Customer Service Centre GmbH, Europaplatz 3, 69115 Heidelberg, Germany. If you have any concerns regarding our products, please contact ProductSafety@springernature.com

Printed and bound by CPI Group (UK) Ltd, Croydon, CR0 4YY
30/09/2026
02225327-0009